Lost in the Crowd

M.J. Santley

Published by M.J. Santley, an imprint of Lakeside Data Services

ISBN: 0995662711
ISBN-13: 978-0995662711

To four friends who all passed far too soon.

Pat Todd
Dave "The Leg" Hartigan
Darren Hickey
Billy "The Egg"

You are forever in our thoughts.

Contents

"IN MY OWN MIND, I AM AN IDIOT.
IN THE MINDS OF MANY OTHERS, I AM NOT.

I'VE BEEN TOLD THAT I AM CLEVER;
I AM INTELLIGENT,
AND EVEN THAT I AM A GENIUS.

I AM NOT. I'M A FUCKING IDIOT."

M.J.Santley

Preface

When I started to write this book, I had no idea what I was doing.

Initially, I just put together some old poems I'd written. I then rearranged them in an order that felt right, and tried to tell the stories behind the poems to make it more interesting. My first attempt at this didn't work, so I put it to bed and forgot about it.

After not writing a single word for eight months, I returned to it and realised almost everything I'd written was just about my own life. It suddenly dawned on me that I had the foundations of an autobiography – of sorts.

It only took me eight months to realise this. This is because I'm an idiot.

I subsequently removed most of the poems, but decided to leave a single one at the very start – a forgotten rhyme that had triggered me to write the book in the first place. This poem then amazingly seemed to define a path for the whole book, but it took the removal of every other poem for me to notice this, as though I couldn't see the wood for the trees.

I forgot about the other poems for a while, concentrating on writing short stories instead. Strangely, one by one, many of those poems slowly began to work their way back in. I'd realised I was still going along with my original idea of writing stories behind the poems, the only difference being that I was also filling in the gaps.

The more I wrote, the more it occurred that some amazing things have happened to me over the years, many hilarious things too, and I've also experienced more than a few strange coincidences.

Therefore, I continued to write about all the good shit, the bad shit, and the weird shit that I've encountered, and it grew into something I never could have imagined.

My emotions took over at times, and the language often grew stronger to reflect this – often influenced by alcohol. I soberly revisited each page but decided to leave in many of the strong words where I felt they were necessary or added to the humour.

At the time those words were written, I was telling myself the story, so they were raw, coming from deep inside. I felt it best not to

1

change many of them; better to leave them raw, because that's how it should be: truthful, honest, and from the heart, even if the odd word might seem strong to some sober eyes.

You may find the book quite sad in parts, but it's more of an uplifting comedy of interesting life events than anything – in which I mostly take the piss out of myself – and I believe everyone will find something in these pages to which they can relate and laugh at; though the more fragile of you might well be offended by some of it.

What I know for certain, though, is that you will enjoy it.

However, there is no money-back guarantee if you don't.

I'm not that much of a fucking idiot.

M.J. Santley

Acknowledgments

Thank you to all the people who have loved, touched, inspired, encouraged, annoyed, hurt, ignored, and drained me over the years.

You might not realise it, but this book comes as much down to you as it does to me.

So many people have had kind words to say about my work, encouraging me to write more, but I can only mention those who have directly influenced the book in some way.

My mum and dad, Ruby Johnston, Janet Higgott, Richard "Yorkshire" Preece, Mark Vanderkamp, Alan/Mike Barrett (thanks for the title), Tim Mullin of Lancs, Dora "The Explorer", James Greaves, Abi, Ling, and my brother – without whom it would only be half a book and it would have no meaning.

You have all either given me your time, encouragement, advice, or just did something that triggered me to write. All this somehow came together, giving me the confidence, the drive, and the content to create this book.

Thank you also to Chris Rivers-Nuttall for your wonderful artwork, and to my editors Ginny Glass, Ash Newsome, and Judith Henstra, of bookhelpline.com, for your great help and advice.

I hope you all understand the part you have played in creating this beautiful thing.

Chapter Zero

Belgrade: The Screenplay

Scene One

INTERNAL. BELGRADE CENTRAL POLICE STATION. DAYTIME.

Old dilapidated building.

Inside a small court behind a locked iron gate.

Two men sit together, both staring straight ahead.

One of the men, Chris, is barefoot and dirty, wearing soiled, ripped jean shorts and a blue Serbian football shirt. He looks disheveled. He has recent cuts to his head and face, and also several large recently-healed scars. One eye is black, swollen, and completely closed. He is also shaking slightly, as if craving something.

The other man, Matt, is much better turned out. He is wearing smart blue shorts, a white collared T-shirt, and shades. Although clean, Matt hasn't slept in over fifty hours. He is exhausted.

Chris turns his head to face Matt.

CHRIS (speaking in a northern-English accent)

   I need to buy some shoes and some shades.

MATT (too tired to give an actual fuck about anything)

   I think we've got more important things to worry about first, Chris.

Matt takes the shades from his own face, revealing his tired and distressed red eyes. He turns to his right and puts the shades onto Chris's face, partly covering the mess he sees before him.

A strict female voice starts to speak as Matt and Chris look on nervously.

THE FEMALE SERBIAN JUDGE

You have been charged with the crime of trespassing - breaking into the Canadian Embassy in Belgrade - and drunk and disorderly behaviour.

CHRIS

But I didn't do it. I wasn't even...

Chris is interrupted.

MATT

Just shut the fuck up and listen to her, Chris.

THE FEMALE SERBIAN JUDGE

The punishment for your crime is a fine of fifty thousand Dinars or spending twenty-eight days in prison. However, I will only fine you ten thousand Dinars. This is because you need medical help and I want you out of my country as soon as possible. I will let you off with only this small fine if you admit your crime and leave Serbia immediately.

CHRIS

But I didn't do anything. I wasn't even there.

The judge looks dumbfounded. She sighs and brings her hands to her face. She seems prepared to send him straight to prison – which would surely kill Chris in his present state.

He has caused her enough trouble already over the past twenty-four hours. She has now had enough of him.

MATT (also dumbfounded)

Chris, can you not see that she's trying to help? Just look at the state of you. I believe everything the police have said, but even if they are lying and you are innocent, the only option is to admit to the crime so we can get the fuck out of here. Just admit it, please. I'm paying the fucking fine anyway!

THE FEMALE SERBIAN JUDGE

Do you admit your crime?

MATT

Yes. He does.

CHRIS

Okay.

Matt pays the fine. The big iron gate is finally unlocked and they are free to leave.

On the way out, Chris strangely hugs the judge, thanking her for everything she has done for him. He seems shocked and confused that he has actually been released, as if not fully understanding anything that has just happened in court or the seriousness of the situation from which he's been saved.

Matt and Chris then exit the police station with big smiles. They are free, when just a few hours earlier neither of them could have envisaged sharing this special moment.

EXTERNAL. BELGRADE. DAYTIME.

In a back street.

Matt and Chris walk to the main road to flag down a taxi. Chris walks like a sped-up one-hundred-year-old man, even though he is less than half that age.

Matt tries to hail a taxi while Chris stands behind him in a trance, but he is being ignored by every taxi that passes. It's almost as though he is invisible to their foreign eyes.

Why are they not stopping for him in his time of need?

Maybe it's the sight of Chris? Maybe it's the sight of Matt – which isn't much better.

Ten frustrating minutes pass and still no taxi.

Matt turns to check on Chris. Unbelievably, Chris isn't there. He's gone.

Matt starts to panic. After all he has been through over the past two days he can't quite believe this is actually happening.

He finds himself lost and alone again in this foreign city, and his already impossible situation seems to have taken yet another turn for the worse.

He is in a state of despair.

The opening scene fades out with Matt looking around anxiously while shouting his brother's name.

MATT (Shouting, screaming, almost crying)

Chris! Chris! Chris!

choose to be optimistic, it feels better.

Dalai Lama XIV

Chapter One

A Blessing in Disguise?

It was a lovely day. The sun was shining. I felt great. I was even singing and smiling on my way to work for a change. Then my fucking car broke down.

Luckily for me, rather than this happening elsewhere on my three-hundred-mile round trip, it occurred just as I stuttered into the office car park, which, rather conveniently, was only a one-minute drive to the appropriate car dealership.

My car had never previously let me down in the five years I'd owned it. In fact, I even felt as though it had looked after me; never more so than on the two occasions I'd found myself skidding out of control on icy roads when the car amazingly appeared to take over the situation, saving us both in the process. I'm sure this was more mechanical engineering than divine intervention, but I know I didn't do anything to change the outcome. Just like the road, I'd frozen each time, seeming to accept my impending fate rather than bothering to put up a fight.

The only other trouble I'd had in the car occurred when a long block of wood appeared in front of me on the motorway. On that occasion, speeding home from work in the fast lane, I held tightly to both the steering wheel and my breath, waiting for the tyres to burst. Burst, they did, before the car momentarily left the ground. Although this happened in a split second, it felt like an age before all four wheels were level again, at which point I remember being bemused and relieved that I'd managed to hold my position in the lane, and then at how the traffic just seemed to part, gifting me a clear exit – through four lanes – to the safety of the hard shoulder.

Obviously, this could have ended differently, but luckily again, my decision to do nothing – apart from hold on tight and accept what was coming – had been the correct choice. My only inconvenience was arriving home late from work after buying two new, expensive tyres.

Funnily enough, those burst tyres had a hand in changing my plans for the evening, and instead of the pre-arranged night at the cinema, me and my girlfriend, Abi, had a rather unexpected heart-to-heart in the pub. This was something we rarely did at the time, and strangely, it turned out to be that little spark we needed to put us back on track.

The random block of wood had been a minor blessing in disguise.

The breakdown in the office car park would also turn out to be a blessing in disguise – one that would affect my life in every way from this day onward.

I popped into the office to let my boss know what happened before I returned to my car – which was stuck in first gear – and rolled it down the naturally convenient hill to book it for repair.

Afterward, I strolled back up the slope and enjoyed a few moments of sunshine on this fine, crisp morning in North-East England. All repairs were completely covered under the car manufacturer's warranty and would be free of charge, so I just smiled at how lucky I was, even in what initially appeared to be my unlucky episodes. I wondered if this was yet another of those small things going wrong in my life that would later leave me even better off than I had been before it occurred.

My car had broken down, but I still felt lucky. I shrugged my shoulders and laughed because it almost felt as though it was meant to happen.

Unfortunately, though, it wasn't all good news. The repairs wouldn't be complete until the following day, so I'd have to spend one more lonely night in a crappy Newcastle hotel – something I'd been doing for most of the year. However, even the nearest hotel was only a five-minute walk from the office, so this really had been the most accommodating of breakdowns.

I'd reluctantly taken this job – one hundred and fifty miles from home – because my computer programming skills were so specialised – or old hat – that they were only required on ancient mainframe systems still used by the UK government. After being out of work for the second time in two years, Big Brother came calling again, so I headed further North for a much-needed injection of cash.

Having initially wangled it so I could drive home to lovely Bolton on this particular Wednesday evening – therefore enjoying the next two days 'working' remotely – my car problems meant that after a long, boring, shit day at work, I instead ended up walking to my nearby hotel, going straight to the bar, and getting drunk.

The optimism I'd felt earlier on that unfortunate morning had slowly been ripped away by another typical day in the office. However, my buoyancy returned when I'd discovered it was happy hour at the bar, not that this had any effect on how much I would drink. I really didn't need further encouragement from anyone other than myself.

"Bollocks!"

– Matthew John Santley, Thursday, 29 October 2015

The following morning, Thursday, 29 October 2015, I bent over to pack my bag, and in doing so, I managed to split my pants at the crotch, exposing all my glory. Then, walking to work with my hangover in tow, I somehow got dog shit all over my suitcase – the suitcase which would normally have been safe in the back of my currently disabled car.

I couldn't cope.

My car was broken, my trousers looked ridiculous, my suitcase was covered in shit, and to top it off, I was freezing cold and walking to work with a fucking hangover.

"Matthew, you are becoming a fat, drunken idiot," I thought. "Please sort your life out."

In the office that morning, with the faint aroma of dog shit lingering, I was bored, eagerly awaiting a phone call that would inform me I could collect my car and drive home. The minutes were dragging, so I needed something to keep me occupied in the meantime.

The nature of my job meant there were some busy days often followed by periods of not having much to do at all, so at the turn of the millennium – the previous time I worked in Newcastle for the government – I'd realised I had to find something to stop me going insane during the quiet times. I therefore began to write poems in my own style about things that were happening in my life.

I didn't know it at the time, but during those dull moments in the office years earlier, I was actually beginning to write the foundations of this very book.

Almost fifteen years later, having come full circle, I was back in Newcastle doing the same boring job on a similarly doomed project, and I'd also recently started to write again, spending much of this particular year penning countless verses about my break-up with Abi.

Maybe we should have just gone to the fucking cinema that night after all.

Anyway, today's painful period of boredom seemed like another perfect opportunity to pour out my heart in bits and bytes, but on this slow day, with my brain hampered by the previous night's shenanigans, I was struggling to write even a single dreary word.

However, over the years, I'd always saved my compositions to hard disk, and now, with the wonder of cloud computing, these were forever at the tips of my unworkmanlike fingers, so I decided to read through my old poems for inspiration.

Almost immediately, something emerged from the cloud to make me sit up and realise how lucky I was even to be alive, lounging there at that miserable desk.

An old rhyme I'd written brought home some near misses and quite terrifying lucky escapes I'd experienced. Ironically, it was my mind which then kicked into gear.

Breaking down the previous day had been much more than a simple blessing in disguise. On this cold, depressing morning at work, when I should have been at home, everything seemed to be going wrong, I couldn't see or think clearly, and I could still smell shit, I somehow came up with the idea to write this book – my greatest life achievement.

Eleven Lucky Escapes

I drank a cup of bleach
When I was a kid
My friend's mum found me
And she saved my life, she did [1]
My mate threw a slate
Heading for my eye
Another mate blocked it, slicing his own hand
I really don't know why [2]

On Bonfire night, some idiot
Fired a rocket straight at me
I turned, and it just missed my face
By a millimetre or three [3]
The week before the Manchester bomb
I was shopping on that road
I chose the week before to go
The reason I don't know [4]

The Friday before the Ealing bomb
I was there visiting my friend
If I was there the following week
That could have been the end [5]
And I was on my way home from work
Driving down the M6
When my next-door neighbour's house exploded
Filling my garden with bricks [6]

The year before the first bombs
Destroyed beautiful Bali's hub
I was there for seven days
Each night frequenting those two pubs [8]
And months before the second bombs
In Kuta were to hit
I was there again
In Raja's destroyed restaurant, I did sit [9]

When I went to Taiwan

Dodging all the crazy cars
There was a sudden outbreak
Of the deadly virus SARS [10]
In Taiwan again
When I was in a lift
A 5.8-magnitude earthquake
Made the earth's crust shift [11]

Months before the tsunami
Destroyed so many lives
I was on Koh Phi Phi Island
Living in beach huts and seaside dives
And on this lovely island
Where ten thousand did reside
So many people perished
Only half of them survived [7]

So now wherever I go
I make the most of it
I take a mental picture
Of any place I sit
And I take in every aspect;
The people, the place, the weather
Because the chances are the place I am
Will soon be changed forever

A Typical Day – Lucky Escape Eleven

In 2004, at thirty-two years of age, I was living in Taipei, Taiwan. I lived with Ling, my tap-dancing Taiwanese girlfriend, but she'd left me alone in Taipei for six whole weeks while she was tapping and living it up with some friends in New York.

I hadn't been invited this time, unlike the previous year when I'd gone to meet Ling in New York a few months before I moved to Taiwan. I was left by myself to persevere with learning the lingo to prove I was serious about making a life in Taiwan for us both.

You see, in late 2003, the first time I'd gone to live with Ling, I don't think she'd really taken me seriously. She'd formed an opinion that I was a lazy English bum who needed looking after – something she did a great job of, by the way.

This was my second chance, and I was going to do anything to make it work.

One typical morning, I attended the Taipei Language Institute for my daily two-hour Mandarin Chinese class, and then I did a bit of shopping. I bought mainly cheese, bread, and many other unhealthy Western foodstuffs which the locals generally didn't eat in this country, plus all the things I didn't eat when Ling was at home. We only ate healthy dishes, such as fish, vegetables, rice, and loads of fruit, and although it was often delicious, I really did miss the unhealthy stodge of my English diet.

I arrived home and parked in the underground car park before entering the elevator and selecting floor number seven – the top floor – where Ling's apartment was. The doors closed, and the lift slowly started to rise. Seconds later, the unthinkable happened.

The metal box in which I was encased suddenly started to crash against the walls, swaying back and forth and throwing me into the sides like a frightened drunk — with shopping bags.

I was petrified, and this seemed to go on for ages, hearing the loud clatter and screech of metal on brick while I tried and failed to keep my balance. I didn' t even start to think what it might be. I had no idea. I just presumed I was going to die on my own in a fucking lift in Taiwan.

Eventually, the doors thankfully opened at the top floor, and I can' t explain the relief I felt inside. With the lift still swaying and banging, I quickly leapt out onto what I thought would be the safety of solid ground.

I was wrong, because when I landed on the concrete, that was moving too. It was awful.

Having never experienced one before, I had no idea that I was in the middle of an earthquake, and I didn' t have a clue what I was supposed to do.

I saw steps to my right. These led to a door which I knew opened onto the roof. I ran up the steps — when I probably should have been going down — smashed the door open with my foot, and burst outside into the blinding sunshine and onto the baking roof.

It was absolutely amazing.

We lived up in the mountains — more like big hills, but the Taiwanese like to exaggerate a bit — so you can imagine that my view from the roof was spectacular.

I found myself gazing into the distant beautiful green scenery, while the building was slowly swaying from left to right in pure silence.

I' d always expected an earthquake to be noisy, and it was in that fucking lift, but this was completely silent. It was eerie.

However, it was so, so peaceful, that the fear inside me faded away, being replaced by a feeling of what I can only describe as love. It was as though I found peace up there, high above the ground while there was an actual earthquake going on underneath me. Work that one out if you can.

It was so surreal.

At that very moment, I looked down.

For some reason, I was still clinging to my shopping, and I couldn' t help but wonder, "How the fuck did I end up on the top of a building in Taipei, overlooking some mountains, in the middle of an earthquake, holding some shopping bags, after attending a Mandarin Chinese language class, while my tap-dancing Taiwanese girlfriend is dancing in New York City?"

I didn' t even try to fight the smile that came with the thought.

I wasn' t smiling for long, though, because after the swaying had subsided, I couldn' t even open the door to our apartment due to damage caused by the movement of the building.

I had to kick that fucker open, too, at which point I was greeted by picture frames and glass all over the floor, plus loads of shit and piss from a terrified Old English Sheepdog called Snoopy.

Welcome home, Matthew.

Chapter Two

Where Do I Begin?

Initially, I had no intention of making this book a full-blown autobiography. Let's face it, who wants to read the life story of some unknown idiot from Bolton? However, it soon became obvious that I couldn't just write tales about my later years without giving some background on where all the nonsense began. So, after penning versions of all the other chapters, and thinking the book was almost finished, I reluctantly returned to the start to add some foundation.

It was amazing how going back to my youth then brought so much more out of me. One old memory or emotion seemed to trigger another, and soon, writing about my past became the glue to bring this whole book together; the final piece of the jigsaw. Subsequently, the book doubled in size and I was still writing the fucking thing twelve months later. However, it all finally started to make sense, unlike some of the stories involving my family.

Growing up in the dull, grey, cold, wet, English industrial town of Bolton, Lancashire was a joy to behold – mostly. I have happy memories of playing football in the snow with my brother and riding my BMX bike through the streets, using self-made ramps to jump over kids who would put their lives in my hands by lying trustingly on the tarmac. This was fine, because I returned the favour and did my odd stint on the tarmac myself. I was mainly a happy kid, and I didn't seem to have much fear.

I did have the odd accident, though, such as when I rode my bike into a wall – teeth-first. You might think this would have knocked my two front teeth out, but as my dentist implied at the time, my teeth were fucking massive, and they probably ended up doing some damage to the wall instead.

His actual words were, "Was your father a Viking warrior?" Even my dentist was taking the piss out of me, and I wasn't even a teenager yet.

I lived with my mum, dad, and brother, in Great Lever, a district of Bolton bordering a small place called Farnworth. Typically, many kids and teenagers from both areas enjoyed getting into the odd fight, and there was more than the odd bully hanging around the streets looking for trouble. I managed to avoid the bullies, but it was only a matter of time before I would get into serious trouble if I continued to hang around with the same people.

My brother and I were friends with some much older lads. When I was five years old, a boy named Colin – twice my age – was the leader of our little gang.

One day, he took a few of us into his house where he lived with his father. He guided us upstairs and into his bedroom. I remember being sat on the bed when Colin suddenly plucked a large air rifle from somewhere and aimed it at my head. My face was then violently forced flat to the mattress, with the butt of the gun being pushed into my temple.

Being a small child, there was no way I could possibly fight this. I just closed my eyes and expected the worst.

While I was waiting for him to pull the trigger, Colin paused, and then said, "I should probably check if there's a pellet in here first."

He removed the butt from my head and aimed at the wardrobe, pulling the trigger. A pellet terrifyingly pinged into the wooden door. He laughed. I was already crying. I don't know what damage a pellet shot at point-blank range could do to a five-year-old's head, but as it made a hole in the solid wooden door shot from ten feet away, I doubt the outcome would have been in my favour.

When Colin was in his late teens, he was a heroin addict who was in and out of prison. That was the last time I heard anything about him.

Hanging around with people like this obviously did not make for the best environment a kid could grow up in, and thankfully my mum realised this before it was too late, though she never knew of this incident until reading it here forty years later.

My mum, Patricia, is probably the only real sane member of the family. In the early 1970's, with two young children, little money, living in an area that was quickly going downhill, and seeing her young kids hang around with pricks like Colin, she decided that she had to do something about it. She had to get us away from there.

My dad didn't earn much money at the time, so she would need to get herself a career. In her late twenties, going to college to study nursing was just the beginning, and she had to start right at the bottom by revisiting her O-levels – or high school exams.

As a young child, I can even remember sitting next to her in the classroom, drawing pictures while she was learning with the younger students. I really can't see this being allowed today, and it's something I can't really comprehend. How can you study and look after a child at the same time?

She later qualified as a nurse, gradually moving her way up the ranks, and we managed to move homes when I was around eight years old. We only moved a couple of miles away, but it was just far enough to have a major positive effect on our lives.

In her forties, she studied for her degree, becoming an expert in palliative care, and now retired, she still works part-time and volunteers her help to the needy. She's the rock of the whole family. If anyone has a problem, they call Pat – my mum.

My mum – Patricia Mary Santley, at seventeen years of age.

A Cup of Bleach, Sir? – Lucky Escape One

One of my earliest memories happened when I was around six years old. I was playing football with my big brother, his friend Ian, and some other older lads.

It was a hot summer' s day, and after chasing a ball around for hours I needed a drink, so I nipped to Ian' s house around the corner.

On my return, I suddenly felt sick, and had sharp pains in my stomach. I tried my best to continue playing but decided I needed to go home, which was around a ten-minute bicycle ride.

I headed back past Ian' s house, and was just about to turn the corner and disappear when I heard a woman shout, "Matthew, have you drunk that cup of bleach?"

I turned to see Ian' s mum, Anne, with a familiar cup in her hand.

When I' d been to Ian' s, there didn' t seem to be anybody home so I' d just let myself into the kitchen and drank a cup full of what I' d thought was water. I' ve no idea why I didn' t get it out of the tap. It seems I was an idiot from a very young age.

I stuttered back at Anne, nodding. She immediately called my mum who would know exactly what to do, and she was there to pick me up within minutes with a pint of milk waiting for me in the car.

My mum told me to drink the full pint as we headed to hospital, so I gulped it down like my life depended on it. Thankfully, the doctor said I was fine, though he also said I was extremely lucky because I would have needed my stomach pumped if it hadn' t been for the milk.

What were the chances of Anne realising that someone had drank the cup of bleach rather than just having poured it down the sink? What were the chances of her popping her head outside just as I was about to disappear out of sight? If I'd turned that corner a few seconds earlier, who knows what would have happened on my way home?

Like many other days in my life, it felt as though someone was looking out for me - and I don't just mean Anne and my wonderful mum.

The Family

My mum's side of the family were coal miners, while later in life her parents owned their own pub – Uncle Tom's Cabin in Great Lever. Their pub had a darts team, for which my dad and grandmother played, while my dad also played for another team, consisting of himself, a man with one eye and an eyepatch, and a midget, who even needed help getting his arrows out of the dartboard.

The midget was married to a tall woman until one day she left him for his brother. You might think that his brother was a taller, more handsome version of himself, but no, he was also a fucking midget, and believe it or not, he was called Little John.

This is one of my dad's tales, and it is actually true, but it can be difficult to know what is and isn't true when it comes to my family.

My grandfather on my mum's side, Ken, I remember mostly as watching cricket with a pint of strong lager in one hand and a cigar in the other. I'd often see him at the bus station in the morning when I was on my way to school, and he was off to watch his team – Lancashire – play at Old Trafford in Manchester, or sometimes by the coast in Lytham St. Annes.

One day, Ken was supposed to be looking after the pub, but he couldn't be found anywhere. People were getting worried, and because there was no one else to run the pub, my mum had to cover for him while also looking after me.

Late in the afternoon, with him still missing, cricket appeared on the fuzzy black-and-white TV in the pub, and to everyone's amusement, there was my grandad, in the cricket crowd, on screen, cigar in mouth and beer in hand. For some reason, he'd slipped out early in the morning and jumped on the bus to Old Trafford without telling anyone.

Ken spent much of his time travelling to cricket on the bus, and this is probably why he developed a kind of affection for buses. Once, he even stole one – passengers included.

He'd joined a coach party of friends for a night out, and at the end of the evening there was no sign of the driver. Rather than wait for him, Ken agreed to drive the bus and his friends back home.

The police later caught up with him, and subsequently charged him with stealing the bus. However, the passengers were also charged because they didn't try to stop him; many had encouraged him. Ken decided to get his own lawyer, while none of the passengers bothered.

Ironically, and ridiculously, all the passengers were later found guilty and received a fine, but Ken, the bus thief and probably drunk driver, somehow managed to get off without any charge because he had a lawyer. I wouldn't be surprised either if he actually drove all the way home with a beer in one hand and a fucking big cigar in the other.

My other grandad, George, was a grumpy old sod, but I remember him doing something amazing for me once. I'd had a wart on my middle finger for ages, and no amount of medicine would get rid of it. Then, one freezing-cold Saturday lunchtime, after I'd enjoyed a bowl of his home-made broth and dumplings, he said to me in his broad Northern English accent, "I'll buy it off thee."

George was as tight as he was grumpy, so I wasn't expecting much by the way of cash, and I wasn't surprised when he gave me ten whole English pence. He was doing me a favour, though, by buying the wart off me.

Hang on a minute. What the hell did he mean? How could he "buy the wart off me"? It was part of my finger. What kind of old wives' tale is that?

Anyway, miraculously, though I don't know why I should be surprised, the wart was gone within a week and it never returned. Not only that, but the next time I saw him he showed me a wart on his finger, implying that it was the one he'd "bought" from me. Now then, his wart was obviously already there before he came up with this plan – I hope – but for years I believed he'd magically done this.

This is the kind of ridiculous thing my dad would also do – a trick – and I wouldn't be surprised if my grandad actually slipped some special cream on my finger at the time, though maybe just putting the thought in my mind was all that was required; a sort of placebo if you will. Maybe this was my first experience of positive thinking helping me out, because he convinced me that it would disappear. Who knows? Maybe it was just another one of those strange coincidences that keeps on happening – as you'll soon discover.

Grandad George used to make incendiary devices during the Second World War, and my dad, also George, who could also be described as tight, but not quite as grumpy, must have also taken a shine to explosives. One day he bought a fucking hand grenade from his mate.

This grenade was quite obviously a dud. You could even unscrew the top and look inside it, something I did regularly, and it was just meant to be used as an ornament of sorts.

I was intrigued by this grenade, and as kids, me and my brother used to play with it. We'd even take the pin out and throw the heavy metal lump at each other, shitting ourselves at the thought of what was about to happen. We were very aware that it wasn't a live grenade, though, mainly because it hadn't fucking blown up when we took the pin out, and that's why we were allowed to play with it. However, all this didn't matter when the authorities got involved.

I was seven years old, and with my mum working, my grandma walked me to school. I'd decided that I wanted to take my grenade to school to show my friends, and my grandma didn't object. Why should she? What's wrong with taking a grenade to school?

When we arrived in class each morning, we'd first pray to the Lord our God, before drinking a free bottle of government-provided lukewarm milk. As we stood for prayers, I placed my grenade on the desk next to my milk, thinking nothing of it. It might as well have been a cuddly toy to me, but come to think of it, there's something quite sinister about a young child praying in a full class of other kids, with a hand grenade sitting right in front of him.

As we were praying – to something or other – I noticed my teacher, Mrs. Greaves, suddenly fixate her eyes on the grenade. Her mouth slowly opened wider and wider, and her eyebrows rose up in apparent disbelief – and no doubt fear – as the prayers gradually faded earlier than expected, but maybe took on a higher meaning.

The whole class stopped when she asked, "Matthew, what is that?"

I replied, "It's a hand grenade, Miss."

Mrs. Greaves then nervously said, "Please take it to Mr. Scott right away."

Mr. Scott was the headmaster, and I can still see him now.

He was talking to another teacher, Mr. Marr, in the main school hall when this small child closed in on them with a hand grenade. They actually jumped backwards as I approached them and tried to hand it over. They were visibly shocked. It was hilarious.

What wasn't hilarious, though, was that they then passed my new favourite toy to the police, who in turn passed it to the bomb squad, who in turn blew the fucker up. All I can say is that things were different back then – I think. Just imagine this happening nowadays; a seven-year-old child taking a grenade to school. It really doesn't bear thinking about.

I remember Mr. Scott calling my parents that evening to let them know what I'd done. Not knowing who was calling the house phone, my dad decided to answer in his own ridiculous manner by greeting my headmaster in a deep, sinister monotone voice, with just the two creepy dark words, "Bolton morgue." Mr. Scott must have wondered what kind of deranged family he had within his quiet holy school, St. Williams.

A few years later, Mr. Marr told me off for wearing my watch on my right wrist, saying that only girls wear their watch on their right wrist. He even made me stand up in front of the whole class to tell me, embarrassing me and making me a laughing stock to them all.

Ever since that day, because of him, I've worn my watch on my left wrist. If I'd known at that moment what I know now, I'd have shoved that grenade up his fucking arse.

Grandma and Grandad Santley with my brother – notice the bloody cap.

My dad is quietly the funniest person in the world, and at least part of my sense of humour comes from him. Also, seeing his many dark and mysterious poems published in the local newspaper when I was a teenager probably prompted me to start writing my own.

Nowadays, having retired from his manual job in a chemicals factory, a job he held for over forty years, he does what he says is the most dangerous job in the world, that of a lollipop man, or for those who don't know what this job entails, he helps children cross the road. Since taking this job, he's been hit by cars on three separate occasions – twice while working in the rush hour and once whilst on holiday in England.

The accident on holiday happened when he was walking to the shop, and he was knocked flying by a young woman who couldn't see him in the bright morning sunlight. With people rushing to his aid, he somehow just jumped up off the tarmac and asked the driver if she was OK.

He then realised that the stupid cap he always wears had fallen off in the impact, spotting it sitting pretty on top of the car roof. He collected it and put it back on his head, just as if it had blown off in the wind. This ridiculous situation ended with him consoling the distraught young woman who'd knocked him down; hugging and chatting with her for ten minutes to calm her because she was in bits. Yes. He consoled her.

Afterwards, he continued on his merry way to the shop to buy his newspaper and fags as though nothing had happened. It's not his job that's dangerous. It's the fucking family, but I must also get some of my strange luck from him too.

Not everyone in the family is lucky, though. My great grandad – yet another bloody George – was knocked down in Bolton by a car in 1936. He lost his leg on that day and, sadly, died the following week. Considering the number of cars on the road in Bolton at the time, I think this is probably as unlucky as you can get.

Eye-Eye – Lucky Escapes Two & Three

These two incidents were within a few years of each other. The first occurred when I was around ten years old, and it was all a bit daft really. I've no idea what it was all about.

It involved me and my two best mates at the time, Mick and China. I must have really pissed off China in some way, because he threw a fucking piece of slate at me from a few feet away. I think he was as shocked as me that he'd actually done it, and I'm not sure he really meant to hit me. It was just one of those things kids do sometimes without thinking, and we were actually laughing about minutes later.

Luckily, Mick was standing right next to me, and without thinking, he stuck his hand in front of my face, stopping the slate in its tracks. It was heading straight for my right eye.

I still don't know how Mick managed to stop it, because it was thrown from so close that there wasn't any time to think. The sharp slate sliced Mick's hand quite badly, so if it wasn't for him, that would have been my eye. It was an amazing, instinctive act of bravery for which I'm still so grateful to Mick.

The next incident, I managed to save myself, though it was from another ridiculous thing kids do without thinking: the kind of thing that can ruin lives.

One winter's evening, I was walking through the estate near my home. I'd been to the shop for some chocolate and was heading back home when I could see a group of laughing teenage boys and girls across the road. I recognised some of them because they used to be my friends a year or two earlier, until I decided they were the wrong kind of kids to be hanging around with – again.

They seemed to be egging each other on to do something. I tried my best not to look at them – because just looking at other kids on the estate seemed to invite trouble – but as I passed them, I just had to have a glance to my left.

As I turned, I saw a blinding bright flash, and then what looked like fire speeding towards me. I instinctively turned my head back to the right, expecting to feel the full force of the fireball heading directly for my face.

It was a firework. It was an actual fucking rocket, and it brushed my left eyebrow before screeching into the wall of the house to my right.

It shit me up so much my balls almost dropped. They hadn' t, though, so I screeched back, "You fucking wankers!" and ran home, hearing more laughter behind me.

If it had blinded me, though, they wouldn' t have been laughing for long, because it would have ruined their lives too.

These two incidents just show how easily and how quickly your life can be turned upside down by someone doing something daft without thinking. Both were just stupid things that many of us do as kids, but they could have seen me blinded in both eyes from a young age – and for what?

The Family – Cont.

Into my late teens and early twenties, many of my friends from Farnworth and Great Lever would still be involved in this rather strange past-time of fighting, especially on drunken nights out. It was never organised. It just seemed to happen when they enjoyed a few drinks too many, though it did often feel like certain individuals were looking for it.

I was rarely present when any fighting took place. This was either because I was just lucky enough not to be there or because I had the sense and presence of mind to walk away when I could sense something brewing. One night, my football teammates at the Brooklyn pub had a Christmas night out at the Bolton greyhound racing track. I couldn't join them that night, but my dad just happened to be there at the same time with a different group.

Not surprisingly, there was a huge brawl involving my teammates, another group of lads from a rival team, and almost every other punter in the vicinity. The fight took place indoors, and it happened to kick off at the same time my dad was on his way to collect his winnings from what was probably a very small bet. Unfortunately, he got himself caught up in the trouble, managing to drop his betting slip in the mayhem.

I was later told by a friend that in the midst of the fight, with punches being thrown, kicks being aimed, shit being shouted, and flat beer being spilt, just one lonely man could be seen on all-fours, searching frantically through the thousands of identically strewn betting slips. This man was successful in his search, because the tight git was my dad, and he was more bothered about saving a £5 winning bet than saving his own fucking life.

My dad's mum was called Gladys May Plaw, and she apparently came from a bit of a well-to-do family. By "well-to-do" I mean that her mother wore a hat every day, and they lived in a semi-detached house with an indoor toilet and hot water; almost unheard of in Bolton at the time.

My grandad wasn't her first husband. She'd been married once before, but sadly, her first husband died from tuberculosis in his mid-twenties. She then met George and bravely left the comforts of her "indoor toilet" life for a small terraced home in which I can only remember sitting around the small coal fire, eating broth while trying to keep warm.

At thirty-eight years of age, Gladys May gave birth to my dad. Thirty-eight was very late in life for having a child at the time, so with this and the early death of her first husband, it's a wonder these pages happened at all.

Isn't it strange? If TB was eradicated in the UK just fifty years earlier, my grandma's first husband may have led a full life, and my dad, me, my brother, and his two great kids wouldn't have had a life.

The fact that we are all here is the miraculous result of an unimaginable number of past events, twists, and turns. You are a miracle, so make the most of it.

Grandma – Gladys May (Plaw) Santley

38

My grandma on my mum's side, Mary, is the person responsible for my brother and me being fanatical Bolton Wanderer's football fans as kids. From around seven years of age, we'd sit with her, using the season tickets she'd buy us each year. These years coincided with the worst ever period of football hooliganism in English history, when fighting often broke out inside the grounds, and not just outside like nowadays.

There were many Saturday afternoons when drunken away fans managed to get into our section at the old Burnden Park ground. My brother and I were often left cowering, not from the hooligans, but from my grandma. She'd stand up, shout, and wave her finger at these thugs, telling them to "sit down and watch the bloody match". They often listened, while we just sunk into our seats with embarrassment.

There was one time in the mid-1980s when she was especially vocal, and this time her barrage of words wasn't aimed at any of the supporters. It was aimed at the few police officers on duty that day.

There'd been an awful lot of trouble during this game, and the main reason for it was the lack of police presence. Normally, there were hundreds of officers keeping the peace, but this was the time when Margaret Thatcher's Tory government had decided to close all the pits, so the police were needed elsewhere.

Many mineworkers, including most members of Mary's side of the family, were striking by now, soon to lose their livelihoods, but there were also those who weren't on strike, and to give those few a clear and safe passage to the pit, it required thousands of police.

Daily, there were violent clashes outside the mines, with angry picket lines baying for the blood of those breaking the line, so the majority of the UK police force had been sent there to keep the peace – if that's what you want to call it.

The miner's strike was obviously a little more important to Maggie than a second-tier football league game, so the football fans suffered, much to the disgust of my grandma. The fact that the government was in the process of ruining the lives of her family may well have had something to do with her reaction that day, though, and who can blame her? She really laid-in to the police, like an Iron Lady herself.

Maggie

She sold off our assets
For not much in the pound
But a lot more was lost
With that stuff from the ground
Like the butchers, the bakers, and the candlestick makers
While the only ones thriving
Were the undertakers

How could she not see?
Selling off our coal
Would kill those poor towns
And put more on the dole
A short-sighted vision?
To make a quick buck?
But what about those people?
For whom she didn't give a fuck

Together they coped
With help from each other
But while King Arthur led his troops
It was to get much tougher
Cracks were born
Friends and family divided
The power of the union
Then slowly subsided

The fight was soon lost
The battle was over
But at what the cost?
With each and every pit closure
Things were never the same
But opportunities were found
Though they didn't expect
What was soon to be inbound

Young men with big balances
Travelled the seas

And returned one week later
With white powder and Es
This was soon distributed
Amongst those with more time
And the need for the high
Introduced much more crime

Now this just goes to show
That the government's plan
Was not well thought out
For every child, woman, and man
And because the clowns in charge
Are not the brightest of folk
It wasn't our coal, but our towns
That went up in smoke.

Grandma and Grandad – Ken and Mary Pilling

Big Brother.

There's one person in my immediate family who I have yet to mention – my big brother, Christopher. Chris is almost three years older than me, but we used to do a lot together as kids, and into my late teens I even went on two holidays abroad with him and his mates.

As kids we used to play football with each other all the time. We'd play anywhere; from the cricket field facing our home – until chased off by the groundsman or the resident glue-sniffers – to the back garden, the road outside our house, the hallway, the living room. Anywhere we could conjure up some goalposts, we played, with often the "football" being something as simple as a rolled-up pair of socks.

Being brothers, we also had the odd scrap. This was made slightly worse when my mum bought us a pair of boxing gloves each for Christmas. What on earth was she thinking? I can remember her often shouting at us, telling us to stop fighting, so why she bought us those gloves I've no idea. One day she really snapped, though.

After a long day at work, having done her weekly shop, she walked through the door, exhausted, carrying her many bags. She was then greeted by the pair of us going at it in the hallway, so she took the first thing out of her shopping bag, which happened to be a large tin of Heinz baked beans, and fucking threw it in our direction.

Luckily for everyone involved it missed us both and smashed into the front door, leaving an almighty dent. Shocked, we stopped fighting immediately, and I don't think we had many fights after that at the thought of what she might throw at us next. It obviously worked.

When I was around eleven years old, in an attempt to learn how to throw a proper punch and protect myself, I joined Bolton Lads Club. I'd just finished my first-ever boxing session when a much older lad asked, "Do you fancy going in the ring with me?"

Being my first time, and not being totally stupid, I obviously declined his kind offer. Then, minutes later, he came up to me and punched me in the fucking face, unprovoked. Sadly, because of this one pathetic incident, I never returned for another boxing session; a blessing in disguise, maybe?

Speaking of punches in the face, my brother could have done with a few of those over the years. In his early twenties, he married

Deb and had two children – Sam and Olivia – and I think he did start to grow up for a while. However, when he got divorced after fourteen years, he started to live the younger years which he felt he'd missed out on, and he's never really grown up since, even though he is now forty-eight years old.

He has a particular sense of humour which I can only describe as being an acquired taste. He takes things a little too far. He's just a little too daft, just as when he left his first job to begin a career in sales, and he left a leaving-present for the management.

After using the toilet, and not flushing, he took the toilet roll and laid a trail of paper, all the way from inside the soiled toilet to outside the main toilet door and into the corridor. At the clean end of the trail was a message which read, "Goodbye from Chris." Therefore, anyone following the trail would end up being lead to an almighty dump at the other end.

Now, this is quite funny, but it goes too far. You just don't do things like that. To make things worse, my mum later had to call his ex-manager to apologise for him, because there was a chance Chris was not going to be given a job reference after what he'd done, which could have affected his new job. It seems as though he has lived his whole life like this, with other people sorting out the problems he created for himself.

He used to watch me play football quite often, and once, with my team leading 6-5 with seconds to go, the referee gave the opposing team a penalty. For some mad reason, Chris then decided to run on the pitch and jump on the referee's fucking back. Who does that? My team was almost kicked out of the league for that, and I can still remember the disciplinary meeting we had to go to. The referee's report read, "A wild animal jumped on my back!"

We're not anywhere near as close as we used to be. This is mainly because it gets to a point where you have had enough, and you have to get on with your own life rather than worry about someone else's; otherwise they bring you down, and you die along with them.

It just seems as though there's always something wrong in his life, and where I would just get on with it and try to work through whatever problem I have, he puts his problems on other people – his family and mainly my mum and dad. He's become a bit of a dick. He doesn't know when to stop – especially on a night out – and after so many years of it, he's become very annoying. What can you do? Sometimes, there is nothing you can do to help, and, rightly or wrongly, that is what I have started to tell myself.

Me (left) and my big brother, Chris

Mum and Dad – George and Patricia Santley. You can't help but love them both..

Karma Chameleon

As a teenager, I captained a local football team called Bradford Rovers. We often played heated matches against Farnworth Boys, a team made up from some of the bullies and other pricks I've previously mentioned.

Being a goal scorer myself, the opposition defenders often tried to wind me up. After seeing me play previously, they knew this was the easiest way to get under my skin and put me off my game. I was always easily sucked into a verbal battle, but I was often the instigator too. This was quite odd, because I was reserved and quiet off the pitch; even shy.

One particular game, two Farnworth players were constantly threatening to "kick the fuck" out of me. Normally, these threats were often forgotten when you left the field, but after this game, these two clowns cornered me away from my teammates. The huge one stood over me while the other, smaller lad punched me in the face, giving me a black eye. If only my first boxing session had ended differently, I might have had a response for him. As it was, I didn't even attempt to fight back – choosing to do absolutely nothing again – and that one punch was the end of it until I finished school a few years later, which I will get to shortly.

In my early school years, I thought I was quite clever, without being outstanding, but I later seemed to get distracted. I don't know if this was because at my school, Mount St. Joseph's – a convent school – the boys were made to study needlework and cooking, while the girls were doing woodwork and metalwork. It was all a bit upside down for the time really, though we were eventually given a choice of what subjects to study. I think it was already too late for me by then, though.

The school had been all girls previously, accepting boys into the fold just four years before I joined. Unfortunately, some of the nun teachers couldn't come to grips with the influx of unruly young male pricks. I suppose there were only a few idiots, but that's all it took to spoil it for the rest. When you've got teenagers telling nuns to "Fuck off!" something is just not right. I even used to feel embarrassed and quite sorry for the nuns.

I did lack interest in most of their classes though, especially religious studies, which I believe should not be taught in any school. It's just one more thing to divide people. My concentration in this nonsensical religion class dwindled week by week in my exam year, not only because we studied subjects as "interesting" as St. Mark's fucking gospel, but because I actually had six different supply teachers for the same class. I think my original teacher – an ageing nun – had a nervous breakdown. It was a shambles, and just imagine what I could have achieved that year, if only I had been given the choice of a different subject, plus one good teacher to go with it?

Maybe not much, but I can only remember having one good teacher in my final two years at school – Mr. Barton, my maths teacher. Although I didn't like him and I was scared of him, he extracted the best out of me. The grade B I achieved in maths was my best grade, when one year earlier that had looked like a pipe dream until he became my teacher.

I subsequently received grade U for religious studies – un-fucking-interested. These two vastly different grades obviously weren't down to the teachers – nuns or not. They came down to me.

Many of my friends did well in all subjects, and they had the same teachers as I did. It works both ways, and the answer is black-and-white. I struggled because I had no interest in most of what I was learning. I started acting the fool, concentrating more on football than learning. Due to this, the majority of my final grades weren't good, and I decided to leave school at the age of sixteen to find a job, instead of going to college with most of my schoolmates. This left me feeling a bit thick and stupid at the time because I'd always wanted and assumed I would go to college.

I applied for one job only, that being a youth trainee at British Gas, Spa Road, Bolton. This was a two-year training plan where the successful candidate would learn various roles in each department. It seemed like a fantastic opportunity for any teenager. They even gave you one day off per week to study business studies at college – perfect.

When I arrived for my interview, I was shocked to see someone from my past in the waiting room – it was the Farnworth Boys prick who'd punched me in the face.

We just about acknowledged each other. He almost looked as though he wanted to say something to me, but there were many other worried-looking virgin interviewees in the room, and he probably didn't want to break the uncomfortable silence with an even more uncomfortable "hello".

I was just thinking, "Where's your fat backup now then, you prick?"

It was strange how small and meagre he looked, packed on the sofa between all the other nervous hopefuls, while I felt as though I was towering over him. This was only because I was late and all the seats were taken, so I had to fucking stand up on my own.

However, after feeling quite pathetic and helpless at our previous meeting a few years earlier – when he and his big mate seemed to tower over me – I felt as though the tables had turned. I felt that I could do something about the situation in which I now found myself, and I suddenly became convinced that I would get the job before him.

I can't remember a thing about my interview, but this day happened to be my first wonderful experience of karma, because days later, I was over the moon to be offered the job. The next time I saw him, he was cleaning windows outside in the freezing cold.

I couldn't help but think again that there was someone upstairs on my side, guiding me through life. I also believed I was offered this job before him because I was a decent kid, and he didn't deserve it because he was a bit of a tit. I had also believed that one day I would get my revenge over him, and what a way to get it.

Then, months later, I came across the other party who had been present when I was punched – the fat bastard. I was with my brother in the Ritzy nightclub in Bolton, when I spotted him with around twenty other lads. I'd once seen some of this group jump a lad in the same nightclub, and the victim's face that night was an absolute mess.

When fat boy spotted me with my brother, and looked me in the eyes, I said, "All right, mate?"

He continued staring at me, saying nothing, so I turned around. I then became quite concerned when I overheard him say, "I'm going to fucking kill him!"

I suggested to my brother that we walk away, so we did, quickly, past the DJ console and up the steps to the second floor. As I looked over my shoulder, and down to the dance floor, I saw this idiot and his entire group pointing upstairs. Worryingly, they started to run our way.

Our fast walk quickly turned into a run. I remembered there were some rarely used steps in a far dark corner of the club, which could be dangerous if they cornered us there, but happened to be our only chance at escape, so we ran towards them and managed to get downstairs, making our way to the only exit that wasn't a fire exit, avoiding the group just long enough to find a doorman in the foyer.

Seconds later, the door burst open. It was the idiot and his cronies, so I pointed them out to the doorman.

Without the doorman we would definitely have been in big trouble, but although he warned them off, he didn't throw anyone out of the club – probably because he hadn't witnessed anything, though it should have been obvious to him what was happening.

We all then bizarrely hung around in the foyer for a while. Everyone was just looking around, pretending they were waiting for a fucking bus or something, but it was obvious they were waiting for me to leave so they could twat me outside.

I waited a few minutes until the group of not-rights eventually piled back inside. I then ran like mad for the exit and escaped. My brother had slipped out unnoticed by this point. They weren't after him so he left to give me a better chance. At least I think that's why he left.

Just a few weeks later, me and this idiot encountered each other again, in the sister club of the Ritzy – Central Park – which was underneath the main club. For some reason, he was very different this time, even buying me a drink.

We actually had a good chat, and he told me that he was soon joining the army.

However, he then said some disturbing things.

Firstly, he told me he had an appointment with his dentist the following week to have one of his front teeth extracted; not because it needed to come out, but because he wanted to look "hard".

He then congratulated me on getting the job which his friend didn't get, and as we parted company, alarmingly, he said, "Good luck mate, it's been great talking to you, but just remember, one of these days you'll be walking down the street and I'm going to fucking kill you!"

The next time I saw him was around five years later. This was at the christening of my cousin's daughter, and it turned out that my cousin, Paul, was his fucking boss. Here we go again – karma. Not surprisingly, he then wanted to be my best friend, and I hadn't done anything other than let nature take its course.

Jokingly, I asked Paul to sack him, but it was enough for me to feel like I had that control over him.

He'd left the army after little more than a year. I never asked him why he left, but I just imagined him being bullied for having his front tooth missing, and him not being able to handle being on the other side of the hard men.

I often wonder in what situation the phrase "What the fuck!" was first ever used. I need to ask my mum this, because these are the first three words I can actually remember saying, probably because I've said them so many times in my life that they're just permanently branded onto my brain.

This prick should have had those words branded onto his fucking forehead.

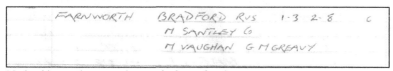

Maybe this was the reason he punched me after the game.
We won 8-2 that day and I scored six. My dad kept a record of every game.

Bang, Bang, Bang – Lucky Escapes Four, Five, & Six

These three incidents are more about not being in the wrong place at the wrong time, but writing this, it's just occurred to me how many explosions I've actually been close to.

In 1996, I was walking along Deansgate in Manchester city centre on Saturday afternoon the week before the IRA bomb was detonated, and that was probably one of the first times I'd ever walked down that road. Deansgate was cleared, and no one was hurt, but I was there exactly one week before, which is also the case with the 2001 bomb in Ealing, London – a place I've only visited once.

This Ealing bomb was apparently planted by the Real IRA, not the fake ones from 1996.

Me and my mate Andy had gone to visit our friend Simon in Ealing, and on that Friday night we caught the train to London from Ealing Station.

Around midnight the following Friday, the Real IRA bomb exploded outside Ealing Station. Again, no one was killed, but there were several casualties, and again it was exactly one week after I walked past the location of the bomb.

The third, and hopefully final explosion, happened next door to my mum and dad's where I lived at the time.

Our next-door neighbour, Frank, lived alone. He was a private chap who did nothing but tend to his beautiful garden all day long. The outside of his house really was perfection to look at, and it made the area around our home look so lovely, rather than the concrete shithole it has since turned into.

A few weeks before it happened, something awful, but also quite comical, happened with Frank.

My dad had gone into our back garden and, over the fence, had noticed Frank in his greenhouse. This was quite normal, but this time there was something weird about Frank – he was tending to his plants while not wearing any clothes.

My dad also noticed there was something else not quite right with Frank, so after trying and failing to get some sense out of him, he called the emergency services.

This is when the situation took on an even more ridiculous turn.

The police arrived first. My dad told them the situation, and they gained entry to Frank's home and entered his back garden. Frank was standing there in the greenhouse, stark bollock naked, holding a trowel in one hand and a plant in the other.

When my dad made his way in, the police officers were standing outside the greenhouse, making no attempt to get in and speak to Frank, so my dad thought he would try.

A police officer shouted at my dad, "Don't go in there. He's armed."

They made it sound as though Frank was holding a deadly weapon, but in reality he was just potting a fucking plant in the buff. It doesn't sound like the most dangerous situation now, does it?

Thankfully, the ambulance soon arrived, and the paramedics quickly took control of the situation. It turned out that Frank had recently had a bad fall, banging his head, and this had obviously caused some internal damage. This explained his odd behaviour, and may have also had something to do with what happened a few weeks later, which wasn't funny in the slightest.

I was driving home from work, and was around ten minutes from home when I heard on the radio news that there had been an explosion on Bishop's Road, Bolton.

My mum's house was the first house on Lakeside Avenue, which led onto Bishop's Road, so my heart was obviously in my mouth when I heard the news.

When I first started to work at British Gas, I'd discovered that there was a huge gas main running below this road. I remembered quite clearly that one of the engineers had said, "Fuck me, lad. If that goes up you're in trouble."

This had obviously stuck in my mind. Had the engineer been joking? I didn't know any better at the time and just laughed it off, but here I was realising my worst fears. I thought the whole fucking road had gone up.

As I got closer, I drove, tentatively, wondering what on earth I was going to see. I had no idea if my mum and dad were home. Mobile phones didn't exist back then, so I had no way of finding out anything until I arrived on the scene.

I turned left onto Bishop's Road and immediately saw Frank's bungalow — or what was left of it. It was in bits. It was actually completely flat, with debris all around it, including some in our garden.

We sat out in the garden that night with the neighbours — something that my mum and dad did most nights during the summer — and I remember it being a surreal evening. Our back garden, in which for almost twenty years living next to Frank we'd spent so much time playing football, having barbecues and parties, relaxing and the rest, was now filled with bricks from Frank's bungalow. We were all so lucky that the explosion happened at a time when no one was home. However, not everyone was so lucky. Frank's bungalow was rebuilt, but he was never to return to it. Although he somehow survived the blast, he sadly died months later.

I think something else died that day too. The area never quite looked the same again without Frank's perfectly trimmed lawn and beautiful colours surrounding it. Isn't it amazing what a bit of colour can do to your mood, and to a community?

Mum and dad looking much more affluent than they actually were.

Proud of Bolton?

Proud of the yobs
That run riot in town
Proud of the thieves
Who keep getting me down
Proud of the drugs
Which are rife amongst teens
Proud of the thugs
You must surely have seen?

Proud of the numerous
Slappers & tarts
Proud of their clothes
That set them apart
Proud of the girls
That work on our streets
Proud of their parents
I'd just love to meet

Proud of the roads
That ruin my car
Proud of the council
Who used up all the tar (on useless bumps)
Proud of the litter
A beautiful site
And of garbage collection
Once every fortnight

Proud I left Bolton
For distant shores
Proud I discovered
A place I love more
Proud of Bolton Wanderers
For putting it on the map
And proud that I realise
That Bolton is crap

Back to Work

After little over one year in my job with British Gas, I was offered a permanent role as a customer service representative with them. I sometimes even struggle talking to myself, so why they offered me this job full-time, I've no idea. It involved me constantly talking to other people – my worst fear.

Not surprisingly, I wasn't very good in this job, and I hated getting up in the morning for it. In fact, I remember feeling a tight knot in my stomach every day as I drove my little black rusty mini to Manchester. That's really not the way life should be.

One morning – around nine depressing months into the job – in-between trying to talk to angry customers, I saw an internal job advert for trainee computer programmers. Anyone could apply for the first stage of the interview process, which was an aptitude test. I decided to apply because it was something different, and I thought it would at least get me out of the office for a few hours; relieving the stress for part of the day.

When I arrived for the test, I noticed everyone was much older than me, and they all seemed to be taking it very seriously, whereas I just saw it as a morning off work. After completing the test, which I found extremely difficult, I sat around for half an hour waiting for everyone else to finish. I assumed I'd messed it up.

Two years earlier, at sixteen, I'd received a grade E – a fail – in GCSE/High School computer studies. I did like computers, and being a programmer was my dream job at the time, but I didn't think I was really cut out for a job in computing after the total failure in my exams. I also thought nothing had changed in the two years since leaving school.

However, I was obviously wrong. I was offered a job at the north-west headquarters of British Gas in Altrincham, near Manchester, and was over the moon that my life was finally being mapped out – somehow.

I'd failed at school, but within two years I'd ended up in a roundabout way, and partly by extreme chance, working in the exact job that I'd wanted to do. This was no doubt in a much shorter time period than if I'd have passed all my exams and gone to college and university. It was ridiculous really. I would soon be earning good money in a career with good prospects, while many of my "cleverer" school friends still had another five years or so remaining of study.

Fast-forward five years to my early twenties, and I was an experienced COBOL computer programmer, albeit one who still didn't know what the fuck was going on half of the time – it does take a while for some of it to sink in. By now, British Gas had decided that the impending impact of the government's ending of British Gas's monopoly – by opening up the gas industry to other suppliers – meant that it couldn't survive in its current state. Therefore, in the subsequent few years, they decided to close many regional headquarters, leaving just one central building in the place that never wakes up – Solihull, near Birmingham, over one hundred miles and a two-hour drive from Bolton.

A job here was not an option for me because I didn't want to leave home at the time, so together with my two colleagues – and good mates – Andy and Dan, after seven years working at British Gas I decided to take voluntary redundancy. After leaving one Friday in April 1995, I started a contract role on the Monday with the central government in Lytham St. Annes, Lancashire.

Getting the role in Lytham wasn't straightforward, though. After we all had our telephone interviews, only Andy and Dan had been offered contracts. After not hearing anything for a week, I decided to call the job agency to see what was going on. I was distraught to be told that I wasn't being offered the role due to my poor performance in the technical part of the interview – surprise, surprise. I was so upset, and almost embarrassed, but rather than accept this as I normally do, I told them that I was excellent at doing my job, and that I would have no problem in the role if they only gave me a chance. When the managing director heard about this, he invited me in for a chat, after which he then offered me a contract.

It seems that sometimes doing nothing isn't always the best thing. Sometimes things are worth fighting for.

Lytham is forty-five miles North of Bolton on the way to the beautiful Lake District, and there were many contractors who travelled South from places such as Kendal in the Lakes. Just a few weeks into my new role, a few more new starters arrived – all from Kendal. We got chatting, and when they heard that I was from Bolton, one of them asked if I knew of a place called Farnworth – it keeps coming up, doesn't it?

I lived about two hundred metres away from Farnworth at the time, so I, rather hesitantly, just said that I knew of the place. One of them lifted a copy of the local Kendal rag from his briefcase. On the front page was a headline that, I think, read, "It's just not cricket!" The main story was that of a cricket match that had taken place in Kendal the previous weekend, a cup semi-final tie between Kendal and – wait for it – Farnworth.

Farnworth had taken a large group of supporters with them, and after drinking all day in the sun, there was an almighty brawl. This even involved many of the players who were on the pitch at the time, and the game was eventually quite comically abandoned when the police arrived. I even knew many of the idiots who played for or supported Farnworth Cricket Club, but never in a million years was I going to admit this to my new, rather well-to-do colleagues. Many of the lads at the cricket that day were actually my friends who I played football with at the time too. I've never understood this drinking and fighting culture; drinking yes, but fighting? Idiots.

Stepping away from Farnworth again, for now, there also used to be a big drinking culture in computer-related jobs in the early years, and this first time in Lytham was no different. Just like at British Gas, they even had a club on site where you could go for a pint, which is quite unbelievable thinking back. In fact, in my first computing role at British Gas, I worked with a team of around thirty men, all mid-twenties to late-fifties. There was something odd about these men, in that, quite bizarrely, every single one of them wore an earring in one ear. Being the young kid in the office, it took me a while to ask them about this.

Ridiculously, one day, British Gas had amended their employee terms and conditions, stating that male employees were not allowed to wear jewellery above the neck. Therefore, my whole team, manager included, left work at lunchtime the same day and had their ears pierced as one big "fuck off" to the company. I thought this was absolutely brilliant, though I often wondered if it came about during a lunchtime drinking session in what was called the "Gas Club," a place we often visited at lunchtime.

Like most, I'd only been offered six months in Lytham, thinking that I would be lucky to get one year's work, but I couldn't have been more wrong. It went on for over two and a half years before I left to work for IBM. I then returned to Lytham for another two years, before working for Barclays Bank. In 2001, I accidentally ended up back in Lytham again when the previously mentioned mind-numbing Newcastle project was scrapped. Bored out of my tree in Lytham again, I wondered if I was ever going to escape the place and, more importantly, if I was I ever going to escape fucking Farnworth?

Whatever the case, the foundations of this book had now secretly started to be formed with a couple of crappy poems. However, after a number of rather sedate years, I wasn't quite prepared for what was about to happen next.

SILENCE

DALAI LAMA XIV

is sometimes the best answer

Chapter Three

Life Is a Journey

For a while, I'd planned to go travelling on my own. I just hadn't decided where or when to go.

It was the turn of the century, and I was feeling a bit lost. I'd been in a relationship since my teenage years so it was strange being alone, not having my partner-in-crime next to me. Although life was now much more peaceful, and I had a lot less to worry about without her family in my life, things just weren't the same. I was really unhappy – especially at how things ended between us.

I broke up with this girl in 1999, after a ten-year relationship, and in 2000, I started to go out with a great girl from work named Karen. However, this all happened too soon for me – even if I did instigate the whole bloody thing. To this day, Karen is one of only two girls I have ever asked out – the other said no. That's how serious I was.

We'd only just started going out when Karen travelled to Australia for six months – a trip that was planned well before we met – and it just didn't happen after that. However, I did visit her in Australia for four weeks, and we even flew to Bali while we were there. This was the trip in which I first caught the bug for travel, so you could say I have Karen to thank for the next stages of my life. It's amazing how the people you meet determine your future, because if I hadn't met Karen, the following chapters in this book would all be so different, even though she doesn't figure in them once.

For some reason, I broke up with Karen on the final night of a romantic break to the ancient Roman city of York, and this obviously didn't go down too well at the time. The morning after, I awoke to find Karen had left the hotel, taking her clothes and the car keys to my ride home with her.

There was also a note which read something like "I've driven home. I hope this teaches you to treat your next girlfriend a bit better!"

However, as I am such a lucky bastard, one hour later, when I was really flapping, Karen turned up at the hotel. She'd just been shopping and left this note to wind me up. That's how great she was.

Anyway, the government work had been good to me over the years, but I always knew there must be more to life than the day-to-day bollocks I was enduring. It was dreadful at times, and it seemed that nothing ever got finished on the projects I worked on. It was really shit. I'd often work my arse off on something for months on end, only to see it brought to an end because the money ran out or some top bods in the government changed their minds.

Feeling fed up during my third stint in Lytham, I told myself that the next time my contract wasn't renewed – which could have been weeks or years in the future – I would go travelling alone for a very long time.

Then, on September 16th, 2002, everything changed.

I was only now based in Lytham because of the failed Newcastle project. When that had ended, rather than put me out on the street, my manager found this role for me. However, after only six months, this was scrapped too, so I was thinking I really must be a fucking jinx with every project I joined seemingly doomed. However, although it didn't cross my mind at the time, each one of those failed projects was sending my life down a different path.

Again, instead of getting rid of me altogether, I was offered yet another opportunity in Lytham, on another project, in a different building. That is when I met a lovely girl called Adele.

I quickly became good friends with Adele, and it was to get even better when the chair gods decided that I should be moved to sit with her. We got on really well. I liked her a lot, but she'd been going through a rough time outside work with her ex-boyfriend, and she seemed quite unhappy. One day, she said something about not being able to cope with another Christmas on her own. I didn't really press her on this. I hadn't taken it as a flippant comment, though. The way she said it sounded real, and I didn't know what to say in return, so I just kind of smiled, almost pretending that she hadn't said anything. I suppose it was just easier for me to ignore what she said rather than listen to what more she might have wanted to tell me.

The next day, Adele was almost sacked for sending a joke email at work which happened to 'offend' one of the managers. The electronic trail was tracked to Adele's email address, and she was subsequently given a final warning by a panel of company wankers.

When she returned from her telling-off, she was clearly quite distraught, and this was more apparent when I asked her how it had gone.

Adele replied, "I feel like going into the toilets and hanging myself. That will fucking show them!"

I was obviously shocked by this, but we both laughed it off. I told her to forget about it; that these people weren't worth it. This sad bunch of bullies had no sense of humour and definitely had no life outside work.

She later showed me the offending joke, and it was nothing at all. It was just a collection of photos of various Miss Worlds wearing bikinis, with the picture of Miss Iran showing a woman with quite a bit more pubic hair than everyone else. That was it. Well, it was actually a lot of pubic hair – quite reminiscent to Bin Laden's facial mess – but some people really are too touchy about these things nowadays.

The world seems to be full of people being offended on behalf of others. The way I see it, if you can't make a joke about a certain group of people, then you are segregating them from the rest of us and treating them differently than everybody else, which, funnily enough, you could say is racist. Far too much is classed as racism today, so much so that the meaning of the word has changed and I feel it is almost becoming a dead word. Basically, some people just need to fucking lighten up a little.

Not long after Adele had been through this ordeal, I was gutted to be moved to the other side of the office. I'd just been getting to know her too. After this, I started to see quite a bit less of her, though she would still be the first person I looked for in the morning and we'd have the odd chat during the day – the only part of the day I enjoyed at the time. I never got around to asking her out though – not surprisingly – and whenever there was a night out from work there was always something strangely getting in the way, preventing one of us from going.

Then, one cold wet depressing morning, Adele didn't arrive for work. We tried calling her but there was no reply. This continued all morning. I was really busy that day for a change, so I carried on working, not really thinking about it until later in the afternoon. Around 3.30 p.m., I nipped over to the printer to collect a large listing of a computer program I'd been pulling my hair out over. Two of Adele's friends were quietly chatting nearby, so I rather matter-of-factly asked, "Is there any news on Adele?"

The faint whisper of a reply I then heard was simply, "She died."

Such devastating, quiet words I can still hear so loudly today.

In shock, I dropped the heavy paper listing on the floor, breaking the eerie silence with a thud, and making the whole office look up. I then turned away and walked straight outside in a hollow tearful daze.

I climbed into my car, just sitting there for a few moments trying to comprehend what had just happened. What had just happened?

I eventually started the engine, and a song gently began to break the silence; it was "Where Angels Play" by The Stone Roses. I listened for a while as I wiped the tears from my eyes.

Eventually, I set off on the sixty-minute journey home. The unavoidable drive past Adele's house was the worst part. I just stared at the car in front of me, not wanting to catch a glimpse of anything happening to my right. This was the point at which I realised the music was still playing. I turned it off and drove the rest of the lonely journey in silence – straight to my mum's.

Adele had committed suicide. She'd drunk a few bottles of wine and taken some pills. Was this a cry for help? I don't know. I just remembered the words she'd recently said to me and wondered if she'd been crying out for help days earlier.

Maybe this was one of those occasions on which I should have actually tried to do something, rather than doing nothing at all. Could I have helped? Maybe; probably not; but maybe. This is something I asked myself over and over again, for years.

She was just twenty-five years old.

It would be a decade before I could bring myself to listen to that Stone Roses song again.

The Aftermath

This obviously hurt me and everyone in the office, though it hit some more than others. Things like this can be difficult to move on from, and it was quite clear afterwards that some people only dealt with it by completely blocking it out. One of those people was me.

I had to miss Adele's funeral because I was in Florida with my family. I would have liked to have paid my respects and met her family, but I wasn't too gutted about missing it. Selfishly, it would have been a horrendous personal experience, and it would have made it feel more real to me. In my mind, I could still treat it like a dream – nightmare – if I didn't see her being laid to rest.

On my return to work, I joined a few other colleagues and friends of Adele for a night out in Blackpool, mainly to chat about her and to toast her life.

One of these people was someone I worked closely with called Andy Paps. He was a great laugh, a good friend to me, and also close friends with Adele. They weren't close in a romantic sense. He was just a friendly bloke, and because he worked away from home, he used to pop round to Adele's house for a chat while she ironed the lazy bastard's shirts.

Sadly, Andy was the unfortunate soul who found Adele on that dreadful afternoon. He'd opened her bedroom door to find her slumped behind it, and he was obviously traumatised by this. He described to me what he saw in graphic detail. Though I didn't want to hear it, he must have felt the need to try to release some of the pain he was feeling – so I reluctantly obliged.

I just can't imagine what it would be like to find anyone like that, never mind a good friend. There was no way Andy could block this awful event out like I could. He would have those images with him forever.

On our night out, Andy gave me a card from the funeral. This had a beautiful picture of Adele on the front. He said that he'd like me to have it because he couldn't stop looking at it, and because it kept reminding him of the horrible scene he'd discovered. While I was looking at this stunning but heart-breaking picture, Andy began to tell me that he'd had some close chats with Adele, and she'd told him that she'd been really lonely since breaking up with her partner the year before. Adele obviously missed what they'd once had together, and she'd wanted to find someone to share her life with. She'd just really hated being alone.

Then, Andy said, "Matt, I need to tell you something. I really don't want to tell you this. I just have to. A few days before she died, Adele was saying how she just wanted to meet someone nice, and I asked her, what about Matt?"

Adele had replied, "I really like Matt, you know."

Adele.

"THERE'S NOWHERE
YOU CAN BE ...

THAT ISN'T WHERE
YOU'RE MEANT TO BE."

JOHN LENNON

Chapter Four

The Escape of a Lifetime

After the nightmare of September, the office became an even more depressing place. I needed to escape this environment and attempt to put the sadness behind me. That's how I cope with things like this. I shut them out and get the hell away from the situation. I mean, what's the point in going over it again and again, reliving it every day? I've never understood that, and although this might work for some people, it certainly doesn't work for me.

I told myself that I'd definitely be going travelling at the end of my current contract – whether it was renewed or not – and I did exactly that. In March 2003, I embarked on a South-East Asian adventure. I booked a flight to Singapore which was due to return six weeks later, though my ticket was flexible and open for twelve months, so I was almost prepared for anything to happen.

My special trip didn't get off to the best of starts, though. In the midst of take-off from Manchester Airport, as the Singapore Airlines jet left the runway, a fucking drinks trolley came hurtling down the aisle next to me, throwing bottles of red wine around which smashed on the floor.

This was obviously unnerving for everyone on board, with two flight attendants leaving their seats during take-off to secure the potentially deadly random trolley. Thankfully, no one was injured, and we continued without any further hitches, but how the hell did this happen? It almost seems impossible. But it did. Someone had obviously made a major cock-up before take-off.

However, this cock-up was almost a wonderful act of fate.

My flight was first stopping in Mumbai, so the plane was full of Indians. My good friend from work, Usman, had previously done this journey to Mumbai a number of times, and he'd warned me that when I was boarding the plane, there would be dozens of pathetic, able-bodied men in wheelchairs, all being pushed by their wives. They apparently do this to get to the front of the queue.

He was right too. Before I could board, I first had to fight my way through countless abandoned wheelchairs. It was ridiculous. They were everywhere. I couldn't quite work out why these pathetic men would do this, or why their wives wouldn't just tell them to fuck off. Why weren't the men at least pushing their poor oppressed wives?

After that heavy metal trolley had shot down my isle on the plane at speed, I pondered on the irony of it hitting one of those wheelchair-bound losers and crippling him for life. Maybe that would have swayed my opinion about there being an actual personal God looking over us. He didn't deliver on this occasion, so my logical mind remained unaltered – God does not exist.

I'd booked three nights in Singapore and three nights in Malaysia, but the rest of my trip was still totally unplanned. I thought I'd just take it day by day, though I had plans to visit Thailand.

While in Singapore, I became friendly with a couple from Newcastle – the place I used to work in England. Singapore is English-speaking, so funnily enough, these were the first people I'd met on my trip that I couldn't fucking understand.

I eventually grasped what they were saying, and it was rather important. They'd also planned to go to Malaysia and Thailand, but due to the threat of terror in both places, and after advice from their travel agent, they'd changed their plans. They were now travelling to Australia instead.

I had no idea about these terror warnings, but even after hearing the advice I still decided to stick to my original decision. I wasn't going to let some terrorist wankers dictate my plans. In any case, if I went somewhere else instead, I'd probably get knocked down by a fucking bus or something.

After surviving three days of basically just getting pissed in Singapore, I flew to Langkawi, a lovely, quiet Malaysian island. I stayed at a wonderful, peaceful hotel on the beach called Barjaya Beach Resort, spending my days lying in the sun and relaxing. I was using my time here to recover from the Singapore overindulgence and plan my next move. I didn't actually have any clue how I was going to travel from here though, or where I was going. That's what made it all the more exciting, albeit a bit of a ball-ache and quite scary.

On my second night here, when I was having a quiet drink on my own in the almost-deserted bar, I was asked by two mature English gentlemen whether I'd like to join them at their table. They were from Norwich, and I sat with them for a while, but soon became a bit uncomfortable in their presence. I nipped to the toilet to gather my thoughts, then returned and had a sip of my drink, and I soon started to feel different: I felt drunk immediately and things became a touch blurry.

I'd only had a couple of beers before this, so I assumed they'd slipped something into my drink. With both men being quite obviously gay – and that overpowering gayness now standing out much more than before – my blurred mind assumed there was only one reason for what they'd done – they wanted to take turns in bum-raping me.

Writing that line has just sent a big fucking shiver up my spine by the way, and then for some reason I also clenched my arse muscles.

When the drug hit me, I suddenly started to remember strange and quite forward questions I'd been asked by this couple of old pricks, such as, "What number is your cabin? Do you like sleeping alone?" There were more things that they just seemed to be saying about me to each other and then laughing about between themselves.

The moment I felt slightly dizzy, I didn't touch another drop of my drink. I quickly made my excuses and exited the bar in a shot, managing to get a lift to my secluded cabin in the forest by one of the hotel porters. I immediately locked and barricaded my door, and then used my camcorder to record everything I said. This moment then became the start of a wonderful video diary I kept for my whole trip. The footage from that night wasn't wonderful, though. I was visibly shocked. I was even talking about going looking for the pair of them and "torching the fuckers' cabin". That's the state I was in. Maybe that was the drug talking. Maybe it was the fucking anger.

This is the worrying part of travelling alone in today's world, because things like this can happen to anyone, and when it happens there is generally nothing you can do about it. I think I was just lucky that what they slipped into my drink only affected me a little, so I was still able to do something about it and get the hell away.

I didn't see those two men the next day. I think they'd left the resort. I didn't even consider reporting them to the police. Was this because I doubted myself? Did I feel embarrassed or even stupid at what happened? I have no idea, but the thought of reporting them never actually crossed my mind. What proof was there anyway?

The thing about this night is that I would always have denied it, or tried to completely forget about it, but for keeping the video diary.

Now I know why many people don't come forward in situations when they've been drugged, and even abused, because there can be an element of it in which you feel daft, or even that you must be partly responsible. If you've been drinking too, it's so difficult to be 100 per cent sure that everything happened as you initially thought.

Even after watching the video from that night, in which I was visibly upset and groggy, I still have about 5 per cent doubt that those two men actually drugged me at all. It's hard to explain. I know it happened, but I would have struggled to stand up in court and say it happened.

This night frightened me quite a bit, and being right at the start of my holiday I did wonder about the dangers of travelling alone and what else might be in store for me over the next weeks and months. I had to block it out, though. I had to keep trusting people; otherwise I'd just end up spending all my time alone, and what would be the fun in that? Not much fun at all, though I suppose it would be more fun than being dry-bummed by two old wankers from Norwich.

Phuk Off

From Langkawi, I decided to catch a ferry to Satun, Thailand. This journey didn't turn out quite as scenic as I'd thought. I'd pictured myself lying on the top deck of a large, shiny white boat in the sun, waving goodbye to the mountains of Langkawi in the distance, but in reality I was stuck inside a small shitty old ferry with a load of peasants and dirty travellers, while cockroaches crawled around my flip-flops. It also stank of piss. It was disgusting.

In Thailand, I stayed one night in a weird dirty town called Hat-Yai. I read that Snake Street was a popular place to visit here, where drinking snake blood is the thing to do. Apparently, the snake is hung on a hook before being slit from top to bottom to drain the refreshment from its unfortunate slithery self. I decided not to explore this rather bizarre and inhuman pastime. Instead, I chose to have a pizza, a beer, and a quiet night, and the next day decided to move north by bus to a place called Ao Nang Beach, Krabi.

I had a really nice few days here, but on my final day I happened to lose most of my clothes – and all of my underwear. Because I'm a dick, I couldn't quite find the place I'd taken my dirty laundry to. The owners had told me they'd send the clothes directly to my hotel, and in the unbearably hot and sticky confusion, I hadn't taken much notice of the place at the time. I had no reason to. I had my receipt, and that's all I required, though I'd failed to notice this was just a fucking raffle ticket without the shop's name on it.

Everything looked the same to me, and because I was on the last minute – having to catch a boat to Koh Phi Phi Island – I decided to leave all my things behind and go commando for the next two months. Every other traveller I met in Thailand was a dirty bastard anyway, so I figured this might even help me fit in – not that it bothered me that I didn't fit in. I was happy on my own, being myself, away from the many pricks I'd already observed around me.

The laundry loss happened the day after my mobile phone had stopped working, so little things had started to go wrong early in my trip. With these unfortunate incidents coming just after I'd avoided being bummed by Norwich, and I'd been away less than two weeks, I was obviously thinking the worst about the rest of my holiday. Then, I had a nightmare time on Koh Phi Phi Island, where I was very sick for three days, before a visit to Phuket really put me off Thailand altogether. I was constantly being pestered here by all the local slags and dickheads; everything and everyone annoyed me.

I'd actually paid for one whole week in Phuket, but before the full week was up, I decided to leave Thailand altogether. I needed to find a nice quiet place for a while; somewhere I could relax, gather my thoughts, and ponder my next move. I therefore booked a flight from Phuket to Bali, where I'd spend one week relaxing at the Hard Rock Hotel in Kuta – the place I'd stayed with Karen in 2001.

This spur-of-the-moment decision to go to Bali, and especially to go to that same hotel, was to change my life forever.

Koh Phi Phi – Lucky Escape Seven

While in Thailand, I spent three days on beautiful Koh Phi Phi Island. However, I didn't take many fond memories away with me.

I was staying alone in a basic hut just a few metres back from the beach. This all sounds like it looked in the brochure - amazing - and at another time in my life, it might well have been wonderful, but it was absolutely roasting in this hut, and while I was there I just happened to be very ill.

Before travelling to Koh Phi Phi by boat, on my final night in Ao Nang, I remember being in a reggae bar, drinking the local Chang Beer, when I noticed something written on the wall in chalk.

It read, "If you think the bottom is falling out of your world, drink Chang Beer, then you'll think the world is falling out of your bottom."

The following night on Koh Phi Phi island, I knew exactly what this meant. I had really bad stomach pains all night, and I was up and down to the bathroom for hours on end. During this time, the unthinkable happened: the toilet stopped fucking working, so you can just imagine the mess building up in there.

Then, I started to be sick too. Every time I'd get up to be sick, I had to go and throw up in the same toilet in the same bathroom, which, having not been flushed for hours, and being on the edge of a jungle, was attracting all the creatures of the night – of which there were thousands. I had to stick my head down that toilet over and over again, each time adding to the existing mess while all the ants, flies, cockroaches, and whatever else there was all fed on that same sick, piss, and shit which had been there for hours.

As you can envisage, it was hell, and it was the moment I decided that huts on beaches were definitely not for me, vowing to stay in hotels with minibars for the rest of my trip. I just wanted to get off this godforsaken island as soon as possible and never return.

On my final day, just one hour before leaving for Phuket, I had a stroll along the beach. I ended up climbing over some rocks which went further out to sea, finding a secluded place away from everyone. I sat there in silence for a while, admiring the beauty right before my eyes.

I was then surprised to notice a young girl appear behind me. She smiled and started to chat, telling me that she lived just behind the rocks where we were sitting. She was so friendly, and she brought the first smile to my face for a few days.

Then she did something amazing. She invited me to her house for tea. I was quite shocked by this because I felt it was such a nice thing to do. I mean, I was a total stranger. However, I had to decline her kind offer because my boat was leaving shortly.

If I did have the choice, though, I don't know if I would have accepted her invitation. I'd obviously think twice about going anywhere with a complete stranger, but why would I have my reservations about going to the house of a young girl who seemed so genuine and kind? Shouldn't it be the other way around? Shouldn't she be wary of the odd-looking foreign man thirty years her senior?

I always try to trust people because the world is a horrible place to be if you can't trust, but isn't it a sad reflection of the world we live in that this meeting, which first filled me with such warmth, later led me to become suspicious of a little girl who probably just wanted to make a new friend?

Soon after this brief encounter, we said goodbye and went our own way, myself completely unaware that I would be in Bali in five days' time, changing my life forever.

In 2004, the year after my stay on Koh Phi Phi Island, the Indian Ocean earthquake and tsunami changed many more lives. Approximately half of the ten thousand people on Koh Phi Phi island were killed. I was at my mum and dad's house that Boxing Day, and when I heard the news, my heart sank. I'd obviously had yet another lucky escape.

My heart sunk even further, though, when I thought about that little girl.

I didn't really make any friends on Koh Phi Phi, mainly through being ill the whole time I was there, so this little girl was the only person I can really remember talking to. With her saying her home was just behind the rocks, it seemed as though she literally lived on the coast - the same coast that felt the full impact of the tsunami.

I will never know what happened to that little girl, but what I do know, is, if I'm not having a minor disaster of my own, then a major disaster is usually not far behind me.

Another Slapper (Tart, Whore, Slag)

The Hard Rock Hotel, Bali – the island of gods – was a lovely place, but the seaside resort of Kuta itself was not so special. When I walked outside I was continually being asked if I wanted a woman or if I wanted drugs, and all this mither was the sole reason I'd escaped Thailand and travelled all the way here in the first place. I'd just wanted some peace and fucking quiet.

One evening in Kuta, I was even asked if I wanted an injection; an injection of what I don't know. I didn't ask.

Then, after turning down these offers one hundred times and more, I was actually asked, "You want boy?"

I think this last one was said in jest, because it was the same bloke who was sick to death of me rejecting him and his ladies daily, and he was laughing when he said it. However, it doesn't bear thinking about what would happen if some freak actually said yes to this question.

I decided that I couldn't be arsed with all this nonsense again. I just wanted to be left alone in peace. I therefore made the decision to stay around the hotel complex for my remaining few days in Bali. This hotel had a great live music bar, a nightclub, and a wonderful swimming pool with waiter service. I didn't need anything else at the time. It was just what the doctor ordered after putting up with the constant ear-pecking of the street sellers and loose slags.

With three nights remaining in Bali, I ventured down to the nightclub for the first time, where I met a beautiful lady from Java. There I was, thinking I'd been lucky to meet her, but then, just like the dozens of other women I'd already met on my travels, she gave me one of her business cards.

She tried to persuade me to go to my room for a "drink", and there I was in that position again – another slapper masquerading as a non-slapper had entered my life. In fact, she wasn't masquerading at all. She was just being a very obvious slapper. It's just that I'm a bit slow sometimes. Actually, I'm always a bit slow when it comes to women.

She told me that I should call her to arrange a date, and I did actually ponder on this all night because she was absolutely stunning, but I stuck to my principles and refrained.

Late the following night, I returned to the same club. I'd had a bit of a crappy day and not really spoken to anyone, so I was overjoyed to see the same beautiful girl from Java standing out from the rest. At that moment I cracked, and I thought, "Sod it! I'm just going to take her back to my room and get it over with."

I sloped over to where she was, semi-confidently moving my way through the rowdy group surrounding her, and proceeded to tempt her back to my room – with nothing more than dirty cash, obviously. However, to my shock at the time, and now to my utmost pleasure and amusement, she apologised, saying that she couldn't join me on this particular evening because she already had a 'partner'. She enquired as to why I hadn't called her earlier, and then glanced over to a fat, hairy, greasy, Mexican-looking character in the corner. This was her bloke for today, and he was a right fucking sight.

For a second, I was slightly embarrassed, but as I sheepishly exited the club alone, a smile began to form on my face. I felt relief, and then started to laugh. I felt as though I'd had another lucky escape because seeing her with that bloke brought it home to me what she was. When I saw her alone, she looked just like any lovely girl, but when I saw her with dirty Pedro, I started to wonder how many more of these greasy blokes had gone before over the years, and I really didn't want to go next.

I quickly decided to go back to the hotel bar. I had nowhere else to fucking go.

I sat at the bar alone for a while, as usual, when out of the blue two German men invited me over to have a drink. Now then, you will remember that I'd recently been invited to join two English pricks for a drink in Langkawi, and that had ended quite badly. It was a scary experience, and being just a few weeks later, you might think I would be a bit wary of joining two more strange men in a quiet bar. However, that thought didn't cross my mind. I'd completely blocked it out and moved on. I also felt that these two Germans had a genuine look about them, and anyway you can't stop trusting everyone just because you meet the odd couple of twats in your life.

Thorsten and Alexander were really good blokes. I could just tell. They could hardly speak a word of English, but they drank beer and laughed a lot, and that's all that mattered to me.

At the next table were two Chinese-looking girls, and after a while Thorsten also invited them to join us. I'd previously spotted them and thought they were just another couple of local prostitutes, now taking the approach that every female I met on my trip was a tart until I was proved otherwise. However, it turned out they were both just on holiday from Taiwan, and I was wrong again. One was called Aline, and the other was called Ling.

We then enjoyed a really amazing few hours together. It was one of those nights you look back on and wonder how these five individual souls travelling alone all came together in a certain place at a particular moment in time, altering the path that their lives were about to follow. It was special.

When the bar closed, I even nipped back to my room to empty the fridge of all the alcohol so that we could carry on the party at the pool. None of us wanted it to end. Before the night eventually did end – in the middle of the morning – we all promised to meet up for breakfast. Ling and Aline were leaving to go to a different hotel before lunchtime so it would be our only chance to meet up again.

Not surprisingly, I overslept and didn't make breakfast. This is because I'm an idiot. I later returned to look for them by the pool, but unfortunately, they were nowhere to be seen. I was so annoyed at myself at the time because I had no contact details for any of them and I really wanted to keep in touch. I lay down in the burning sun for a bit, but I was so rough from the night before that I decided to go back to my room to cool down, knowing this meant I'd probably never see my new friends ever again.

Now then, there were two ways to get back to my room, both using the same corridor which went in a complete circle. If I turned left, this would take me by the reception, while turning right would take me straight to my room, and that was the much quicker route. I initially turned right because it was the obvious choice, but then, for some unknown reason, I decided to stop to look at a picture on the wall. I paused for a moment, and when I finished looking at the picture, I turned back on myself and walked the other way. I have no idea why.

When I arrived at reception, to my pleasant surprise, Thorsten, Aline, and Ling were all sitting there waiting for a taxi. Alexander had already left.

Before I go on, I will be honest. My "pleasant surprise" was half pleasant, and half "Oh fuck, why have I come this way?" I was so rough that I really just wanted my comfortable cool king-sized bed at the time.

Ling, who was being paid by the Taiwanese newspaper *Apple Daily* to write about her experience in Bali, had already invited Thorsten and Aline to her next hotel, which was in some other – nicer – part of the island. She then invited me too, and within minutes we were all in a car on route to a mystery hotel. I didn't even know where we were going. Even today I have no idea where that hotel was. How lucky I had been to see them again, though. Their taxi had pulled up outside just as I was walking towards them. If I had been seconds later I would have missed them forever.

That second day with them was very surreal. We stayed in a beautiful hotel on the coast, miles away from anywhere and with hardly any guests apart from the four of us. How we all ended up there together I'll never know. The events that had occurred in my life, not just the previous night at the nightclub and hotel, or that morning in the corridor, but the things that had occurred in the past weeks, months, and even years, for me to be there with them at this particular moment in time were too strange.

We shared another quite bizarre but perfect night, somehow managing to communicate with each other.

In addition to their native tongues, Ling spoke very good English and French, Thorsten spoke a little English and French, Aline spoke a little English and German, and me, well, I am English, so I just spoke English. We, therefore, sat by the sea until the early hours, chatting a mixture of English, German, Chinese, French, and shite, while watching the stars in the unblemished, glamorous night sky, before the rain suddenly came down and pissed us all wet through.

We all then slept in the same room. Thorsten and I had a small sofa each, for which we'd both given up the comfort of a king-sized bed at the Hard Rock Hotel. Neither of us regretted that decision in the slightest. It was perfect.

The next morning, we said our goodbyes, and I promised to email Ling because she'd said she'd be happy to show me around Taiwan if I ever visited.

Taiwan? That really didn't cross my mind at the time. I didn't even know where the place was.

Starry Night

Starry, starry night
That night we met on holiday
Our troubles seemed to fade away
The island gods were smiling on our souls
The sunset on the sea
So beautiful for you and me
And soon again there we will be
Side by side holding one another's hand

Was hard to understand
What you tried to say to me
My English versus your Chinese
Not the best match there can be
I listened, and I heard somehow
And just look where we are now

Starry, starry night
When we look back it's all a daze
Gods mystify me with their ways
And how on earth did I come to meet you?
So what did I do?
To deserve to meet my one true flame
To have the sun replace the rain
And have this special person in my arms

Was hard to understand
What you tried to say to me
My English versus your Chinese
Not the best match there can be
I listened, and I heard somehow
And just look where we are now

And though I did not know you
And that our love would soon come true
Something touched me deep inside
On that starry, starry night
And it stayed with me the day I left you

It didn't take us long before we realised
Our love would be so wonderful and true

Starry, starry night
That night the rain began to fall
So hard it soaked us one and all
Brought to an end a night I can't forget
There we were all so wet
So desperate for a change of clothes
And in the morn when I arose
I saw your smile and didn't want to leave

Now I want to know
All you have to say to me
And one day I will, you will see
And you too will understand me
I will work so hard for you, I will
And I just know
Soon our dreams will be fulfilled

The Bali Bombs – Lucky Escapes Eight & Nine

I chose to return to Bali in 2003 due to what had happened there the previous year.

In 2002, the main drinking haunts of the town Kuta - Paddy's Bar and the Sari Club - were both destroyed by terrorist bombs. I'd been in Kuta with Karen just before it had its heart ripped out, and we'd visited both of these bars seven nights running.

I felt the need to go back and have a look at what had happened, and maybe say a prayer - to who I don't know. Kuta wasn't the most beautiful place I'd ever been to, and I probably wouldn't have ever returned if it wasn't for those bombs. I was just tempted back there for some reason.

During this second visit to Bali, before meeting Ling, I walked out into the town and enjoyed a lovely meal and a few beers at a restaurant in Kuta Square called Raja's, a place I hadn't visited previously. Shockingly, in 2005, Raja's restaurant is where the bomb was placed in the next terrorist attack to hit Bali.

To this day, I'm sure there have only been two terrorist attacks on Bali, and I was lucky to avoid them both. Can you see a terrible pattern appearing here?

Paddy's Bar, Kuta, Bali. Seven nights running, Karen and I sat at the bar on the right.

Taiwan?

On that blurry, starry night, Ling had told me that Taiwan was "an amazing place". In the years to follow, I was to learn that Taiwanese people tend to say that almost everything in their country is "amazing", and to be fair they are right about many things. Taiwan is a wonderful country, but the people can sometimes get overexcited about the most basic of things, and they often over-exaggerate.

While in Bali – before meeting Ling and the others – I'd already decided that I was going to extend my holiday past the original six weeks. Realising I wasn't too far from Australia, I'd thought that returning there was too great an opportunity to miss, so I booked a flight to Brisbane, and put my return flight to Manchester back a couple of months. I also told Ling that from there I might try to visit Taiwan, though in the back of my mind there wasn't really any thought I would do so because that would just be ridiculous; though the seed had been planted.

After two wonderful weeks travelling up Australia's Gold Coast, and with two more weeks remaining, I decided to ask Ling about the mad possibility of visiting her in Taiwan. There was something about her that I couldn't get out of my mind. She didn't seem like your typical girl and I just had to see her again.

However, my many attempts to contact her were all fruitless. Seven days and six emails later, I'd had no response. Devastated, I gave up.

Then, I suddenly remembered I also had the email address of Ling's friend, Aline. They'd only themselves met at the airport in Bali, and they didn't live near each other in Taiwan, but I knew this was my only hope to contact Ling. I emailed Aline to ask if she could try to contact Ling for me, and amazingly, the following day, I received an email from Ling. God only knows what the problem was, but she hadn't received any of my emails, and yet another act of fate had almost ruined everything.

Surprisingly, she seemed really keen for me to visit. There hadn't been any romance between us in Bali at all, but there was definitely a mutual feeling that we should see each other again. However, quite typically, at this particular time, the deadly SARS virus had just broken out in China and Hong Kong, and there was also a real threat to Taiwan, so Ling was a little wary of me going. I was a bit more than a little wary. I still didn't even know where the place was. Nevertheless, I nervously booked a flight from Sidney to Taipei, where I would be spending two weeks at Ling's home. This did seem more than a little crazy. I didn't really know who this foreign girl was at all.

By this point I'd been away on my travels for two months, and I'd probably been drunk – or at least tipsy – on all but just three days. However, I was now hopefully going to change this unhealthy nonsense for two weeks of green tea, fresh fruit, fresh fish, and colourful vegetables. This was much needed.

I was so keen to make an impression in Taiwan, that I even bought a book about the place to try to understand some of the customs and culture. My thinking was that I would turn up with all this knowledge and blow everyone away with what I knew about their country. However, there was only one small thing that stood out from reading the book.

It mentioned a national custom involving a group of men in a room, all bonding while drinking copious amounts of alcohol together over a number of hours. The text finished by saying something like, "When the time is up, if a man is able to walk out of the room unaided, then he is either a liar and a cheat, or a man with the capacity of an ocean".

I thought, "For fuck sake, here we go again."

Nob-Head

Before I get to Taiwan, I need to mention Australia, or more importantly, my mate Jamie.

From Bali, I flew to Brisbane, and the day I landed I found a travel agent to sort out my next couple of weeks travel up the Gold Coast. My first stop on this journey, Hervey Bay, was just a few hours away. I was booked on a two-night trip to Fraser Island nearby, better known to many as "Death Island" due to it being full of deadly creatures.

On this trip, I became quite friendly with Jamie, his girlfriend Zoe, and their two friends Laura and Jane, all of whom lived quite near to me in England. Jamie had been travelling with the three girls for months already, so he was glad to have a male friend to escape them for a bit, and over the next couple of days we shared some funny times. Then we went our own ways, thinking that would be it.

Two days later, after a fourteen-hour journey, I arrived in Airlie Beach around 9 a.m. As I was getting off the bus, I noticed four people across the road having a stroll. Quite unbelievably, it was Jamie and the girls. I shouted over to them, and they responded, saying that they were going on a yacht for a few days – something I was also doing the following day. As they were going on their boat trip in a couple of hours, we didn't think we'd get chance to meet up again so we left it there and said our goodbyes again.

I smiled at the coincidence of meeting them again, the minute I arrived in Airlie Beach after a journey of over fourteen hours. I had no idea they were even going to Airlie Beach.

The next day, I prepared for my three-day trip on the yacht. I was told to take my own booze, and while on the yacht I could get involved in as little or as much work as possible. It sounded perfect, so I thought I'd just relax for a few days, as if I hadn't done enough relaxing and drinking over the past couple of months.

It was beautiful on the yacht, in the middle of nowhere, with the stunning scenery, and the sun and wind on my skin. It was such a lovely experience. We'd dock at a small island, do some snorkelling, and then set sail to find a place for the night. There, still on the yacht, we'd have a bit of a party and then sleep there before waking up at dawn with the sun rising over the vast ocean, the yacht gently bobbing up and down on the water. It was wonderful.

The second day, a bit hungover again, we'd been sailing for hours with no land in sight. We hadn't seen one soul since embarking on our trip almost two days earlier, so I was quite surprised to see another yacht coming up behind us. This was a smaller yacht, looking like there were just half a dozen people on board.

I spotted three girls sitting with their legs hanging over the side. I was again shocked to see that it was Zoe, Jane, and Laura, so my eyes wandered to a figure sunbathing on top deck that looked like Jamie. For some reason I then decided to shout, "Oi! Nob-head!"

He immediately popped his head up and looked over to me across the calm water, almost as though he was quite practiced in responding to the name "Nob-head".

Realising it was me, he shook his head and gave a wry smile that seemed to say, "I don't fucking believe it."

So we had met again. This might not sound like too much of a coincidence, but considering the sheer scale of the place, the fact that they left on their yacht the day before I did, and the lack of absolutely anything around for miles, it certainly was a massive coincidence, and it didn't end there.

After leaving Airlie Beach, I travelled over ten hours to Port Douglas. I'd booked a couple of nights in a secluded hotel overlooking the sea, and after unpacking I had a stroll along the beach. There was nothing but coastline to my left, and there was nothing but coastline to my right. I decided to go left.

I walked in the blazing sun for over one hour before coming to the end of the beach. As I was shagged, I thought about turning back, but I then decided to turn left and walk up the only road at the end of the beach. I'd hardly seen anyone again since I'd been walking, but I suddenly saw life. There were four people cycling towards me down the hill. They had helmets on, so I didn't realise at first, but, yes, quite unbelievably, it was those four idiots yet again. We were obviously meant to be in each other's lives, so from this moment we saw a lot of each other over the following week – especially me and Jamie.

I did play golf on my own one day, though, just to get away from the prick for a bit. When we were together, it was always carnage at the end of the night, and I needed a rest. However, the day before this, Jamie had wanted a break from me, but fate made sure he didn't get one. I'd texted him to ask what he was up to, but a couple of hours later, I'd still had no reply. I was then walking out of a shop in Port Douglas when I bumped into Jamie again, and he told me that he had just nipped out to buy food for the girls. It was around lunchtime.

He then said that he hadn't received my text message, which I had no reason to doubt. I happened to mention that I'd heard of a little bar called *On the Inlet*, which I was going to try to find, so rather than buy food right then, he accompanied me to find the bar first. I'd had no intention of having a drink until the evening – I'd just wanted to find the place for later – but we then somehow ended up sharing seven bottles of white wine and two buckets of fucking prawns. Quite late in the evening, he reluctantly owned up that he'd lied to me earlier. He received my text message after all. He just really wanted a night off from me because he couldn't be arsed getting in a state again. I fully understood this.

However, on that unplanned day when we were sitting there sipping wine, chatting, and laughing for hours on end, overlooking the inlet into Port Douglas, a bloke playing guitar and singing live behind us, and the sun setting before us was probably the most memorable day for us both of the whole trip. Well, it was for me. Jamie had something else that might have topped it. It was though, one of those days that you think you don't want, and you even try to avoid by lying, but it ends up being the time of your life. It was a day we both made a really good mate.

The four of them were next going to Ayers Rock, where Jamie was proposing to Zoe, and then they were off to Sydney, where he was buying her an engagement ring from Tiffany's. I was kindly invited along to Sydney, so I joined them for an extremely special week before leaving on my mystery trip to Taiwan.

A number of years later, I ended up going to Jamie's wedding. However, he married a different girl than the one he'd proposed to on Ayers Rock. You'd probably think I was making all this up if he'd married the same girl.

Lost in Translation

On the way to Taiwan, I first had to stop in Bangkok to change flights, and it was there that the seriousness of the SARS situation first hit me. Almost everyone at the airport wore a mask, and there were many other controls in place where they were checking each passenger's body temperature to see if they had a fever. If you had any signs of SARS at all, then, quite worryingly, you would be prevented from flying and placed in quarantine for the foreseeable future.

Then, on the flight to Taipei, which was eerily quiet, we were all made to wear a mask for everyone's protection, though I'm not quite sure what this mask did apart from give me a sore throat. It was all quite farcical really, because when I was being asked what meal I wanted, I had to take my mask away from my mouth to speak, and then when the food arrived, well, what were we supposed to do?

I eventually arrived at Chiang Kai-shek Airport – renamed Taoyuan Airport in 2006 for political reasons – feeling excited, and maybe a little scared. Let's be honest; it was pretty crazy, flying to Taipei to meet a Taiwanese girl I hardly knew.

I waited anxiously at Terminal One where Ling was supposed to be waiting for me, but she didn't appear to be around. As my phone didn't work in Taiwan, I couldn't even call her to find out where she was or whether she was actually coming to meet me at all.

At least SARS hadn't hit Taiwan yet apparently and not everyone was wearing a mask. I therefore decided to take mine off because they really are uncomfortable things to wear. I waited and waited, thinking up all sorts of possible, terrible outcomes, and wondering what on earth I would do if she never appeared. This place was as foreign as it gets for me, and I started to feel quite uncomfortable after a while.

I'd had almost two hours of waiting around worrying when I was really starting to panic, but I was suddenly relieved to hear a female voice with a slight American twang shout, "Maatt! Maatt!"

When foreigners learn English they generally speak it with the same accent as their teacher. Ling's teacher had obviously been American, like the vast majority of English teachers in Taiwan, but her accent only sounded slightly American. It was a beautiful mix; very clear, very commanding, but also very soft and peaceful, until she shouted, that is.

I couldn't see her. I heard it again, "Maatt! Maatt!"

There she was walking towards me with that beautiful friendly smile of hers. We hugged like the strangers we really were, but I soon felt comfortable and relaxed in her presence. It wasn't just her smile, but her calming nature that seemed to relax me. After only a few minutes in her company I no longer felt worried. I felt at peace. I felt happy.

You'll never guess where she'd been all along: terminal fucking two. This was a sign of things to come. I remember thinking, "If we get confused between the number one and the number two then what fucking hope is there?"

Ling then drove the ninety-minute journey to her home in the mountains while my eyes jumped from one place to another, trying to adjust to my new strange, fast-moving surroundings. There were a few more cars and bikes on the roads than I was used to, and there also didn't seem to be any rules. Why does it always seem like this in foreign countries? Is it only us English that actually follow a highway code? Or does every foreigner also feel the same about driving in a different country?

We finally arrived at Ling's home in one piece. It was quite a way outside the city, up in the "mountains", and was quaint with beautiful views. It was lovely and unexpected. I was so excited. I was actually in Taipei with my new friend. How? Just how had this happened? Only weeks earlier I'd been at work in Lytham feeling sorry for myself, dreaming and hoping for something good to happen.

Things again started to flash through my mind; the many random events occurring over recent weeks and months to bring me to this foreign place with this foreign person on this particular day. Sometimes it's just fate, and however it came about, fate is what led to the next truly wonderful, interesting, and most amazing part of my life.

Jon Bon Who?

I was a little nervous and overwhelmed when I first arrived in Taipei, but I was so well looked after that I really needn't have worried. In the following two weeks I had dinner with so many of Ling's friends, and was even invited into many of their homes. I was also personally guided around the city's many wonderful sites, and I really was treated like a king. They were all so welcoming and so interested in me.

One evening, we had dinner at Mr. and Mrs. Du's home. They'd been Ling's friends for many years, almost like another mother and father to her. They lived on the next to top floor of an apartment block in the city centre. They had this whole floor to themselves. Amazingly, the complete top floor of this building was a music recording studio, and it was owned by Mr. Du. It appeared that he was a very rich man, and his son managed the recording studio which apparently had many famous visitors over the years.

While we were having dinner, Mrs. Du, who was in and out of the kitchen all night, came over to the dining table with some dumplings, and then started to say something in her mother tongue which obviously meant nothing to me. However, somewhere in the middle of her sentence I picked out the words, "Bon Jovi".

It just so happened that the last foreign person invited into their home for dinner, who had actually been sitting in the same seat as me, was none other than Jon Bon Jovi. I couldn't help but feel like I'd let them down slightly. I mean, one week, Bon Jovi; next week, Matt from Bolton.

The night became even more interesting when Mr. Du started to show me his collection of laserdiscs. Yes, laserdiscs, remember those? If you don't know, a laserdisc looked like an overgrown CD, or like a silver version of a twelve-inch vinyl record. These things existed before DVDs, and they could store thirty minutes of video and sound on either side. They were more popular in Japan than anywhere else, and I'd never seen one in my life until this evening, apart from on *Tomorrow's World* on BBC1 in the early 1980s.

Mr. Du looked like a child on Christmas Day when he was showing me his collection, and so did I, if I'm honest, though I never even began to wonder what was actually on the discs. He played the first disc, which was a karaoke video, and they all started to laugh in tandem. Meanwhile, Ling looked a little sheepish. This was because Ling just happened to be the beautiful young star in the film.

Mr. Du then proceeded to show me many other films. In fact, I think he had the whole remaining catalogue of fucking laserdiscs on the planet. All these videos starred Ling in her prime, dancing around, looking beautiful, and doing a bit of kung fu here and a bit of tai chi there. They were all singalong karaoke – or KTV – videos, and the three of them were all singing along at one point – just imagine my face – until Ling gasped at the sight of one particular scene.

This scene was filmed in a special room at a museum in Taipei, and it showed Ling with a Japanese sword, doing some other martial art along with a handsome Japanese chap. By an amazing coincidence, Ling had taken me into that same room just a few hours earlier. It had been the first time she'd returned there since filming this scene almost twenty years previous. She had no idea that Mr. Du even had this film. These videos were filmed so many years earlier that she hadn't seen them for years, and for Mr. Du to have them all on laserdisc was a bit of a shock for her.

But the fact that we were shown this film, just after we'd been in the room it was filmed all those years ago, was an amazing coincidence. Mr. and Mrs. Du were quite visibly shocked when Ling mentioned it, and I was also surprised to hear each of them utter the words, "Oh my god!" in the midst of all the Mandarin they were speaking. Are the English words "oh my god" actually used in the Chinese language to express surprise? That was even more bizarre.

It turned out to be an extra-special evening with some extra-special people. They were all so welcoming to this complete stranger from the other side of the world, and this day really summed up the whole two weeks I spent there. I was made to feel so special during my time in Taipei. It was as if I was the first foreigner many of them had ever seen, and it was amazing how well they looked after me. I didn't want to leave.

Who Really Was Ling? – Part One

From day one, I knew there was something special about Ling, but having only known her for less than two days before travelling to Taiwan, I had no idea what I was getting myself into.

One day in Taipei, Ling took me to see some special sights, even climbing a mountain full of snakes with her friend Mr. Du and his daughter – I can't remember her name so let's call her Miss Du. After this we had lunch – on Tofu Street, of all places. I'd never eaten tofu before, and I'd never really fancied trying it either. Here, I had no fucking choice, and maybe if I hadn't started my tofu experience with the Taiwanese specialty that is "stinky tofu" then tofu and I might have had a different story to tell. It stinks like bad eggs and vomit, and it tastes like it smells.

Something then happened to get me thinking there was even more to Ling.

While I was still crying into my bowl of stinky tofu, Ling asked the owner of the restaurant for the bill, but he refused to take money from her. Our meal had been "on the house". Later that evening we enjoyed dinner at another restaurant where we ate real food, and exactly the same thing happened again. Why was this?

Ling was a tap dancer. She owned her own small tap dance school, and she lived for dance. In my first two weeks with her, we went for dinner several times with some of her students, and there was more to this than met the eye. She taught many different classes, with students at varying levels of ability, but her late Saturday class was different. This class contained a complete mixture of abilities, and it was basically just a collection of her favourite students, or rather, the people she liked to go to dinner and have drinks with on Saturday evenings. She wasn't daft.

While in Bali, Ling's friend Aline had also mentioned a particular song she was amazed to learn was written by Ling. I remembered Aline had gasped when she'd heard this, uttering that popular Chinese phrase, "Oh my god! *Every* Taiwanese know this song." It turned out that Ling had written many songs, even having several number ones in Taiwan, and she'd written many more hits and album songs for some top artists.

Ling was working part-time for Sony when I met her, and one of her jobs – which she didn't really like due to the pressure – was rewriting the words in songs for a number of artists. She didn't like this job because there was always a twenty-four to forty-eight-hour deadline, and no artist wants to work like this. This is the job that she would later give up for me – not that I wanted her to. She just wanted a simple life, and though this job sounded like a dream to me, it had obviously drained her over the years.

She was now in her mid-thirties, a little over a year older than me, and after half a decade of writing under pressure, she just wanted to dance, paint, and maybe write a bit, but write what she wanted to write – for the pleasure of it.

Her love for music and dance were evident the night before I left Taipei for the first time. Ling and her students treated me to a night at KTV – Karaoke TV – drinking beer and singing Chinese/Taiwanese songs that I obviously didn't know. Therefore, I just drank, until one of them put on the classic "Leaving on a Jet Plane", for me to sing. Unfortunately, the battery died on my camcorder so the world will never experience this special moment in history.

Ling's students mainly kept choosing songs written by her. She was even in many of the pop videos, similar to the one's I'd seen at Mr. and Mrs. Du's but more recent. She was obviously well known, but after my first two weeks with her in Taiwan, I still felt as though I was left with more questions than answers.

Severe Acute Respiratory Syndrome (SARS) – Lucky Escape Ten

This was probably not much of a lucky escape, but more of a bloody stupid situation for me to get myself into. However, I think this is a good opportunity to discuss the China-Taiwan relationship and how the bullying buffoons that are China could have prevented many more cases – and even deaths – by SARS in Taiwan.

China's ridiculous policy even put me in danger - as if I really needed any outside assistance in getting myself into these perilous positions. However, without China's mishandling of the SARS situation in Taiwan, I might never have actually gone there to visit Ling. In fact, I suppose you could say that their mishandling of the SARS crisis played a part in me and Ling getting together, because if it had been handled properly, it may well have driven us apart before we'd even got going.

Over eight thousand people eventually died from the sudden outbreak of SARS, and many of these cases were before I visited Taiwan. However, there hadn't been one case reported in Taiwan when I entered the country in 2003, although, after appearing in Southern China and Hong Kong, it was almost inevitable that SARS would eventually break out in Taiwan.

I just mentioned that there were no cases "reported" in Taiwan. However, there were definitely cases in Taiwan before I arrived, and they were known about, but due to China's hold on Taiwan, the world hadn't been made aware of these cases until much later than was necessary.

China sees Taiwan as part of its own territory, with Taiwan's official name being the Republic of China – named by China. Taiwan is therefore not recognised by the world as a country in its own right, and because of this, China doesn' t allow Taiwan to be registered with the World Health Organisation (WHO). Therefore, the WHO was not permitted entry into Taiwan to report on SARS, leaving the reporting up to China.

The breakout in Taiwan was kept quiet from the whole world for a while, and during this time, the disease continued to spread there while people travelled freely without taking the necessary precautions that were advised by the WHO in all infected areas.

Would I have even gone to Taiwan if I had known this? Being me, I probably would, but it' s possible that I wouldn' t have. It was a real problem in Taiwan the second week I was there. Everyone – including me – had to wear a mask over their mouth and nose when in public. If not, you were sent to prison.

There were also whole apartment blocks quarantined, with the buildings surrounded by soldiers making sure people couldn' t leave or enter. It was a frightening time because there was no known cure for this disease, and as it mutated faster than anything known previously, it made finding a vaccine for it extremely difficult.

When I was leaving Taiwan, I arrived at the airport to find it almost deserted due to the vast majority of international flights being cancelled, including my own. I had no idea about this until that moment, and it even looked like I might have to stay in Taiwan past my visa end date for a time, before they managed to find me a flight to Bangkok with some dodgy Chinese airline. This plane must have had a total of ten passengers on board, and I was even allowed to carry my luggage onto the plane and put it on the seats next to me. It was all a bit strange, as though all rules were dropped. It almost felt like the end of the world or something. Maybe that was just me though.

To this day, no further cases of SARS have been reported since 2004. However, you might be shocked to learn that there is still no known cure or vaccine for SARS.

That's fourteen years past and still no vaccine. Isn't that quite worrying? Just imagine what affect a similar, but more deadly and contagious virus could have on the world, especially when we have countries like China preventing the WHO from doing their vital work at the most critical stage of an outbreak, just to save face.

Flower Needs What?

Those two weeks in Taiwan, albeit a bit scary, were the most special of my life. I made so many friends, learnt so much, and I even fell in love. I felt frustrated at times due to not being able to eat what I wanted and because I couldn't understand the noise being shouted around me – and also because they wouldn't leave me alone for five fucking minutes – but memories were created that would live with me forever.

Also, the Mandarin Chinese language, although more than annoying to listen to at times, has something special about it. It is very artistic and beautiful.

On the day I left Taiwan, many people wished me a pleasant journey home using their mother tongue, uttering the phrase, "Yī lù shùn fēng" (一路順風). Translated word for word, this means, "One road, favourable wind." Beautiful, I'm sure you'll agree.

However, nothing explains the beauty of the language, or rather how well the Chinese and Taiwanese people use their words poetically, more than when Ling's good friend Suri had something to say to me. She assumed Ling and I were just friends, and she wanted us to be a couple, so Suri's special words to me in English before I departed Taipei were simply, "Matt. Flower needs water. You are the water."

Flower Needs Water

She craved for water
And how hard she tried
But the only drops came
From the tears that she cried
She searched far and wide
But the rivers were dry
And when the floods came
They flowed from her eyes

Just one drop would help
From the mountain spring
To help her buds blossom
To make her heart sing
But it just wouldn't come
For so many years
And so she continued
To pour out the tears

But in the distance
Water flowed her way
And she soon felt a kiss
Of the ocean spray
You could see her flower
From the day it arrived
And she thanked the world
For all those years she'd survived

It'd been worth the wait
And all of the pain
To finally feel
Those few droplets of rain
With each drop she grew stronger
And her colours so true
A tidal wave of happiness
Flowed in through her roots

With the water came sunshine

Like never before
That reached in and touched her
Right through to her core
And the future looked bright
That these feelings would last
So she reached for the rainbow
And waved goodbye to her past

One Road, Favourable Wind

After leaving Taiwan, I still had two more weeks of my holiday remaining. My plan was to travel back through Thailand and Malaysia, where my return flight to Singapore would be waiting for me on the Island of Legends – Langkawi. I was constantly thinking of my time in Taiwan, wondering if I would ever return. We always have bright ideas and good intentions when we meet people on holiday, and it rarely turns out how you intend at the time. This did seem different though. Then again, doesn't it always?

I'd been away from Taiwan just a few days when Ling was working on a video for a new song. This song was to raise money for SARS, and it was similar to the charity songs you will have endured in the past, like "We Are the World" in the United States and "Do They Know It's Christmas?" in the United Kingdom.

While I was in Koh Samui, I chatted online with Ling and one of the singers she was working with. Ling was choreographing something for the video, while the girl was one of the stars apparently. While chatting to them both, I couldn't help but feel a little out of my depth. I wanted to write something for Ling to show her that I was thinking about her, but writing for an actual songwriter felt quite daunting, especially when it wouldn't even be in her native language.

The second day after leaving Taipei, I'd had a near-death experience while crossing the road. With my iPod booming tunes into my ears, I'd stupidly looked left instead of right, and was just about to walk into the path of a fast approaching un-roadworthy truck, when, typically, I was suddenly stopped in my tracks by a stroke of luck. At the perfect moment, my new second-hand Nokia 6210 suddenly buzzed in my pocket, as if to warn me of the impending danger. I stopped to check it, and the truck sped past my nose with an inch to spare.

It was a text message from Ling – the first one she'd ever sent me – and it quite possibly saved my life. The timing of that message was staggering, and I was subsequently overwhelmed by the urge to return to Ling as soon as I could, before I did myself any lasting damage. I needed looking after, and she was the obvious person for the job.

Two More Days

It's only been *two days*
But god it seems so long
And in *two days* I've realised
Where I finally belong
It's been *two days* of torture
With just you in my thoughts
I feel love's finally hit me
Like a speeding juggernaut
Two days might not seem long
To your average Mr. Wu
But to me it's like an age
That I've been missing you
Two days more of this pain
To start again tomorrow
And after that *two more days*
Of heartache sure to follow
But as *two more days* pass
And I wonder what to do
I know I'm *two days* closer
To the day I next see you
For that day will be upon us
Much sooner than we think
And I will share *two more days*
With my beloved Ling
And those *two days* we will wonder
How we ever were apart
And from those *two days* onwards
We will share each other's hearts
Then *two more days* will go by
And *two more* after that
But the days won't really matter then
As I will be with you, love, Matt.

Fully Booked

After three months away, I was finally aboard my flight home from Singapore. I was so excited about getting home, but also with a view to coming back out to Asia soon.

While I was reflecting on the previous three months, thinking of all the wonderful people I'd met, the amazing places I'd been to, and all the fantastic experiences I'd had, one of the cabin crew surprisingly asked me to follow her to the front of the plane.

She then told me that the flight was overbooked, and asked if I'd mind getting on the next flight, which was just one hour later, and meant I'd still make my connection. Suddenly, in my messed-up mind I thought, "Oh my god! This plane is going to crash, and I've just been given an opportunity to save myself at the last minute."

You hear about things like this all the time, don't you?

I therefore agreed. I was happy to get off the doomed jet, thank you very much. So there we were, walking away from the plane with me feeling mightily relieved, but also feeling terrible for those who would remain on the plane. How awful for them, this was. God only knows why I was thinking this.

I was then asked, "You don't have any bags checked in, do you?"

I said that I did have bags checked in, but that it wasn't a problem. I could just collect them as normal when I landed.

To my utter horror, I was then informed that it is illegal to leave bags on the plane if you're not flying on it. This woman had incorrectly been informed that I hadn't checked any bags, which changed everything. It was now too late to take bags from the hold, so I would have to get back on the fucking plane and join all the other doomed passengers. No!

I was now absolutely terrified. Walking back to my seat I felt as though I was walking to my certain death. How unlucky I'd been. I'd almost escaped, but now, what a way to go? It was the most terrifying flight I have ever experienced, but, surprise, surprise, we landed without a glitch.

The only glitch was in my fucking head.

GEORGE SANTLEY

HOW LONG IS A CHINAMAN

Chapter Five

A One-Way Ticket to Taipei

In late 2003, I decided to take up Ling's invitation to join her in Taiwan – permanently. This was around six months after we'd first met. I hadn't worked since returning from my travels, though I'd been saving myself for a job that was promised to me by a friend of a friend. I was let down badly on this, after thinking for three months that the job was mine. This other act of fate made up my mind about going to live in Taiwan. I decided I had nothing to lose.

If I'd gotten the job, I may well have never gone back to Taiwan. At the time, I would have struggled to make a big decision like that – giving up good money and a good opportunity for almost the complete unknown. I think this is a fault many of us have. We prefer to stay in the relative safety of what we know rather than take risks – even though it's shite. We must take risks every now and again, though. Otherwise, we don't get anywhere. We just stand still; we stay dormant. We fucking die.

For some daft reason, I bought a one-way ticket from Manchester to Taipei. I suppose this was because I had no plans on returning to England any time soon. However, after weeks of planning, this resulted in me being stopped at the very first hurdle – the check-in desk at Manchester Airport. I wouldn't be allowed into Taiwan without first being booked on a future flight out of Taiwan, so I had to arrange another flight before I could even check-in. I hastily booked a return flight from Taipei to Hong Kong (the closest place to Taipei), and I finally started to relax. I was finally on my merry way; excited, sad, happy, and nervous.

The journey was a lot more relaxed after this, and my arrival in Taipei was so much calmer than the previous time. My two other visits to Chiang Kai-shek Airport were awful – first the no-show of Ling and then the SARS debacle causing all the flight cancellations. This time, it was perfect. Ling was already there waiting for me. We jumped in her car and then just smiled and laughed our way through the journey to Ling's home, or as Ling put it, "our home."

We kept looking at each other and giggling like kids. Neither of us could quite believe what we were doing, especially me. I was about to begin life actually living in Taiwan, when six months earlier I didn't even know where to find the place on a map.

Who Really Was Ling? – Part Two

Ling had been to a special school from a young age. This school was a government experiment, with only one class, made up of a dozen specially selected, extremely talented kids. This group were taught mainly artistic subjects, but they also studied the standard subjects at a vastly accelerated rate to everyone else. This meant that when she was fourteen years old, Ling was years ahead of everyone else of a similar age in most general subjects while she had also mastered many artistic disciplines.

She played piano, danced, and painted almost every day, while also passing her general exams years before the rest. On state visits, as a young girl Ling had often been selected to dance for the presidents and prime ministers of visiting countries – so she obviously had a number of talents. She was special.

Ling was born in Taiwan, though the Taiwanese government at the time didn't recognise her as being Taiwanese. They recognised her as being Chinese because her father was born in China.

While living in China, her father had been quite an important politician in the Chinese Nationalist party – the leader of which was Chiang Kai-shek – but when the Communists took control of Mainland China in 1949, he escaped the Red Army and travelled to Taiwan with Chiang Kai-shek and most other Nationalists. This was their only hope of survival.

Remember the name of the airport in Taipei? Well, Chiang Kai-shek imposed martial law on Taiwan, and for years he led Taiwan under a one-party authoritarian rule. I'm sure you can see why the airport was originally named after its leader – or to some, dictator – and then why its name was eventually changed in 2006 when 'democracy' had finally hit Taiwan.

In Taipei, Ling's father had become the manager of a top bank, and was very successful. The family lived in a large house and had everything money could buy. However, when Ling was fourteen years old, this world was turned upside down.

She arrived home from school one day to find a note from her mother and father. Her father had apparently been illegally cashing cheques for his friends, and had been charged with fraud. Quite unfathomably, rather than stay and face the consequences, her mother and father both absconded, leaving Taiwan and everything behind, including Ling and her nine-year-old sister. Hard to believe, isn't it?

Incredibly, Ling carried on as though nothing had happened for a few months, maybe hoping her parents would return and things would get back to normal. She continued with school and even looked after her younger sister at the same time.

To this day, I don't know where Ling obtained the funds to survive. Like me, you'll have to assume that her father's banking past had something to do with it and he'd left her a bundle of cash under the futon or something. I mean, he must have also had to do the same for himself because I'm sure his bank accounts would have been frozen in the circumstances. Then again, I'm only guessing.

Amazingly, she hadn't told anyone for months because nobody had asked. This was until her uncle, who lived in the Philippines, called one day. There was no other family in Taiwan, so Uncle Philippine arranged for her and her sister to go and live with him in the Philippines, and they lived there for two years before returning to Taiwan.

It's difficult to understand how people can act in such an irresponsible manner, like Ling's mother and father, especially when they've shown so much love previously.

Ling had been in a terrible accident when she was just eight years old, being hit hard by a car while riding her bike. That day, her father arrived at the hospital to be told the devastating news that there was no option but to amputate Ling's leg, but he refused to accept this.

His little girl's whole world was dancing, and he couldn't bear the thought of not seeing her dance again. In his eyes, her life would be over. He sought the opinions of three more doctors from different hospitals, but unfortunately, they all agreed that her leg would need to be amputated. He still refused to accept it.

As a last resort, he had Ling transferred to a military hospital, just to get one final opinion. He had to try everything in his power. Sadly, they also said that it would need amputating. But, even then, he pleaded with them to at least try to save it first.

They finally agreed to try, first making him sign a waiver in case anything went badly wrong. They were going against the advice of every doctor they had seen so there was obviously a lot of risk involved in what they were doing.

Ling was operated on for fourteen hours, and she now has a huge scar on the outside of her right hip – but that is all. As of today, she has danced for almost another forty years since, and all because her father wouldn't take no for an answer.

This is why Ling never showed any bitterness or anger towards him, even after he'd abandoned her. He saved her life, and that is the part of him which Ling wanted to remember him by, not the part of him that left her alone at such a young age to fend for herself and her little sister.

On her return to Taiwan, in her late teenage years, Ling started a promotions business with her two best friends. This was successful for a few years, until the sad day that one of these friends suddenly passed away. Ling and her other friend closed the company shortly after this tragic event, and Ling decided to travel to Paris to study fine art and French – like you do.

After returning home two years later, she found a role in television, becoming the face of a financial news TV programme, similar to Bloomberg, and she told me that she had no idea how she'd gotten the job. She'd known absolutely nothing about the financial markets, and for the first few months her questioning of experts in front of millions of viewers went something like, "So how are the markets looking today?" She was just one of those people who always looked like they knew exactly what they were talking about. You just admired her and trusted what she said, mainly because she more often than not knew what she was talking about.

When I started to learn Chinese, one of her friends told me that Ling would be the best teacher of Chinese that anyone could possibly have, though Ling said she didn't have the patience to teach me for some strange reason – I did kind of understand that. She even used to win state competitions as a child for being able to write more Chinese characters than anyone else her age in the country. She was a fucking know-it-all.

Anyway, the financial news programme on TV was the reason her face was so well known wherever she went in Taipei. She's had other jobs over the years too, such as writing about food and drink, running her own fruit juice shop, singing and dancing in clubs, plus I'm sure there are others I've forgotten. She was a busy woman, trying her hands at everything and showing that she could do anything. Then, in her late twenties, another tragedy struck. Ling was diagnosed with leukaemia.

She suffered for two years, hardly doing anything but spending her time in hospital. She was eventually given six months to live if she carried on with her treatment, and was told she would live a much shorter life if she decided to stop the treatment. Typically, Ling decided on the latter and left the hospital.

She then chose to have some natural Chinese treatment, mainly just to try to improve the quality of her remaining months. This included chi massage from two different chi masters – one for bone and one for muscle. She saw each of these every other day, and she slowly became stronger, and started to believe that she was healthy, no matter what the doctors said. Amazingly, this went on and on, until years had passed, so she decided to visit the doctor again. To everyone's astonishment her leukaemia seemed to have disappeared. Her blood was normal again, somehow.

The Chinese believe in many things that we don't even try to understand, one of which is that people can have an unlucky name. During her treatment, Ling changed her name due to all the bad luck she was having. I never asked if she believed this miracle might have something to do with changing her name. I didn't want to know if she believed that because it is just ridiculous; isn't it? Maybe the positive thoughts had something to do with it, though? Who knows?

I, maybe, believe that the chi masters helped cure her, but while I was in Taipei, I saw each of them numerous times for treatment to help ease the back pain I'd had for years, and they seemed to make that fucking worse. However, on one occasion, the "muscle woman" was doing something strange with my right arm and she asked me if I often had a sharp pain there. For a few years I had often received a shooting pain in that arm, and I'd never mentioned this to anyone.

She then twisted my arm one way, and then the other, for thirty seconds, and then she said, "It's OK now."

114

I haven't felt that pain in my arm for the past fourteen years, and my back has actually improved a lot too over recent years, though I don't know if this has anything to do with the treatment I had; it might just be a coincidence – a bloody big one. Make your own mind up about it all, but Ling is still healthy in 2017, over twenty years after being told she was dying.

Ling's previous name was "Si Ning", which doesn't mean anything to me. However, her new name "Ling" is the Chinese word for the number zero, and there is apparently nothing bad that can be associated with this word.

The Chinese are superstitious with words that sound similar to another word that has a bad meaning. For example, you will never receive a gift from a Chinese person containing four of anything. Rather than receive four plates, you will either receive three or six. This is because the word for number four is "si", which sounds like the Chinese word for "death".

Shit, I've honestly just this second realised why Ling changed her name all those years ago; it only took me fourteen years to work it out. The reason it took me so long was that I'd actually forgotten her old name. She told me this name when we first met and never mentioned it since, so I had to look it up.

What I've just spotted is, just like the number four, Ling's previous name sounds like the word for "death". This is obviously why she changed it. I'm not surprised she changed it either.

That wasn't the story I was going to write – it just came about while I was writing. What I was going to say is that if Ling ever visited my apartment, where I lived at the time we met and I still live today, then she would have had an almighty shock.

The number of my apartment is 204. Using the Chinese language of superstition, this actually says "Two Lings Dead". After all she's been through, could you really see her moving in?

On continuing her miraculous recovery from leukaemia, Ling married a well-known Taiwanese music producer, and they moved into a big house in which they had their own recording studio. Ling had written many hits by this time, and for tax purposes, she'd put fifty percent of the royalties to these songs into her husband's name. Sadly, the relationship broke down quite quickly, and during the separation her husband was being difficult with the financial situation. Ling had everything tied up in the house, plus, he had half of her royalties, and it seemed that he made it very awkward for her.

One day, after having had enough, Ling decided to get out, leaving him with everything. She couldn't be bothered arguing. She just wanted a simple, peaceful life, and that is what she chose. She actually told me that this was the reason she was with me – because I was a "simple" person. Whatever she meant by that.

After she left, Ling decided to open her tap dance school, beginning to build her Saturday class from her favourite people. She managed to create life just as she wanted it, surrounding herself with the people that looked up to and loved her, and the people whose company she enjoyed the most.

She was a master of everything, including me.

Ling the tea master. A tea house in a place north of Taipei called Jiu Fen.

The Piano

At one time, Ling was friends with many famous people, but she could never accept most of them as real friends. To her, many seemed false, and this was one of the reasons she later created that simple life for herself, with simple friends, and simple people, like me.

One day, a famous female star she'd known years earlier passed away. Ling was later shocked to be left something in her will – an extremely expensive piano. This piano had been the prize possession of the star in question, and although Ling was a musical person herself, and played the piano, she really couldn't quite understand why it had been left to her; she hadn't seen her for years.

Then, it clicked. The girl who died had secretly been a lesbian, and although Ling knew this, she was one of few people in the loop. None of her family had any idea. The star had a female partner for years, but to continue hiding her sexuality from her parents, her long-time love was sadly excluded from the will.

Ling then put two and two together, deciding that the piano had only been left to her as a means of it finding its rightful owner, the secret lover. Therefore, as soon as Ling was in possession of it, she contacted the girl to make sure it was soon with her. It was a lovely gesture that not many people would have carried out, and this showed me that she really did have a heart of gold.

At the time, Ling really would have loved to have owned that piano because she'd not owned one for years. I would have loved to have it too, but when Ling asked me what I thought she should do, there was no doubt in my mind either. It just felt like the right thing to do; not that the decision had anything to do with me, though it was nice to be asked my opinion for once.

This situation influenced me to buy my own piano years later. Ling's musical, lyrical, and creative nature really did inspire me in the years that followed, especially with my writing, but it even resulted in me studying music. I bought the piano and a number of other instruments that I felt a desire to play.

Unfortunately, although my writing and learning have continued to flourish, I am yet to master any of these instruments, and I haven't touched the piano for years.

Dusty Mandolin

There's dust on my piano
And my violin
My didgeridoo
And my crazy mandolin
I've shown them disrespect
Can't even find my plectrum
While my lonely guitar
Is longing for its next strum

Where is my harmonica?
I don't even know
Is it with electronica?
Hoping for a show?
They don't get the practice
That they really need
They just long for a new master
That can take the lead

I've tried so hard to learn
And master all the notes
But all I can do
Is sit here writing quotes
My head is full of music
But my fingers don't respond
So I'm now wondering
Where do these instruments belong?

I'm longing for the day
That my fingers do the talking
And I hope that's before
I look like Stephen Hawking
But I live here in hope
That I will find the time
And one day you will hear
The music to my rhymes

What Do I Do with This Big Dead Dog?

Just one week into the Taiwan experience, Ling's best friend, Toto, her Old English sheepdog, became ill. Toto was the mother of Snoopy, the one who'd pissed and shat everywhere during the earthquake when I was on the roof with my shopping. Toto was the clever one who had been with Ling for many years, and Ling was devastated to lose her.

Toto was at the veterinarian when Ling received the heart-breaking news that she'd gone over to the other side, so we had to make a trip to the vet's. Now then, I was just going to stay in the car, but I thought I'd better pop in to support Ling during this sad time. However, I was not prepared in the slightest for what happened next.

The vet disappeared into the back of the clinic, only to reappear holding a large heavy-looking object wrapped in a black bin liner. I then, reluctantly, felt obliged to put both my arms out towards him, only because Mr. Vet was passing the thing to me.

What was it? You might ask. Well, it was Toto, the big heavy lump of Old English sheepdog, in a fucking bin liner, and I was now holding her.

I remember thinking, "What the fuck! What the fucking fuck! What do I do with this then? Is this going to be our fucking tea tonight or something?"

We said goodbye and left, myself in shock. Ling then opened the boot of her car, and I tried my best to put the fucker in there gently, while all the time I could feel my left hand in Toto's mouth, her cold dead teeth digging into my warm naked fingers. It was horrendous.

I then drove in silence, following directions from Ling. We ended up at what must have been the "crematorium for dogs" or something, and I didn't leave the car this time. I just sat there in more deadly silence and disbelief. I was more annoyed and shocked for Ling rather than myself – I think.

Toto really didn't mean that much to me because I'd hardly spent time with her, but she was Ling's beloved pet of many years, so having to do this must have been horrifying for her. Then again, is it normal? I don't know.

I think it was the shock of it that hit me more than anything. The last thing I was expecting when I walked into that vet's was to be passed a big, fucking, dead dog.

Imagine for a minute, you walk into a shop thinking you're just saying hello, and within seconds someone passes you a big, heavy, fucking, dead animal in a bin liner. How would you feel about that? This is why you need to learn the language when you live in a foreign country. Otherwise, you have no idea what the people around you are saying, and it can lead to ridiculous moments like this.

However, Ling could have helped me and eased the situation slightly by saying something like, "We're going to the vet's to pick up Toto's corpse in a bin liner, and you might have to carry it to the boot of my car."

That might have prevented this event from ever occurring, because I would have just said, "Fuck that, love."

Have You Been Drinking (Again), Sir?

I used to drive Ling everywhere when I was in Taiwan. At first, I thought it was about the only thing I could do for her. You're supposed to pass a driving test if you want to drive there legally. Apparently, this test required you to reverse round an "S" bend. What you are thinking right now is exactly what I thought. Why? There aren't even any "S" bends on the roads. This is why the test had to take place indoors on a special track.

It was also quite bent apparently, with bribes needed half the time to get your licence, so I thought I'd just take my chance and drive without one. I could always play dumb. My Colombian friend Alejandro had told me that he'd once even got away with running a red light in Taipei by pretending he was French. He spoke perfectly good English and Spanish, but there were often police who spoke one of these two languages, whereas French was a different matter. After trying to converse with him for five minutes, they just gave up and told him to go. This was another option I had, though I wasn't planning on doing anything to get noticed by the police anyway.

Then, one late Sunday night, about one year into living in Taipei, Ling and I visited a faraway mountain spring – something we did every other week. While driving home, we were stopped by the police for no other reason than they'd spotted a foreigner at the wheel. I was signalled to wind down the window, and then asked, "Have you been drinking, sir?"

I replied in almost perfect Mandarin, "No, but when I get home I'm going to have several large beers."

He then questioned Ling about my license. She gave him some Chinese bullshit and a smile, and he just asked us to swap places. Then, a few minutes later when we were out of the way, Ling burst into uncontrollable laughter.

I asked what was so funny, and she replied, "The Chinese police officer used English language to ask you if you'd been drinking, and then you, an Englishman, replied to him in perfect Chinese."

Come to think of it, that was quite funny, and ridiculous, us both speaking to each other in the others' mother tongue, but after months of trying my best to learn Mandarin, this was a special moment for me. Although I was asked a question in English, I actually replied using Chinese without thinking about it. It was as if I was thinking in Chinese, and not having to first translate each English word one after the other to make a sentence.

It was a major milestone, and it was an amazing feeling when it happened, so when we returned home I had a celebratory beer – just one though, because I hardly drank at the time, and one small can of Tsing Tao was actually enough to knock me out. Those were the days.

The 645 Bus

For a short time, Ling was working in what she called a "normal" job. She worked for Fubon Bank as an art director, whatever an art director does for a bank. During this period of around one year, I would meet Ling after work for dinner almost every Tuesday and Thursday – the two days she worked a full day.

On both days, I'd catch the number 645 bus from home to the other end of the city, and we'd often find somewhere amazing to eat each evening. This excludes the one time I was eating my beef fried rice and I saw a big fucking rat crawling across the pipe right above my head.

Anyway, forget the rat; you can imagine my shock one Wednesday evening when the number 645 bus was hit by a fucking train. Yes, another near miss. This didn't happen on Tuesday or Thursday, but *Wednesday*, the day in-between when I didn't use the bus. Luckily, no one was seriously injured, but the bus was always quite empty, so maybe that's why. Whatever the case, I'm just glad that I wasn't on the thing at the time.

As bus number 645 had the number "four" in it – the Chinese number of death – I'm surprised that Ling was even happy for me to get on it in the first place. Not surprisingly, I never saw her on it.

Another Typical Day in Class

For a few months, after I'd been learning Mandarin Chinese for a year or so, I shared my class with five others – four American lads and one Brazilian. It was quite funny at times, like being at school, with some of the lads even acting the fool and pissing the teacher off every now and again. Whatever the case, it was a laugh, and I was happy to have a bit of normality while learning the language that I really wanted and needed to learn. I attended class 10 a.m. to 12 p.m., Monday to Friday, in an old city centre building, completing the weekly ten hours of study necessary to meet the requirements of my six-month student visa.

One morning, as we were beginning our lesson, the building shuddered. I looked up at the teacher, and she looked shit scared. This rubbed off on me, so I started to panic a bit.

The room shook again, like a jerk, with noise. It was horrible. I knew it was an earthquake, but this was nothing like the previous peaceful wobble I'd experienced at home on the roof. This was fucking terrifying, the difference being, the previous time, the building swaying calmly was due to Ling living in quite a new building which had special qualities enabling it to sway rather than shudder.

Just to explain this, in 1999, when the building Taipei 101 was being built, eventually making it the tallest building in the world for a time when finished, there was a major earthquake in Taipei. This earthquake killed over two thousand people, destroyed over fifty thousand homes, and crushed Ling's fucking car. This destruction prompted the government to bring in new laws demanding owners of certain buildings strengthen them to specific standards, and making builders of new property follow strict guidelines that would make the buildings almost shockproof.

On this occasion, my Chinese class was in an old "modified" building, and the result was totally incomparable to the much bigger earthquake I'd experienced at home. There was a shake, a shudder, a pause, another shudder, screams, shouts, a jerk, all the while everyone is looking at each other, holding on to anything they can. Everyone was petrified; well, almost everyone.

In the midst of all this, one of the American blokes sitting next to me shouted with excitement, "Whoooooooooah! Yeeeeaaaaaaah!"

What a nutter. What a star.

After an initial unbelieving pause, everyone laughed, and we even calmed down a little before the shaking actually stopped. This is the reason why I can't help but love many Americans.

To top it off, I used to see this bloke in a toothpaste advert on TV almost every night before I went to bed. He'd managed to blag his way onto that advert while he was teaching English out there. He was a star, just happy to be alive and so positive absolutely all of the time.

I wish there were more people like this bloke. How amazing that he could be so positive in a situation in which everyone else was frightened for their lives. I think he was actually also scared, but he refused to show it and just wanted to do something to calm everyone else in the situation. What a wonderful quality to have.

The Taipei 101 building, Christmas Eve, Taipei, 2004.
The statue is Sun Yat-sen – the founding father of Taiwan.

Mastering Chinese

Chinese is obviously not the easiest language to learn. However, you might be surprised to hear, once you get past the early stages there is a beautiful simplicity to much of it. For example, the Chinese word for volcano is "fire mountain". If you know the character for "fire" and the character for "mountain", then you can probably guess the character combination for volcano all by yourself. There are many similar examples.

However, there are different tones used in the spoken word, and to add to the confusion some characters even have the exact same sound as others but have a different meaning; the only difference between them being the written character.

I'll use the Chinese word 'ma' as an example.

1. Mā (媽) – Mum – The sound of the word Mā is a constant tone.

2. Mà (罵) – Abuse – The sound of the word Mà goes down at the end.

3. Má (麻) – Hemp – The sound of the word Má goes up at the end.

4. Mǎ (嗎) – Morphine – The sound of the word Mǎ first goes down, then up.

5. Mǎ (馬) – Horse – Again, the sound of the word Mǎ first goes down, then up.

As you can see, some of these characters are ever so slightly different, but the sound is almost the same, apart from the last two characters, where the sound is exactly the same. If you're reading the characters, you can maybe work out what the subject is, but listening to the spoken word is very different. If there are a dozen Chinese people all talking at full pelt, and you are not involved in the conversation, it can be impossible to work out what the fuck is going on.

As the word for "morphine" and the word for "horse" sound exactly the same, you might only be able to work out which word is being used from the context of the conversation.

It's very difficult for Westerners to recognise these individual tones, so to me, a particular group of Chinese gangsters on the next

126

table uttering the word "ma" could either be talking about entertaining your mother, riding their horse, abusing their spouse, smoking weed, or injecting fucking heroin. As I mentioned, the context of the sentence guides you to the correct meaning, because they surely wouldn't be talking about smoking their horse, abusing their heroin, or riding your mother, now would they?

Maybe they happen to be a particular type of messed-up gangster who could actually be doing all of these, and that is where the main difficulty in understanding Chinese lies: Are they messed-up people? Are they joking? Or are they being extremely sensible? It really is an art form for a Westerner to understand sometimes.

It is a beautiful language though, and it's not difficult to see how Chinese speakers intentionally alter their pronunciation as a form of comedy. I love it. I just don't like listening to it because it gives me a fucking headache.

Also, if you've ever wondered why Chinese people speak English the way they do, with back-to-front sentences, this might go a little way to explaining it. Below is a conversation between two Chinese men, Mr. Du and Mr. Dong. This conversation did not take place. I made it up. There are four parts to each translation:

- My English

- Pinyin – a phonetic language used to help foreigners learn Chinese

- Traditional Chinese

- Chinese translated into English by me

You'll find it much better if you read the fourth line of each with a Chinese accent, and you are really only interested in the first and fourth lines of each.

Mr Du

Hello Mr. Dong.

Dǒng xiānshēng, Nǐ hǎo.

董先生你好。

127

Dong Mr, you OK?

Mr Dong

Hello. I'm good thanks.

Nǐ hǎo. Wǒ hěn hǎo xièxiè.

你好。我很好謝謝。

You OK? I very good thank you.

Mr Du

What are you doing?

Nǐ zài zuò shénme?

你在做什麼。

You are doing what?

Mr Dong

I'm looking for my mobile phone.

Wǒ zài zhǎo wǒ de shǒujī.

我在找我的手機。

I am searching my hand-machine.

Mr Du

We are in a phone shop. That's like looking for a needle in a haystack.

Wǒmen zhèng chù zài yīgè shǒujī diàn. Jiǔ niú yì máo.

我們正處在一個手機店。九牛一毛。

We in one hand-machine shop. Nine cow, one hair.

Mr Dong

Correct. Also, this shop is a mess (at sixes and sevens).

Duì. Yǔ cǐ tóngshí, zhège diàn shì luàn qī bā zāo.

對。與此同時，這個店是乱七八糟。

Right. At same time, simultaneously, this shop is disorderly seven, eight bad.

Mr Du

Where is your toilet? I'm going to go for a shit while you look for your phone.

Nǐ de cèsuǒ shì zài nǎ lǐ? Ér nǐ kàn kàn nǐ de shǒ ujī wǒ yào qù dàbiàn.

你的厕所是在哪里。而你看看你的手机 我要去大便。

Your toilet is where? And you look-look your hand-machine I want go big convenience.

Mr Dong

The toilet is broken. Sorry.

Mǎ tǒ ng huàile. Duìbùqǐ.

馬桶壞了。對不起。

Horse bucket broken. Sorry.

I really hope you attempted to say the word "simultaneously" with a Chinese accent.

Trying to Help

The whole time I lived in Taiwan, I wasn't working or making any money. This didn't go without trying, such as spending hours each day learning the language in an attempt to fit in, and trying to create opportunities for myself which never seemed to work out. I did have a little money, but I was mainly supported financially by Ling. Due to this, I often felt the need to try to help her with little things whenever I could, but when I did they tended to go spectacularly wrong.

One day when Ling was out working, I decided to give Snoopy a wash, because she constantly stank of piss. Unlike her late, intelligent mother, Toto, Snoopy was a bit slow. After Toto left us, Snoopy just pissed and shat everywhere in the apartment, whereas beforehand, she just followed the lead of her mother. Without her mother, Snoopy was clueless. She was totally lost, even pissing and lying in it sometimes. She was a very slow dog, bless her.

I'd washed Snoopy in the past, and I remembered that there were two different bottles of stuff to use on her coat. I think one was probably shampoo, while the other was something to protect her from fleas. However, on this occasion there was a third bottle in the shower room, and with everything being in Chinese, I couldn't quite work out which was which.

It was only when I poured the contents of bottle number one all over her that I realised I'd really messed up. It was fucking bleach. I did my best to wash it off quickly, and Ling failed to notice that Snoopy's white bits were just a bit whiter than normal, but it was a silly mistake, and typical of the kind of thing I would do all the time.

It's not always my fault, though. Some things just happen to me, and some things just attack me without warning. Ling had mentioned that she wanted me to take a lampshade down from the ceiling upstairs in the apartment because it needed cleaning. This wasn't your typical lamp shade, though. It was a heavy, expensive crystal shade.

I walked over to it, and with the ceiling being quite low, I just reached up and touched it, very gently. Guess what? The fucking thing fell off. I had literally only given it the slightest of touches, and this heavy lump of crystal fell, hitting the ironing board – which just happened to be directly below – and then breaking into several large shards, a number of which then attacked my uncovered legs.

When she heard the loud smash, Ling screamed my name from downstairs. I wandered over to the top of the stairs, just standing there, while Ling appeared at the bottom, looking up.

Both of my legs were almost completely covered in blood.

She screamed again, panicking, and saying that we needed to go to hospital immediately. However, it looked a lot worse than it was, and when I washed all the blood away, there were just a load of really small cuts, and one biggish one, which wasn't really big enough to go to the hospital (again) for. However, I was really lucky because the size of some of those thick sharp shards that hit me could have done some real damage. Some were 10 cm long and 1 cm thick.

Lucky or not, it was still yet another thing to go wrong.

This continued for quite a long time, me feeling like I couldn't contribute anything, though it didn't seem to bother Ling. It just bothered me. However, things suddenly changed after we travelled to Japan.

While in New York, Ling had met a Japanese tap dance teacher named Hiro. In 2004, Hiro was hosting a big show in Hamamatsu, a coastal city in Japan, and she invited Ling to take some of her students over to join in the show. The invitation was gladly accepted.

Ling and all her students were so excited about this trip, and especially for the show itself. Many of them had never performed in front of an audience before, and those who had only performed for a few a small audiences. This was new to them all, as there would be hundreds in the audience for this show in a wonderful large theatre.

I was kindly invited to join them, though I didn't know why at the time.

This meant there were over thirty Taiwanese tap-dancing girls, one Taiwanese tap-dancing man, and one accident-prone Englishman on this trip. I wondered what I was going to do while we were there. I really didn't like tap dance, and all they would be doing is rehearsing and preparing for the show in a place in Japan that was in the middle of nowhere. It was therefore decided by Ling that I would be the cameraman/videographer/filmmaker.

I had no real idea what I was doing with this video camera, so I just decided to record everything I could, even when they didn't know

I was filming. It was quite draining at times, just watching and listening to them rehearse all day. There is no noise in the world as irritating as a tap dance studio; believe me. A room with a wooden floor full of tap-dancing girls, shit loud music blasting out, and people shouting unintelligible language for hours on end. It wasn't my idea of fun, though it would all be worth it.

On returning home to Taiwan, I painstakingly edited the many hours of video and then created five short films which surprisingly turned out quite brilliantly. I'd accidentally discovered that I was quite good at this film-making lark. Isn't it funny? You have no idea what you might be good at until you try it; that's why you should try as many things as you can. You might be pleasantly surprised.

When the films were complete, Ling arranged a party in her studio where her students could watch the films together on a big screen. They had no idea what I had created, but I knew it was good because even the biggest critic in the world, Ling, who seemed to do everything perfectly, was amazed by what I'd produced.

At the end of the screening, which took place in front of over fifty of Ling's students, everyone was so happy and thankful to me because not only had I managed to capture their special moment on film, but I'd created something very touching which they could keep and look back on for years to come. At the end, they gave me a standing ovation. It was a very special, emotional moment.

After this, things seemed to change. I felt accepted because I'd finally contributed something. Everyone seemed to change their attitude and body language towards me, though the idea of not being accepted previously was no doubt all in my own messed-up mind anyway. It wasn't everyone else that changed from that day onward. It was just my perception of those around me.

I think the most rewarding thing about making those films involved Ling's father. While I was there, he was back in Taiwan, although I never saw him and neither did Ling to my knowledge. I don't know if he served any punishment for his crime, and Ling never actually mentioned him until he was in hospital on his deathbed, when she asked me to go with her to visit him.

I refused. I didn't see the point. When Ling returned from visiting him, she told me that she'd played those five films of mine for him. He hadn't seen her dance for so many years, so those films gave him the opportunity to see her smiling; doing what she loved again; something that was only possible because of what he did for her all those years ago.

Spot the odd one out – this was Ling's website back then showing us in Japan.

Bless the Animals

In early 2004, I returned home to Bolton to recharge my batteries. Although I loved many things about living in Taiwan, I found it so tiring and draining at times. I think this was because there were so many differences compared to my usual life in England that I felt the need to work at everything. Nothing seemed straightforward. I also didn't really have my own life – I was basically just following Ling around like her third Old English sheepdog. I also missed my friends and family, and as the conditions of my student visa meant that I had to leave Taiwan every six months, I decided to return home for a few weeks.

Back in Bolton, it hit me that I needed to change something when I next returned to Taiwan; I needed my own friends. I'd always made most of my friends in England by playing football, so I thought I'd have a look online to see if there were any football clubs I could join in Taipei. I hadn't played for a few years, and even for the ten years prior to that, I hadn't played too often. This was due to the pain and days off work caused by the many injuries I received while playing. I'd retired several times by my early twenties, but then I always tried to make another go of it when the pain subsided and I realised how much I missed playing.

These injuries all stemmed from the back problem I mentioned earlier, which even prevented me from jogging for a couple of years. It was just too painful. Now in my early thirties, my football days in England were well and truly over, but I needed a way to make some friends in Taiwan and I thought if there was football out there, then the standard would be quite basic and I might just be able to get by.

Searching online for football in Taipei, the first team I came across were called the Taipei Animals. Not only did I like the sound of the name, but I could see it was made up of a complete mixture of nationalities, and by chance, they were sponsored by the Tavern pub – a pub in Taipei city centre where I'd already been to watch football on TV a few times.

I emailed them, and on my return to Taipei, I joined their training sessions. I learnt that they played in the best league in Taiwan – this league was also the only league in Taiwan and was rather shit, as expected. That was apart from the team that won the league every year, who were the previous Taiwan fucking national team. They might have been older than most of us, but they were just a bit better and fitter than us. I bet they even stayed in the night before a game too, whereas for the rest of us it was just a chance to meet people and make new friends.

Anyway, joining the team had worked out exactly as I'd hoped. I made many new friends from all over the world, and I finally had a life of my own. This was much needed, because rather than following Ling everywhere and always going out for dinner with her and her students, I could now sometimes do my own thing. I did enjoy the dinners out with Ling; I just didn't want to do that every single week, and I really needed some male friends.

I often felt like my brain just needed a rest too, otherwise it would explode. By this, I mean that I wanted to be able to have a conversation with people in my own language, and not constantly have to think hard while trying to come up with some clever Chinese words, or pull my hair out trying to figure out what someone was saying. Sometimes you just need a release, and I found my perfect release in the pub with my new friends; drinking, watching football, and talking shite without having to think – just like when I was at home in Bolton.

One evening in the Tavern pub I was looking at some pictures on the wall, which I'd always assumed were pictures of previous Animals football teams. However, I'd never looked at them closely before now, and I was surprised to see photos of a rugby team. I had no idea there was a rugby team at the Tavern. Nobody had mentioned them, and I'm sure I would have met them in the pub if the team existed.

When I asked the Swiss-French owner of the pub – Michel – about them, it broke my heart. He told me that the rugby team were no more. They had travelled to Bali in 2002 to play in a tournament, and most of them were killed by the bomb in Paddy's Bar – one of the bombs which I'd just managed to avoid the same year.

Seeing those happy faces in the photos really hit home how lucky I was, and I wondered what had led me here; playing football in Taiwan of all places for the very same club as those unfortunate souls, less than two years after the bomb that killed them could quite easily have killed me. It then dawned on me that, after avoiding both bombs, I only returned to Bali because of them, and that's when I met Ling.

She was the reason I was now here, blessed to be playing football for the only remaining Taipei Animals team.

Those bombs had somehow managed to write the next chapter of my life, and within two years they had led me to Taipei, coincidentally glaring at the pictures of many of the young men whose lives they'd destroyed.

The Taipei Animals Football Team – 2003/2004.

My Dream Job

In 2004, some lads from the Taipei Animals started a football school for kids, the kind of which there was nothing quite like in Taiwan at the time. This school was named the Master Football Academy (MFA), and I was over the moon when one day the owners asked me to help them out in a coaching capacity, with a view to working for them on a permanent basis.

Coaching football to kids in the sun, this was my dream job. What could beat that? It would also fix my main problem – money. I'd tried to find work in the past – with the help of Ling – but nothing had come off. Ling even took me to see people she knew in the computing industry, but it was evident that my ancient skillset, together with the lack of Chinese language skills, meant that this wasn't going to work. What job could I possibly do? I'd really needed to find one, and to find one doing something I loved seemed too good to be true.

I arrived fully kitted out in my MFA coaching gear on what was a scorching Sunday morning after quite a late night in The Tavern. I then attempted to get to grips with my new job. I soon learnt, however, that this football school was just an excuse for parents to get rid of their annoying kids for a couple of hours on a Sunday morning, while they no doubt had a relaxing and much-needed break from the little twats.

I organised a six-a-side game, but due to a lack of authority from the coach, kids were just picking their own teams and ignoring me, so I left them to it. While refereeing the game between these little joys, which were around five to six years old, it quickly became apparent that one team was bullying at least one member of the other team; something which really annoyed me. I immediately started to side with the team who needed me most.

I shouted at the bullying little pricks, but they still wouldn't listen. It was as if I was speaking a different language. I tried again, but was completely ignored. Confused, filling with rage and turning green, I wondered what I could do to get their attention. I came up with a plan, and then set about putting it into action.

The team being bullied had a throw-in deep in their own half, so I positioned myself right in front of the main bully, before asking the thrower to give me the ball. He threw it straight to me, so I controlled it, while wrapping my arms around this little shit behind me, and subsequently throwing him to the ground. I then dribbled the ball all the way up to the opposing goal, before smashing the ball into the back of the net and celebrating as though I'd won the World Cup.

The kid who I threw to the ground then ran up to me and shouted, "Teacher, teacher. You are the teacher. You cannot do that!"

I replied, maybe shouting a little, "Correct! I am the teacher! So I can do what the fuck I want!"

It was just when we were getting ready to kick off again that I looked up to the side-lines. There now just so happened to be a dozen parents all watching in disbelief; their mouths wide open. Not surprisingly, my career as a football coach ended on that otherwise sunny day.

Dream job? I'd rather go and watch Elton John in concert.

Elton John - Fuck Off

I was extremely unfit. I'd probably played less than twenty games of football in the previous ten years, but I had a blank canvass with the Taipei Animals on which to show off my skills, or to blow out of my arse again.

I quickly impressed a few, and I was somehow selected to play in an expats team against the majority of what were the current Taiwan national football team – not the old team who used to win the league every year. These were the very fit current team, and they wanted practice games to prepare for their upcoming World Cup qualifying match against Iraq. Our game with them was to be played at Chungshan, the Taiwan national Football Stadium, which we were all excited about.

Even writing this now, I feel as though I'm making it up, but it gets even worse, or even harder to believe. My team was made up of players from three different clubs; the Taipei Animals, Taipei Dragons, and the Red Lion –or Farnworth as I used to call them. This was because the Red Lion team was full of lads with local girlfriends who all seemed to have young babies, just like the teenage Farnworth team I'd played against in my youth who seemed to have a following of schoolgirls that were either pregnant at the time or mothers themselves.

I was on the substitutes' bench to start, mainly because I was one of the new lads, whereas the others in the team were all players who'd graced the Taiwan league for a number of years. Also, the coach was my French mate David; he played for the Animals, and I'd told him that there was absolutely no way I could manage a full ninety minutes in my condition, especially not against a super fit bunch of fucking Taiwanese internationals.

Coming up to half-time with the score at 1-1, I was thrown on and told to go and play on the right wing. With my first touch, I received the ball on the halfway line and then started to take players on – just like I used to do in my teens when I could actually run. I went this way, I went that way, I almost fucking fell over, and then I attempted to cross the ball, mainly because my legs were about to give way. My right boot didn't connect properly, and although the ball shot like a rocket, it didn't quite head in my intended direction. It skimmed along the ground towards the opposite corner of the penalty area, when it was supposed to be a cross into the six-yard box.

I was just thinking how ridiculous I must have looked out there, when I suddenly saw my Mexican mate Mora from the Taipei Dragons, running onto the ball. He somehow met it perfectly in his path, and it then looked like I'd picked out a fantastic pass to him. He didn't even take a touch to control it; he just ran onto it and curled a spectacular first-time shot into the bottom right-hand corner from twenty-five yards. It was a fantastic goal.

When the half-time whistle blew, with us leading 2-1, I was getting all the plaudits when all I did was run aimlessly and get rid of the ball before I passed out. It was to get even better, though.

I started the second half on the right wing again, and within ten minutes I latched onto a through-ball from our full-back, finding myself one-on-one with the extremely wide national goalkeeper. From the edge of the box I just hit the fucker, but to everyone else, when the back of the net bulged it looked more like I'd placed it perfectly into the bottom corner. That magic moment made the score 3-1, and we ended up winning the game 3-2.

So I set one goal up, and I scored one more, making a major contribution in beating the Taiwan national team, when I wasn't even fit to play in the lowest of all the amateur leagues in England at the time. I only lasted about thirty minutes too. I was so fucked that the boss soon dragged me off again.

I think it was the following Saturday that none other than Elton John was playing a gig at that very same stadium. Elton was headline news over in Taiwan for a few days, not due to his concert, but because when he arrived in Taipei, he was in quite a bad mood. This came to the fore when he started getting pestered by the local press, who are slightly mental over there to say the least.

He aimed a verbal barrage at them, and being in a foreign language (English), this wasn't blanked out on the local news. Hilariously, shown on TV, he shouted, "Fuck Off! You bunch of rude vile pigs." From that moment, Elton John's popularity in Taiwan plummeted, whereas my popularity shot through the roof. I thought about retiring from playing football there and then, and I probably should have.

Chinese Taipei v Iraq

In 2004, Chinese Taipei played Iraq in a group qualification game for the 2006 World Cup.

To digress a little, Taiwan is known as "Chinese Taipei" to the rest of the world when they take part in sporting events. This is down to their bullying neighbours China, who, as you know, believe that they own Taiwan. Taiwan duly abides by some of China's petty demands to prevent the war which China has often threatened. It is a much-ignored boiling point in the world, especially when you realise that Taiwan's biggest ally is none other than the United States of America.

Anyway, this game was played at the same stadium which had recently been graced by Elton John and yours truly, and it involved a Taiwan team who hadn't managed to score even a single goal in any of their previous World Cup qualifying games – ever.

By this time, the previously mentioned Master Football Academy – for whom I was now no longer employed in a coaching capacity – were growing their business by promoting themselves to the small but ever-growing footballing community of Taipei. To do this further, they were to have their members walk out with the teams for this big World Cup game and stand with the players throughout the airing of their national anthems.

I was a busy man by now, becoming a self-taught one-man videographer and film-making service, honing my talents on the one blemished football pitch of the "not very diverse" corners of Taipei, and the odd dance studio. I was a busy man, yes, but I still wasn't making any money. I was only doing favours and picking certain events to practice and promote my business. Having enjoyed my previous video work, which I just made up as I went along, the main men at the MFA arranged a meeting with me – the coach that left by mutual consent after one infamous coaching session. The MFA tempted me with food, beer, and English company, so I happily agreed to the meet in a neutral venue.

At the meeting, I wasn't surprised that they didn't want me to return to their team of "masters" in a coaching role, but was surprised that they wanted me to produce a promotional film for their "academy". This would be a film showing the kids train at the national stadium on a different night from the World Cup qualifier, showing what their football school was all about – having fun while learning to play the beautiful game, and also improving their English language skills.

I gladly accepted the job, and subsequently produced a wonderful ten-minute film for them. This film required a lot of subtitles, and with Ling helping me to add the perfect Chinese to go with my perfect English, it really did look professional. In fact, Ling said I should have charged them fifty times as much as I did – I can't remember what I charged them, but it can't have been much. They were my friends so I wasn't really bothered, though I can now see why Ling, who was supporting me financially, probably was a little irritated.

Before I'd finished putting the film together, the World Cup game against Iraq was played, and as the kids were going to be walking out with the players, I thought I should record this moment too because it would be great footage for my final production. This turned out better than I could ever have imagined. I was even handed a press badge by someone, and I had access to all areas. It was brilliant, even if I didn't actually know what I was doing there.

This game, remember, was played in 2004 when the war on Iraq was in full flow, so I stood in the tunnel with all these players from Iraq, thinking about their situation back home and how they had even managed to get a team together. It was even more bizarre that my country was effectively at war with them. Like me, I bet they didn't care about all that bollocks either, and they were just more bothered about living their lives, doing something fun and positive, like having a game of football. I know we need them –I think – but I fucking hate politicians. I mean, *war*? What the fuck is all that about? Our elected governments have killed millions more people than every terrorist organisation and unelected lunatic combined. How fucked up does that sound? I don't know where this blueprint for the world appeared from, but ask yourself this: "Is it working?" Would life be any worse without governments? All they seem to do is put you down, stop you having fun, and murder people from other countries to protect your "freedom"; and these are the democratically elected ones.

Back to the football: Iraq won the home tie 7-0, so Taiwan weren't expected to win this match. They just wanted to score a goal – their first-ever World Cup goal. Not surprisingly, Taiwan were hammered again, but late in the game, they finally got their wish, scoring the goal they'd dreamt about, the game finishing 4-1 to Iraq.

I also got my wish, because in addition to walking out with the players and walking along the line-ups to film the kids during the national anthems, I somehow managed to catch all the goals from the game on tape, even though I was moving around the stadium throughout the ninety minutes. I was sitting in the stand for thirty minutes, then I stood right behind the goal, and then back up to the stand, so it was a miracle that I managed to capture all the goals.

More importantly, though, I managed to catch Taiwan's first-ever World Cup goal on video. This was more special than I first realised because football was so small in Taiwan in 2004, that amazingly nobody else actually recorded that game. Therefore, I was the only person to record Taiwan's first-ever World Cup goal. A whole country's first-ever World Cup goal only recorded by me? How did this happen? I wasn't even meant to be going to the game.

After noticing my film on the MFA website weeks later, the Taiwan Football Association contacted the men at the MFA, who passed on a message to me, requesting that I send them a copy of the DVD, which I gladly did. It's just a pity there wasn't anyone recording my winning goal against them months earlier, because I would have sent them a copy of that too.

Stills from the video – Taiwan v Iraq

In the tunnel with the FIFA officials before the big match.

The national football team of Iraq.

Standing for the national anthem of Iraq. The manager shared an uncanny resemblance to a certain dictator.

Iraq make it 2-0. It wasn't exactly a sell-out.

Taiwan score their first-ever World Cup Goal.

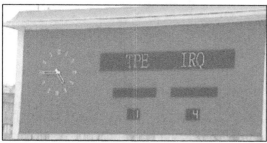

Game over.

145

Fake Taiwanese News

In 2004, I was lucky enough to experience a Taiwanese election. In 2000, an ex-lawyer named Chen Shui-bian had become president, being the first Taiwanese president from what were known as the Democratic Progressive Party (DPP). This victory ended the ruling of over fifty years by Chiang Kai-shek's Kuomintang party (KMT or Nationalist Party), who were, let's just say, pro-China – China being the motherland – and there was nothing democratic about their past victories.

The DPP had the word "democratic" in their name, so to my uneducated self, knowing that China thought they owned the place, it seemed that it was a great thing that the DPP were now in power. The DPP had bided their time and finally fought off the bullies. Well, that was my thinking until I experienced the 2004 election.

Chen Shui-bian had only won power in 2000 by a small majority, and by all accounts, it was going to be a close call again. They therefore had to look for small gains in every group of people. I'd already had my doubts about this bloke after reading the street signs in Taipei, which didn't match the Chinese I was learning. When I'd asked Ling about this, she told me that Chen Shui-bian had spent millions on changing the wording on the signs as soon as he came to power.

The signs obviously displayed Chinese characters for the locals, which are the same throughout the Chinese language, but they also had Pinyin, which is for the use of foreigners like me. Pinyin uses the English alphabet to describe the sound of each Chinese word, as you will have seen previously. However, some of the words in Pinyin used on these signs just didn't look right to me. I learnt that this was because there are two languages in Taiwan – Mandarin Chinese and Taiwanese.

As Mr. Chen Shui-bian was Taiwanese through and through, he changed every sign to match the Taiwanese language. This might sound quite patriotic, but it was actually quite ridiculous because Pinyin is not for the locals – it's for the foreigners. The fact that the wording confused me tells you everything you need to know. The new signs meant fuck all to almost every foreigner in Taiwan, and it often helped me to get lost, so it was an obvious waste of money. Foreigners want to learn Chinese, not Taiwanese, so why do such a thing when there are parts of the country that could have really benefited from that money? It was just something he did to have a go at China, because Chiang Kai-shek had named everything previously.

Before the election in 2004, I learnt that Mr. Chen had banned the military from voting – I might not be 100 per cent correct here. It might have been all, and it might have just been a selection – those abroad.

I then discovered that almost all the military were against Mr. Chen, so banning them from voting might have tipped it in his favour. I couldn't quite believe what I was hearing, and that's me, an uneducated foreigner. I didn't see anyone else in an uproar though. Then again, I suppose I couldn't fucking understand most of them.

However, the next thing to happen was just ridiculous, and I felt like I was the only person to see right through it. The day before the final day of campaigning, there was Breaking News on TV. Breaking News was just normal news in Taiwan, and although I now see this phrase every day in England, I think Taiwan is the place where almost everything started to be breaking news. However, this really was proper breaking news, because President Chen had been fucking shot.

The news in Taiwan at the time was years before any other country. By that, I mean that they had more satellite vans for the size of the place than anywhere else in the world, and they were more in your face than anywhere else – as Elton found out – so they didn't miss anything. Therefore, with the president driving down a street laden with firecrackers, they will have caught every single second on film.

I spent the next twenty-four hours watching the same – and only – twenty seconds of footage being replayed over and over again, while listening to the local newscasters spout Mandarin bollocks over and over. I was drained, but I couldn't take my eyes off it. It was remarkable footage.

That is what happened. He was driven down a street in a carriage of sorts, and like I said, there were firecrackers going off all down this street on either side of the vehicle in celebration of something, and then utter panic. The police surrounded him and then rushed him off to hospital. Then, the fatal shot – a photo of a gunshot to a leg. I say "a leg", because the picture just showed a leg. No body, no face, just a fucking leg. I watched it over and over again, and I came to the same obvious conclusion over and over again – it was complete and utter bollocks.

It was all in Chinese, so I mainly just saw pictures, and I didn't understand many of the words that the locals could, so maybe that's why I saw straight through it – there was no background noise for me. It really just seemed that I was the only one who thought this was the worst faked shooting of all time.

The day after, out of respect for the president, all the other political parties refrained from their promotional antics, and your man with the bullet in the leg was later re-elected by a minuscule margin – a margin that might well have been overturned with the help of the national forces – who couldn't fucking vote. Oh well. It seems that even democracy isn't actually democratic. Who would have thought?

No More Water

Leaving Taiwan for the final time in 2006 was heart-breaking. I'd lived there with Ling for almost three years, but things just weren't right for us. It was very sad. We still loved each other so much, but there was just such a big culture difference, and I did really miss home.

From being calm, friendly, and loving, my daily frustration was slowly changing me. I was becoming angry, antagonistic, and cold. The situation wasn't good for me, and it wasn't good for Ling. When things are not going right in a relationship, it takes courage to be honest with each other about the need to go your separate ways, and it's often easier to just carry on down the same unhappy path together. However, it didn't feel like that for either of us. We both knew, and we found it easy to be honest enough about what needed to happen. This didn't make things any easier, though.

I had embraced everything in Taiwan at first; I tried to go with the flow of Ling's busy life and her many friends, while also trying to create opportunities for myself and make friends of my own, but nothing seemed to go right, and I still wasn't working or making any money. Ling wasn't too bothered about the money. She, like me, just wanted us to be happy, but I needed to be able to contribute more. I think this is why I started to feel more and more useless, and Ling probably thought the same about me towards the end.

We ultimately began to show less and less interest in each other; it was just easier that way because everything felt like it was hard work between us. It was as though we had to work at everything, rather than things just happening and feeling natural – like it should.

I mainly put this down to the language. I personally don't think you can ever be as close in a relationship with someone who isn't a native or expert speaker of your own language. I can't speak for everyone, but I think there will always be something missing – some things that you just don't get, and emotions you just cannot get across. I suppose this depends on the type of relationship you want, because there are probably a lot of fat, bald, middle-aged men in Thailand who couldn't give two hoots what comes out of their girlfriends' mouth (just what goes in), but that type of relationship is not for me.

Ling's English was excellent, and we did share many a joke together, in both English and Chinese, but there was still something missing. I really can't put my finger on it. Maybe it was because she didn't share my Boltonian sense of humour, and I didn't understand half the stuff she was fucking muttering on about.

When we chatted about how we felt, before we both agreed I should leave Taiwan, she told me with a hint of regret in her voice, "I'm just tired."

That summed it up perfectly, because I felt exactly the same. We'd gone from being relaxed and comfortable together to being quite awkward. Everything just seemed even more work than at the beginning, and for me, as I wasn't really the type of person to open up about personal matters like this, it was all just building up inside and I had no release.

On our final day together, Ling drove me to the airport. We sat in silence for most of the journey, but then she looked across at me with a tear in her eye and uttered, "It's just like we are going on holiday."

It was exactly like that. Then it hit me; the thought that this was the last time we would ever see each other, and it hurt. It hurt a lot. It was soon to get much worse, too. Ling accompanied me all the way to passport control, which at Chiang Kai-shek Airport must have about forty booths in a row.

We kissed. We cried. We said goodbye. I then wandered over to a booth near the right-hand side.

After passing through, I then turned left – which was the only way to go. As I started to walk, I looked to my left to wave to Ling, and she immediately started to walk with me, but on the other side of passport control.

Then, for what seemed like minutes, and like a tearful final scene from a romantic film, I was walking, seeing Ling, then seeing a dividing pillar, then Ling…pillar…Ling…pillar…Ling…pillar…Ling…pillar…Ling, and then finally, nothing.

That was it. No more. My heart sunk as the sense of loss punched hard into my stomach. I just sat down and burst into tears. I was heartbroken.

The only time I'd ever felt remotely like this was when I dropped those computer listings on the floor and walked out of the office like a zombie.

What had just happened?

Ling.

"It's never too late to be what you might have been."

George Eliot

Chapter Six

Treadmill Existence

I can't comprehend the logic
Everything here makes me feel sick
I just want time to pass by quick
It's not how it should be
I've seen an alternative existence
Away from all this nonsense
Something we all should experience
The feeling to be free

In our treadmill existence
We show little resistance
While we all keep our distance
Between us oh so far
I watch others contributing
To a world of mass polluting
While on the news another shooting
As I stand here at the bar

I flick through television stations
Watching messed-up generations
Wondering if this configuration
Is what god had in mind
The seventh day that god spent resting
May well have been a blessing
Because with one more day of messing
He'd have fucked things up beyond mankind

In our treadmill existence
We show little resistance
While we all keep our distance
Between us oh so far
I think of future existence
With a lack of real confidence
While I rue my guilty conscience
As I cough on my cigar

It's like the world's circuit has shorted
And I sometimes wish I'd been aborted
When I think of all I snorted
The night before today

And there's a rampant cancer spreading
Since I called off that fucking wedding
Now there's a sad future I'm dreading
If I ever get that far

In our treadmill existence
We show little resistance
While we all keep our distance
Between us oh so far
I hear the ambulance siren sounding
While my heart is merely pounding
I feel a sensation of drowning
As they put me in the car

I start to think of the all good times
Family, friends, chilled beer and fine wines
And wonder who I can blame this time
For the weakness in my heart
Then I realise there is no one
It's just me, and my time has come
There is nothing that can be done
I wish I could go back to the start

In our treadmill existence
We show little resistance
While we all keep our distance
Between us oh so far
Now is the time to do something different
Or you'll regret all that time you spent
And wonder where it all went
So be yourself, and follow your heart.

Back to Reality

It's always depressing coming home from holiday, but the comedown after an amazing three-year life-changing experience, from which you've had to wave goodbye (forever) to your sweetheart, is something else.

I had no job, and I was living with my parents, while I was still letting out my own apartment – otherwise I couldn't afford to pay the mortgage. It was grim.

I'd been trying to develop my video business back in England, but after a little success early on, it wasn't really working out, so I decided to bite the bullet.

I moved back into my apartment without having a steady job or any income, giving me no choice but to find a job soon – that was my only reasoning, to give myself a kick up the arse.

It took me six weeks, while living on credit cards, but I found a job. The role was a business analyst based in Halifax, Yorkshire, and paying one-third the salary of the job I'd had before my travels three years earlier. It was a job, though, and I was happy – for about two hours.

The top boss said he would like to spend thirty minutes getting to know me, so we arranged a slot that morning in his apparently busy schedule. He talked about himself for fifteen minutes, and then said, "Well, that's enough about me. I want to know about you, Matthew."

I started to talk, and then, probably around three to five seconds in, the cunt looked at his watch.

I paused and stared him down with my disbelieving what-the-fuck face. This lasted for around the same time as I'd been speaking, before I made a point of starting again from the beginning.

I kept it short from hereon in. I even made a point of not telling the prick anything interesting that I'd done in the years previous to landing at this shithole – the bombs I'd avoided, the tsunami I'd escaped, the Mandarin I'd learnt, the earthquakes I'd enjoyed, the coincidences I'd experienced, the films I'd made, the people I'd met, the challenges I'd faced, the "goal" I'd scored, the places I'd visited, and the love I'd found, then lost.

I really couldn't be bothered. I felt that none of what I said was going in anyway. At one point I even wondered whether I'd accidentally slipped into Chinese again, and then when I realised I hadn't, I thought about doing it anyway just to see if his blank expression and fat robotic nod changed. I didn't bother. I just bored him to death for about five minutes, and that was it. I'd already decided that I wasn't going to be working here for long.

I never saw him again, so fuck knows what his job was. Maybe I should have listened when he was talking about himself. Sometimes, first impressions mean a lot, and that conversation on my first morning in the job put me in the wrong frame of mind. I just didn't want to be there.

It really was shit, though, and these Yorkshire folk really were something else. I plodded on for a while, and I even joined in the Christmas party to try to fit in. There was a free bar at this party, and also a load of gay blokes dressed as cowboys and Indians for some strange reason. This night probably sums up my whole time in Halifax.

At the time of the Christmas party, I'd only been in the job a couple of months, and at the end of the night, extremely pissed, I wandered into the residents' bar. The main bar was closed, so just a few of those who were staying in the hotel were having another drink here. A dozen or so of my colleagues were sitting in a circle, although I still really didn't know any of these people. It was a big company, so although I knew many of their faces, that's all I knew.

When I appeared, they all suddenly stopped talking and looked at me. One of them, who was a large bald bodybuilding cock of a Yorkshireman, then broke the silence when he kindly asked, "Who the hell are you then?"

I pondered on this question for a moment, and then replied like a typical Boltonian, but with a hint of Farnworth, "I'm not being funny mate, but *who the fuck are* you?"

All hell broke loose. He wanted to kill me. I even had a pink cowboy hat on my head by this point, so you can imagine that the situation was quite comical. It quickly calmed down and I subsequently woke up with three cowboy hats on my head, which isn't a sign of anything other than I was pissed.

One week later, the chair devil arranged for that bald bastard to be moved to sit facing me in the office. I stayed at this pathetic excuse for a company for a further nine months after this, and he never spoke to me once. How very, very sad it was.

Sitting next to me during this time was a pregnant woman – my manager. Sitting behind the two of us in our little cove were two more fucking pregnant women, so you can just imagine how the daily conversations went. One of them even had a calendar on her desk which had a daily picture of a half-naked man. I couldn't help but think how the people working in IT had changed over the years – from the beer-binging ear-pierced jovial blokes of the Page Three era to the era of the middle-aged pregnant "lady" drooling over a young fucking topless man.

I had nothing in common with anyone there, and with me literally having no work to do at all in this job for around six months, time ticked so slowly. I did, however, manage to complete all of my degree assignments at work during this period, which was a bonus, and also the only good thing to come out of working there.

I also became to understand the working of banks too or, more accurately, how they survive by ripping off their customers and selling off their bad debt, which further on down the chain no doubt ends up with certain poor ex-customers getting a knock at the door by local hard men.

Much of the work of maintaining the bank's computer system was also that of adding new rules and fees to their customers' accounts. These new rules and fees were to counteract government laws making the bank remove similar fees they'd added in the past. It was like a game of cat and mouse: they would lose money by being prevented from charging one particular type of fee, so they would just create another fee, using slightly different language provided by their own lawyers.

One day, when a group of bods in senior positions were near my desk discussing one of these particular new pieces of work, I just happened to say, "Well, it looks like I'm the only person working at this company who's still got a clear conscience."

When my pregnant manager asked, "Why is that, Matthew?"

I replied, "Because I've not done a fucking thing since I've been here."

There was no laughter. I don't actually think they understood me.

The company had also refused to contribute financially to my BSc honours degree, which was surprising for a large company of this time, especially when the job I was meant to be doing was directly related to the course I was studying. Because of this refusal, I'd set up a small space on my desk with a plastic cup and a Post-it sticker above which read, "Matt's degree fund. Please give generously." I don't think this went down well with the management, and I'm sure everyone knew I wasn't going to stay at the company long.

I hated it so much, and I couldn't stay awake during the day. For years, I hadn't been living the nine-to-five life, so when lunchtime came, I used to go and have a sleep in my car. Other times, when I wasn't tired, I'd go and hide in my car anyway, and I'd write about how shite I felt at the time.

I was a long way from being over Ling. It still made me sick to think about it, so I tried not to. I also experienced a new low, that of general daily life, which was just so boring after the recent years of almost daily discovery.

The only thing that kept me going at this time was studying my degree, which, when alone at night, would be the one thing to take my mind off everything by keeping me busy. Also, when I received a good grade for an assignment, this was the only sense of achievement I had at the time. If I wasn't studying and learning new skills during those months, I think I would have been totally lost. I would have found it difficult to see a better future and would have felt completely useless all over again. As it was, studying was the only thing that gave me hope of escaping this period in my life.

I know my mum did the same thing in her twenties, but that was slightly different. She did it to support her family and help us survive, whereas I did it to help make a better future for myself, though to me it had the added bonus of keeping me busy and giving me a sense of achievement just when I needed it.

Whatever the reason for doing it, it is clear to see that education is the means to escape all sorts of problems.

The low I felt during my time in Halifax is where the previous poem came from. I think it perfectly sums up how far I'd come, from love and wonder to something dark, uncomfortable, dreary, and depressing. However, you can also see a hint of determination in me to do something other than stay there in that lifeless, soulless, and godforsaken place.

You might wonder whether that soulless place was Halifax, or a place in my life at that moment in time. They were both utter shit back then, so let's just leave it at that and move on.

When East meets West – Christmas party in Halifax. Cowboys and fucking Indians.

Got to Move On

Is this what you want?
Just sitting in front
Of a computer
Feeling almost defunct
You know that it's not
There's more that you've got
To give to this life
So just give it a shot

The same every day
For not enough pay
Working your arse off
Doing just what they say
Is this really you?
Please find something new
You're much better off
Telling them what to do

Should you take the risk?
Or should you persist?
A difficult choice?
Stop being altruist
Think about yourself
It's not good for your health
Sitting there waiting
When you should be somewhere else

You're going insane
But you have the brain
To turn it around
There is so much to gain
From leaving this place
So do it with haste
And soon you will see
A smile back on your face

So the choice is yours

You can stop being bored
Do something you like
You will reap the reward
It might take some time
But soon you'll be fine
And then you will see
Just how high you can climb

But it's not about heights
Or seeking bright lights
It's just about you
Doing something you like
So just seize the day
Do things your own way
No time like the present
So let's start straight away

The Interview

I'd been planning my escape from the dirty shithole that was Halifax for a while, and in the summer of 2007, after working for Halifax and Bank of Scotland for almost one year, I eventually land myself a job interview. It was for a much better job, but it was in Bradford; this is another shithole in an even more distant part of Yorkshire.

It all sounds like a really shit tour of Yorkshire, doesn't it? First, we're off to Halifax, then onto Bradford. Bradford? Bollocks! Someone please pass me a fucking big dead dog.

Anyway, interviews aren't really my cup of tea. I've actually had some really good ones, but I've always suffered with nerves when being in a group of more than, let's say, *one* person. This is why I am often very quiet and feel quite lost in large groups.

When there are two or more people asking me direct questions, this sometimes freaks me out, and my mind often goes blank, or I start talking complete bollocks. Other times, I'm fine. Let's just say I'm a great deal better at doing my job, or writing about it, than I am at talking about it.

My dad summed up the whole interview process for me after he'd retired and my mum wanted him to get a part-time job at a DIY store. On the day he had his interview, he opened a big door and entered the interview room, only to see two people quite far away behind a large intimidating desk. As he walked in, he said, "This isn't fair, two against one!"

He didn't get the job, but that was probably what he wanted – the crafty bastard – just like Spud in the film *Trainspotting* but without the influence of class A drugs – maybe class B, though.

The interviews in my line of work are usually quite formal with the odd exception, and I think this is what trips me up sometimes. In Bradford, I was prepared for this typical formal experience, fearing the worst before it had even started and getting myself worked up for no reason, as usual.

I arrived after the ninety-minute drive, already thinking that there's no way I could do this drive every day as it would kill me. I was, however, pleasantly surprised to find the offices located in old mills by a river, and they were stunning. I immediately decided I would love to work here if it wasn't for the shit long drive every morning and the shit long drive back home every night.

I needed to move on, though, so I really was open to anything at the time. Let's say I was desperate. I would be learning some well-needed new programming skills in this job too, so I thought it could quite quickly lead me to better things.

I was to be interviewed by a bloke (the boss) and a young lady, who was a software developer like me. It turned out, by chance, that she'd even been studying the same computer programming courses as me with the Open University. I'd just completed these courses, but she'd actually pulled out because she'd found them too difficult and too time consuming. Now then, these particular courses were extremely tough – the most difficult I ever studied – but I managed to complete them all, achieving distinctions and merits on the way. I worked very hard on them. I'm no genius.

So, due to this amazing stroke of luck, do you think I've got the job already? I obviously did, and I relaxed for a change. They then gave me some technical problems and questions, not too taxing, they said. However, I somehow managed to mess up every single one. I had no idea what to do with any of them until they put me out of my misery by telling me the answer, when the answer suddenly became completely fucking obvious.

From initially being on such a confident high, I now thought I'd blown it, and I wasn't all that bothered. I was even thinking there and then that the experience will have done me good for my next interview, and that this job in Bradford just wasn't meant to be.

The interview questions then changed to more general, personality questions, and judging by their body language, I thought that they'd had enough by now. They'd just ask me a few token questions and be done with me.

They asked one of those typical behavioural-type questions, which was, "If you didn't get on with a colleague in the office, how would you deal with the situation?"

I replied with the standard answer, "I would be professional, as always, because the office is no place for petty fallouts. Anything like that should be dealt with away from the workplace and not enter your thoughts during company time."

What is that all about? What other nonsense could you possibly answer that question with?

They both fake-smiled and nodded before looking downward towards the desk, putting their pens to the paper and giving me the token tick I had earned.

Let's just pause here for a moment while they are ticking the box.

I already thought that the interview was over due to my incompetence, and I didn't really care whether I was offered the job or not at this point. So what did I do?

At the moment they were looking down, I said, in my own dry tone, "I'd just fucking slag 'em off behind their back."

Those were my exact words. Why did I say that? I have no idea.

However, they both laughed. They actually laughed out loud, and that gave me the confidence to carry on the interview with similar responses, soon having them in stitches. I'd managed to change the whole atmosphere with one daft comment, and their body language towards me changed completely after it.

The next day, I was offered the job, and for some reason they even offered me £2000 per year more than I was asking for, so I accepted straight away.

When is anyone ever offered more money than they ask for?

Just think about that. I know I'd done well in those OU courses which the interviewer had failed to complete, but I failed to answer every technical question they'd asked, and I was still offered the job – with more pay. If I hadn't started being a comedian halfway through the interview, do you really think I'd have still been offered the job? This is why you should always be yourself.

By the way, I'm not sure if this comedic moment has anything to do with me recovering from the dark months I suffered prior to this. I think it is probably more in relation to me not giving an actual fuck about anything at the time.

Carry On, Regardless

I sit here, dejected
I've just been rejected
I wasn't selected
This time
I'm very frustrated
And quite irritated
That time that they wasted
Was mine

I keep on keep trying
Keep laughing keep smiling
But then all the while in
My head
There is much confusion
Even disillusion
Is there a solution?
Ahead

In some desperation
Even deprivation
Hope in this situation
It's tough
But with contemplation
And some education
You will find aspiration
Soon enough

You must not hesitate
But you must orchestrate
And then instigate
Your revival
You will demonstrate
You can subjugate
Overall, it's not fate
But survival

I kept on, kept trying

I looked to the sky and
I prayed for divine
Intervention
I know that it's stupid
But I'm sure I saw Cupid
And my smile was just
Too great to mention

So I now see an end to
The stuff that I went through
I see light at the edge of
The darkness
You must suffer the heartache
But trust me, that won't take
Too long, so carry on
Regardless

Munich, Fake Euros, Methylenedioxymethamphetamine, and Me

After first accepting the excellent job offer in Bradford – a place that would leave you requiring daily intravenous hard-drug injections if you were to work there permanently – I turned it down. I was saved yet again by the wonderful government, who offered me a contract much more lucrative than the Bradford job. Although this contract role was again working on old technology, it paid three times the job in Bradford, and was quite close to home in Preston, so after three years earning no money and one year earning shit money in Halifax, it was a no-brainer of a decision.

The week before, however, I travelled to Germany to watch Bolton Wanderers play Bayern Munich away from home, and I very nearly didn't return to start my new job. This was one of those amazing nights I thought I'd never see, watching my team of thirty years Bolton Wanderers playing in a European competition. As it turned out, I almost wished I'd never even gone.

Me, James Greaves, Gordon Thomas, and the late, great James O'Brien travelled together, and we enjoyed a good couple of days, culminating in Bolton earning a magnificent 2-2 draw with the mighty Bayern. It was a night we would never forget, me more than anyone else, because my night didn't even get started until after the game had finished.

Midnight struck, and it was November 9th, 2007 – my thirty-sixth birthday. I'd lost the other three lads by this point after meeting up with my brother and a different group, most of whom I didn't really know apart from my brother's mate from school, Brownie. Some of these lads seemed a bit dodgy to me, and when one of them gave me a €50 note to get the drinks in, I checked it before going to the bar.

To my untrained eye, the note was obviously fake, and I wondered what I should do. Not wanting to cause a commotion, I just put the note in my back pocket and used my own real money to buy the drinks.

A little later, we entered a pub/club. After being allowed in by the mean-looking doormen, we made our way upstairs where there was a restaurant, and the six of us got a table to ourselves.

Just to add to the entertainment, for some mad reason – and sorry for this, Mum – I had taken half an Ecstasy tablet at some earlier point in the evening, well before we arrived at this place. I'd only done this a few times in my life, and I hadn't done it for about ten years or so at the time. This was the final time I would ever do it. I hope that makes you feel a bit better, Mum.

Anyway, it wasn't as though this night needed anything else to enhance it. I was in Munich, Bolton had just drawn 2-2 at the mighty Bayern in a European competition, and it was my birthday.

We all do stupid things at some point in our lives, but luckily for me, many of my stupid acts seem to have actually worked in my favour, and it's possible that this one daft thing even saved me from months in a Munich prison, and maybe from being bummed by big Fritz.

We ate, we drank, we laughed, and we had a great time over the next hour or so. Then the bill arrived. I was told by someone at the table, "It's your birthday, Matt, we'll sort the bill out between us."

How nice of them, I thought.

We all then got up to leave, and I picked up the tray of cash from the table, before handing it to the cashier on the way out. I had to wait a few moments for the cashier, so as I was handing over the money, I could see the others were just heading out the door.

As I neared the exit, seconds later, I was immediately stopped by two big, burly, German gentlemen. The money I'd handed over had been checked, and there were a total of *three* fake €50 notes in there. The notes were obviously not mine, but it certainly didn't look like that, so the staff had no option but to keep me there and call the police. At first, I thought this was no problem at all for me because I hadn't done anything wrong. However, I then gasped, and suddenly felt sick inside, as I remembered that in my back pocket was the *fake* €50 note which I had previously *refused* to spend.

If you were on a jury, would you believe my story about only having this note in my back pocket because someone gave it to me to get the drinks in earlier, but I'd refused to spend it and used my own money instead? I know I definitely wouldn't. I was innocent, but I was guilty to anyone else in the world.

The two doormen sat me on a stool at the bar, where they kept guard over me. A drunken Irish man then appeared from nowhere. I've no idea who he was, but he asked me what happened, and then started to chat to the doormen while I just sat, wondering what on earth was going to happen to me. Then he said something really frightening. He said, "Two years. Two years in prison is what you get for spending fake money in Germany."

If that wasn't bad enough, the fucking Ecstasy tablet really started to hit me then.

The police were on their way to the scene, I was off my head, and I had evidence in my back pocket that could put me away in prison for two years. What did I do? I stuffed it down the back of my fucking pants.

The police then arrived. There was one woman and one man. He (Mr. Angry) immediately shouted, "Empty your pockets now!" So, I did.

He saw a €50 note and shouted, "This is *fake* Euro!"

My heart sank. I thought, "Oh shit! The note from my back pocket which I put down my pants – was that the fucking real one? Had I somehow mixed them up, ending up with the real one near my arse and the fake one in my front pocket, therefore giving myself a two-year fucking jail sentence in the meantime?"

I really wasn't sure, but I had to say, "This is real money. Why are you so angry? Are you a Bayern Munich fan?"

His face was blank, but funnily enough, I saw half a smile on the female copper's face.

I'd decided in my fucked-up mind that it was a good cop, bad cop situation, and I was already enjoying it, even though I still had evidence on me that could ruin the rest of my life.

For a millisecond, I wondered whether I should hide this fake note up my arse. A millisecond was enough. However, I then decided that I needed to get this item away from my body because I was sure the search at the station would find it on me.

It was all a bit slow motion from then on. The Irishman was talking typical Irish drunken gibberish at a million miles per hour, and for some reason the cops and the doormen seemed to be listening to his every word, while I sat on the stool at the bar pondering my next move.

I knew I had to do something this time. I couldn't just accept what was coming to me; otherwise I was in big trouble.

Moments later, with five people standing right next to me, I slowly slid my arse off the stool and stood up. No one looked or said a word. Tight jeans weren't the fashion at the time, so while the others were all distracting each other, with what I don't know, I slowly stretched, and put my hand down the back of my pants to retrieve the note. However, I only managed to push it further down, and it soon became obvious that I would only be able to retrieve the note from the bottom of my trouser leg.

I manoeuvred it further down by tugging at my jeans, until it was inches from falling to the floor, near my sock.

Then, amazingly, with two bouncers, two police officers, and the mystery Irishman around me, I bent down, pretending to tie my shoe lace, and grasped the note just before it fell to the floor.

I then stood up and sat back on the stool, putting my hand behind my back. With my fingers, I created an opening in the leather underneath the seat I was sitting on, before forcing the evidence into the lining of the seat, while, incredibly, they were still entertaining each other.

It was unbelievable that none of these idiots saw any of this. How? Just how did this happen? I was off my head and drunk, so how did I manage to fool them all? Why would at least one of them not be looking at me?

The feeling of relief that came over me was utterly amazing.

I had always been innocent, but never in a million years would I have been innocent in anyone's eyes if that note had been found on me.

With what I'd just done I'd probably saved myself, but had I done it all alone? There was no way I could have done what I did if it wasn't for the strange, knowledgeable, typically annoying, but also engaging Irishman. He kept me in the bar five minutes longer, and not only that, he distracted the police and the doormen the whole time. It was as if he was put there just to give me the opening that I most certainly needed.

Whatever the case, I somehow managed to see that opening presented to me and grasp it. The high it gave me was the best feeling I've ever experienced.

However, I still had the interrogation to come, on Ecstasy, and this was going to be a long night.

They drove me to the police station and then took me into a room for questioning. This was the first time I had ever been in a police station for being accused of being on the wrong side of the law, so you can imagine that I should be very nervous and quite scared.

However, I had a massive permanent grin on my face the whole time, and I knew that this was really annoying Bad Cop, but I really couldn't help it. I even tried to wipe it off with my hand at one point. I was off my head.

After the body search had produced nothing, due to the miracle in the bar, they took my passport from me and began the questioning.

Why did you have fake euro? How many fake euro did you bring? Where did you get the fake euro? Who are you here with? Where are they staying? Do they also have fake euro? I really can't remember any more than that.

There had been a spate of people using fake euros in Munich over the previous couple of days, and this obviously had something to do with the thousands of Bolton fans who had travelled there.

The police were desperate to catch someone for this, and I got the feeling that Bad Cop really wanted me to be that person. The beautiful brown Stone Island jacket I was wearing, notable for being the designer choice of the football hooligan, didn't help matters, because that alone made me look like a common football thug, which I most certainly wasn't.

I kept repeating myself in my answers; "It was my birthday. It was not my money. The others paid for me."

He just shouted louder and louder, asking the same fucking things, mainly in German, then she would translate everything in a friendly English voice.

Good Cop was great. She spoke excellent English, and she was quite calming. I told her that I couldn't wait to get home and tell my mum this story, and she smiled.

I think it was around 4 a.m. when they said they wanted to search my hotel room. I was staying with the three I had travelled with, who were due to go to the airport around this time. I was a bit worried that we'd arrive at the hotel and they'd be doing something illegal in the room; I'm not sure what I thought that might be, but I know it would have been a nasty shock for them to be woken up by the police. They would have no doubt pissed themselves laughing when they saw me with two police officers, though.

When we arrived at the hotel, I was relieved to find that they had already left for the airport, even though that meant I was now obviously going to miss my flight home. When we entered the hotel room, they did a quick search and found nothing, obviously. They then wanted to take me straight back to the station without all my belongings.

I argued that I would miss my flight if I had to leave my luggage – even though I already had – and that it would be much more convenient if I quickly packed my things and took my suitcase with me to the police station. Bad Cop really didn't want me to waste any more of his time, but his lovely colleague persuaded him to let me pack.

I then completely took the piss for some unknown reason. After packing most of my things with them waiting around trying to hurry me up, I strolled into the bathroom, and started to clean my fucking teeth. They both came into the bathroom and looked at me in disbelief. I just started laughing, and they more or less dragged me out of there. I blame the drugs.

Back at the station, about 5 a.m., they continued with a similar line of shit questioning. This went on for a further two hours.

Then, at 7 a.m., they gave me something in German to sign, and told me I could go if I signed it.

I almost did sign it, but then I realised it could say absolutely anything, so I said, "I'm not signing that. It's in German. What does it even say?"

Bad Cop shouted, "It says you had fake euro!"

I then paused for a moment. I was extremely calm, obviously all down to the Ecstasy that I was still buzzing from, and as I relaxed into my seat, it all just clicked. It was all quite simple really.

There was a fatal flaw in the evidence they had against me, and no court in the land would ever prosecute me unless I admitted it. I had already magically disposed of the key piece of evidence that could have been used to convict me.

After my moment of consideration, I had one of my better interview moments, and I eloquently stated, "I never had any fake euros. It was my birthday, and the group I was with paid for me as a treat. I never touched any of that money with my fingers. I just picked up the tray of cash and handed it over. As there were six of us at the table, how can you prove that any of the money I handed over was actually mine?"

After a chat with Good Cop, who was translating my fine words to him, he immediately ripped up the unsigned statement, threw down my passport onto the desk in front of me, and said those beautiful words,

"You can go."

He then showed me to the door.

As I exited the police station, dragging my baggage into the early morning Munich rain on my thirty-sixth birthday, I thanked him and offered my hand for him to shake.

He refused. I smiled.

I was free, and even though I'd missed my flight home and I didn't know where I was, I felt absolutely amazing.

I looked up to the pleasant grey morning sky with an extra-large grin as the cold rain drizzled onto my welcoming face.

"What a feeling," I thought, before it hit me. "What the fuck do I do now?"

Days later, a lad I know from Bolton named Prawn was locked up for ninety-nine days in a Munich prison for using fake euros. That was how close I'd come.

Me & Chris on the day I was released. We even look dodgy here, and Brownie in the background looks quite fucked.

The Turing Test

In 2007, the week following my eventual return from Munich, I started a new contract for central government in Preston. This was all new to me because I'd only ever worked on government projects in Newcastle and Lytham, so I expected to see a whole load of new faces.

However, during my first week on the job I ventured into one of the other three office blocks on site – the Alan Turing Building – and I was surprised to find many of my old colleagues working there.

While I'd been away, my old project from Lytham had been moved to Preston. Although my new role was now for a different project, my old project was seen as higher priority, and as they were quite desperate to find experienced staff to help out, my old manager quickly snatched me up – again. So, by complete chance, I ended up back in the same fucking job I'd vouched never return to.

The fact that I'd had about five years away from the job and my old programming skills were rather rusty didn't seem to matter. After three years doing not much in Taiwan, almost a year trying to develop my video business back home, and then another year doing fuck all in Halifax, I'd forgotten everything about the job, and I thought it would take me ages to pick things up again. I also figured that they must be quite desperate to get me in so quickly.

They were desperate, and there was a good reason for this.

Much of the work had been outsourced to India over the previous couple of years, and, not surprisingly, it was all going tits up. The majority of development work done in India would come back with problems, and there would be no other option but to rewrite much of it back in England. It was all in a bit of a mess, so my job for the first few weeks was just rewriting the shite from India –even though I hadn't done the job for years. That's how bad it was.

Due to these problems, it was decided that we should have at least one experienced English employee based in India at all times, and after just three weeks back in the job, I was asked if I would like to go to India, so I went. Over one year had passed since I'd left Taipei and I was getting an itch to travel again, so I was actually quite excited about this. I'd never been to India before, so I could also do some sightseeing while I was there, and all at the expense of the government – sorry – and all at the expense of EDS.

When I have mentioned working for the government – I mean I was, albeit indirectly – I worked for a large American company called EDS who had "won" the contract to do this work for the government. From 1995 to 2000, I had contracted directly to the government until Tony Blair's New Labour party decided to outsource all the IT work for government benefit systems. This wasn't a new thing, or even a Labour thing, because the Tories had done this in the past with other departments. However, from what I witnessed, this is how I think the outsourcing of this particular project may have worked at the time. I might be wrong, but something just didn't seem quite right about it to me.

1. The government outsourced the work to EDS.

2. EDS didn't have enough qualified staff for the task.

3. EDS outsourced to Indian company for staff, many of whom were clueless.

4. EDS paid the Indian company peanuts for their staff.

5. EDS charged the government shitloads for the same staff.

6. EDS were quids in.

7. The government was out of pocket.

8. The taxpayer was out of pocket.

9. *You* was out of pocket.

10. Something stinks.

The project had deadlines tied into the introduction of a new system, and if the system was not implemented in time, the introduction of the benefit changes would also have to be delayed, resulting in many more millions of pounds being spent on top of the initial millions spent already.

This is why they needed people like me. I'm not saying I was the only one doing any work, but there was a small team who knew what they were doing, and these few had to get the others out of the shit time and time again. The Indian experience was on a different fucking level, though.

Pune, India

This place is a fucking shithole.

The first time I travelled to India in early 2008, I was very excited. I was flying business class with Emirates, and this was something I'd always wanted to do; be treated like I was important by a company I worked for. I had good intentions, thinking that I would do EDS proud while representing them. I was serious too – I think.

I had a couple of pints of lager in my local boozer, said au revoir to a couple of my mates, and walked home to get ready for my flight, which was four hours later.

I was having a shower, when I thought I might as well give the cubicle a right good clean. It's always nice to come home to cleanliness after a few weeks away. However, after kneeling down to scrub the shower tray, I stood up, and quite typically smashed my head on the fucking chrome tap – *head trauma #1!*

It hurt, and when I looked down the water was blood red. I carried on showering for a few minutes, thinking the bleeding would soon stop, but it just kept pouring out. It obviously wasn't a small wound. With one hand constantly on my head stopping the blood, I exited the shower, dried off, got dressed, and then drove myself to accident and emergency – one-handed.

On arriving at accident and emergency, I explained my scenario: that I needed to get to the airport in the next hour or two. The hospital staff were very accommodating, either that or maybe they just weren't busy for a change. I had six stitches in my wound, and, as is unheard of in England, I managed to get out of the hospital within the hour. I even arrived at the airport with plenty time to spare. However, I was warned that I needed to have these stitches removed within two weeks, so as I would be in India for three weeks, I'd need to find a doctor while I was out there.

I didn't let that bother me at all. I was seat number 1A on an Emirates flight, sitting in business class, so I just told everybody my story, sipped champagne, and enjoyed my first-ever business trip. What a bell-end.

I visited Pune twice over a period of nine months, staying for three weeks each time. Actually, the second time was only two and a half weeks. I left early on this occasion to have a couple of days in Dubai on the way home – at the company's expense. They didn't seem to mind this. They didn't actually know about it, even though I got the company to arrange and pay for all the travel.

I managed to do this because some of these large companies are quite clueless. They sometimes get too big for themselves, with different departments split throughout the world, none of whom seem to communicate with each other, and this was exactly the case here.

For example, I had one particular manager who would sign my timesheet, and he wasn't even in the same time zone as me. I might have abused this situation on the odd occasion. The best example of this was when I was forced to take a 10 per cent pay cut from my daily contract rate. I refused four times before basically being told to take it or get out. I obviously took it, but I decided there and then, from that day forward, I would just work fewer hours to compensate for the rate cut. EDS had just been spouting off about the extra billions of dollars they'd made that year, but they now needed to cut costs? I thought this was complete bollocks, so I worked one hour less every day.

Astonishingly, I managed to do this for the next four years, and nobody said a word, not even my local boss, the one who didn't sign my timesheet. In fact, come to think of it, what the fuck did he do?

I still produced good work during this period though, which is the most important thing. Some people get hung up about the number of hours they work in my particular job when, realistically, quite often, it is a job that doesn't require you to be sat at a desk nine hours each day. I am proof of that. In fact, when I'm away from my desk or driving to work, I am often trying to work out a problem in my head – something that is difficult to do when you're sat in a noisy office all day. However, after reading this, I now expect my manager and fellow workmates to keep a daily fucking record of my hours.

The Dubai situation was similar to the timesheet one. I was authorised to travel business class to Pune, with the usual flights for this trip going via Dubai. The lady organising my trip was based in Southern England, and I just told her that, rather than depart Pune on the Friday or Saturday, I wanted to leave on the Wednesday, spend a few nights in Dubai, and then leave Dubai at the weekend. That was it. I left Pune three days early, and nobody back in the office in England had a clue about it because I didn't tell anyone.

Anyway, when I arrived in Pune for the first time, after being stitched up hours earlier, I made my way straight to the hotel bar. This was for medicinal purposes only of course.

It was a posh hotel in the middle of shit, shit, and more shit. But it was a lovely hotel.

The second time I went to the bar, I mentioned my head predicament to the barman and that I would soon need a doctor to remove my stitches.

He immediately said, "My brother is doctor. He will do for small fee."

Being the well-travelled person I was, and experienced in the consumption of bullshit, I knew that the barman's "brother" could obviously have been anyone, and I might well have been "stitched up" in a different way, so I just took the stitches out myself instead. It was much easier this way, and they almost seem to just fall out anyway after a couple of weeks.

This first time working in India, I realised what a terrible state my project was in. In an office of over thirty local staff, there were just two or three of them doing any work. The rest did nothing, though EDS were still charging the government for every single one of them.

To sum it up, the lad who sat next to me was watching fucking wrestling and reading electronic comics on his PC all day.

Apart from the work, though, of which I did very little in Pune – because there was nothing for me to do apart from answer the odd question – I did manage to have a splendid time.

For security purposes, I had my own personal driver. He would take me anywhere I wanted, at any time, and I generally made the most of him. One night, however, I didn't use my driver, and I almost regretted it.

I'd met a couple in my hotel bar. He was a photographer from Blackburn, near my home in England, and his girlfriend was from Brazil. We chatted for a while, and as I'd bought them a few drinks and some fags on the flimsy EDS account, they later invited me back to their place for a few more.

180

We jumped in a tuk-tuk to their place, which was a large house in its own grounds. It was lovely. We sat out on the balcony for a few hours, drinking whiskey and smoking these strange cigarettes they had. A few hours later, I was completely stoned. This wasn't planned, and it's something that I just don't do because I don't like it. The odd cigarette is enough to make me dizzy.

At a silly time in the morning, and slightly worse for wear, I decided that I had to leave, so I said my goodbyes and off I wandered into the sunrise. One small problem then hit me. I had no idea where I was.

I looked for a main road where I'd be able to flag down one of the thousands of tuk-tuks that were constantly buzzing about the place. At this time of day, however, there were none to be seen, so I walked aimlessly for about an hour, before finally hearing the distant fart of one behind me.

He stopped and I gladly jumped aboard. The driver was a friendly chap who didn't stop talking, and I'm sure he told me that he originated from Afghanistan. Then again I might have conjured this up in my head. I almost laughed at the thought of him being a terrorist on a tuk-tuk, just happening to find his next Western victim by the roadside flagging him down for a lift. This is obviously why you shouldn't take drugs.

We were driving happily along, but then, suddenly, he stopped.

My hotel was nowhere to be seen, so I asked, "Why have we stopped here?"

He replied, "We swap. You drive."

I said, "I'm pissed and I'm stoned, pal. Why the fuck would I want to drive?"

He repeated himself, "We swap. You drive."

I replied, "No."

Quite forcefully, he said again "We swap! You drive!"

Just to shut the clown up, I said, "For fuck sake. What do I do then?"

For some reason he then made me drive all the way back to my hotel. I thought about my company and that they probably didn't have this in mind when they asked me to represent them in India – pissed and stoned driving a tuk-tuk. Just imagine if I'd been stopped by the police – whatever they do over there – and been charged. How could I explain this situation to the top brass on my return? I don't think it would have gone down too well.

I managed to arrive at the hotel in one piece – no crash, no kidnapping by terrorists – and I collapsed on my bed.

The next morning however, I quite worryingly found this poor thing right outside the entrance to my hotel. Now, I know I was in a poor state, but I'm sure it had nothing to do with me.

Tut-tut.

Afghan Man

He's an Afghan man in Pakistan
What is he doing there?
Looking quite suspicious, with his
Upside-down facial hair
He might just be on holiday
With his family
But I'm just glad he's 4000 miles
Away from me

He gets up in the morning
Not sure if he cleans his teeth
And when he puts his robe on
Not sure if he wears much underneath
But this guy he means business
Just look into his eyes
He almost looks as though
He's wearing a disguise

He lives up in the mountains
But he's got a mobile phone
He's probably been to Cornwall
Stayed in a mobile home
He probably goes to theme parks
Just like the rest of us
But you want to see the panic
When he gets onto a bus

He often has a drink or two
But his Mrs is teetotal
It's against all his beliefs, but he
Still pops down to his local
He loves fish and chips
And he's quite partial to a trifle
But underneath that gown
He might well have a fucking rifle

Ask him where he lives

He will say just down the road
When he's really underground
In his not-so-humble abode
He's got a HD TV
And all the mod cons
But there's no electricity
So he just sits there making bombs

When he was in Pakistan
Back home there was a raid
How lucky he was
That he hadn't stayed
Well, that's what you would think
What a lucky man
That the entire US army
Had only killed his gran

Now did he escape by chance?
Or is there some more to it?
Did he give up his gran?
For UK citizenship?
I'm not the one to say
That is not my place
But now he lives in Bolton
Because we don't discriminate

He's an Afghan man in Boltonstan
What is he doing here?
Looking quite suspicious
And filling me with fear
He might just be on holiday
With his family
So why am I not happy?
That he lives next door to me

S.H.I.T.

I've worked in information technology for the past twenty-five years in a number of different roles. In that time, I've worked for ten large organisations, so I think I'm qualified to discuss the pile of complete and utter bollocks that is the IT industry. It's such a strange environment to work in. It's bizarre.

There's so much money flying around, and so much of it being wasted on computer systems that will never be used. Some of these pointless projects go on for years, costing millions, when even most of the people working on them know they will never go live. How can this be?

In a recent interview for a government transformation project, two ways of developing two similar systems were explained to me by the American company doing the work. They were developing both systems concurrently so they would have a comparison between the two and be able to see which method would be the best way to go with the transformation of all the other government legacy systems. This was a massive and important task, because the hardware running their existing systems would cease to be supported just a few years later, and these systems affect millions of people in the UK.

To me, one of these methods sounded ridiculous, if not impossible, so I said to the interviewers, "Good luck. I think you might need a magician like Paul Daniels to get that one done." Then we all laughed.

Even I knew from the little detail I had that it was complete nonsense what they were trying to do, and the interviewers' responses told me that they felt exactly the same.

I ended up working on the other, not-so-ridiculous project, which was successful, but the "impossible" project, not surprisingly to me and many others, was a complete disaster.

Why did I and many others know that it wouldn't work, yet millions of pounds were wasted over two years to keep it going? It's probably because people in high positions with great responsibility are sold these ideas without knowing enough about the technologies being used – or is there some other more sinister reason maybe?

At a lower level, this industry is mainly just a game of bluff most of the time. Often, developers and their managers don't really give anything away about how bad or how well a project is going, not even to each other. On certain projects in the past, if I told my boss that everything was going great, and that I was well ahead of schedule, then he would just pile more work on top of me. The following week, when everything went tits up – as often happened – I then had no leeway, and so by finishing a piece of work early and telling my boss this, I'd put myself under unnecessary pressure the week after.

If I told my boss that I was well behind and would probably not meet a deadline, then this would be highlighted in a report to manager upon manager who would all start to panic unnecessarily, making things a whole lot worse for me. Their plan to deal with this situation of me being behind schedule would then be to micromanage me, inviting me to meeting upon meeting to give them more-than-regular updates on my progress, which was counterproductive. These meetings obviously ate away at the time I needed to do my fucking job, therefore slowing me down, and this has happened to me dozens of times over the years.

It was generally in my best interest to say that I was well on course to meet the deadline on my manager's bullshit project plan. It made things so much easier and gave me a much better chance of finishing my work on time.

Now, that's just me reporting to my own boss, but there can be layers of bosses, all reporting to each other. When you have a situation like I recently had with several external companies "working together", you get additional unnecessary layers of bullshit. My boss and the bosses of the other companies all added their own topping of extra bullshit to the bullshit they'd already been told by their men on the frontline, like me. I think that sums up the IT industry pretty well, really. It's just layers of bullshit. I'm making this up as I'm writing by the way.

On the bottom layer, you have some technical people trying to confuse everyone with technical bullshit. I am a technical person myself, and these few who purposely confuse others are my most hated of everyone in IT, because our job should be to simplify everything: solve a problem in the most efficient or logical way we can find, and then explain what we have done in simple terms that a nontechnical person can understand. Those who don't do this think they are being clever by complicating things and by making someone feel stupid. You are not being clever – you are being a fucking smart-arse, and no one likes you.

One layer up, you have the analysts. There are business analysts, and there are technical analysts, and I have done both jobs. Sometimes, I have felt completely lost doing these jobs because I didn't know enough about the business or technical side to be able to bullshit properly either way. I still managed to get by, though, with minimal bullshit. Sometimes, these people are integral to the project, whereas other times, they just do what the technical people tell them, or type up what the business people say. The job mainly consists of shit, boring meetings, talking bollocks, and listening to varying degrees of more bullshit.

On the top layer, you have managers confusing everyone on the project by speaking a completely different bullshit language. This is usually because they don't quite understand what everyone else on the project is talking about, and they probably can't conceive what the project is actually delivering. They often use ridiculous acronyms, nonsense buzzwords, and other shit terms they've learnt from recent company-funded away days, or what they've picked up in meetings with other like-minded pricks.

Don't get me wrong. There are some absolute creative and technical geniuses developing amazing products for us all to enjoy and "improve" our lives, but this is a small portion of the IT workforce. A few decades ago, the whole industry used to be made up of extremely intelligent, slightly mad people, because computing was something new, and it only attracted the very clever. It now attracts all kinds of clowns.

The above views are all my own, and they are mostly tongue-in-cheek, by the way – just in case I am still employed when this book is published.

I've moved between companies quite a bit, so I've experienced the good and bad of IT in equal measures. I am currently lucky in that I mainly work with experienced people – clever people who have done the job for years, have seen it all, and know what they're doing. I also do a decent job myself nowadays, but this wasn't always the case.

As you know, I fell into the world of computing after not really excelling at school. I was always interested in computers. I just wasn't very good. I have often sat there looking at my computer screen, wondering what the fuck I am supposed to be doing – sometimes for days on end. I then somehow manage to get by with trial and error. In the old days, there was no time for error because you would have to reserve a short timeslot on the mainframe computer, which was the one and only place you could test your work, all of which previously had to be handwritten without the aid of a computer. This is why, forty years ago, the people in my job needed to be a whole lot better at the job than I now need to be. I get a lot more help than they did.

Like many other industries, however, it is now flooded with too many managers. A recent study showed that 68 per cent of today's IT projects fail, which is ridiculous. I'm sure this wasn't always the case, and how can this happen when we now have so many more people "managing" these projects? It is not the whole reason they fail, but it certainly has something to do with it.

The project I worked on for EDS in 2001 was called the Pension Forecasting System (PFS). This was the job based in Newcastle – the one mentioned at the start of the book where I'd started penning poems during the boredom. At the time, EDS had an American CEO who would email us weekly bullshit, signing off his emails with the phrase "Action, Urgency, Excellence!"

Now then, what the fuck is all that about?

He even wrote a book of the same name. This is the kind of nonsense you endure in the IT industry. You get pricks spouting new nonsense buzzwords every other week, for no other reason than they think they are being clever. As you've no doubt realised, I prefer to use simple English words that everyone can understand, because I feel it is important to keep things simple in my line of work, rather than finding every opportunity to confuse others, and ultimately piss them off.

This is now quite a special moment in the book. I can't quite believe it, but it all began with that "Action, Urgency, Excellence" bollocks. This is because the next poem – written in 2001 – was the first thing I wrote that appears in these pages. Who would have thought that two different experiences in Newcastle, fourteen years apart, and that shit phrase, would come together like they did to trigger all this off?

Project Failure Shambles

When I started on PFS some months ago
I was warned that progress was very slow
But I was in for a shock when I got into the swing
As I realised no one knew a fucking thing
I dug in deep for a week or two
Trying to work out what I was supposed to do
But the task became such a painful task
As I didn't know who or what I was supposed to ask

The business, they weren't the most pleasant lot
In fact, if I were in charge I would have had them all shot
They just made it hard for us to do our job
And that Peter? What a fucking knob!
They got what they wanted though in the end
After driving us all around the bend
The project was scrapped after eighteen months
A decision that was made by a complete dunce

They thought they had a contingency to fall back on
But then realised they didn't really have one
For the contingency would take an extra year
And eventually work out twice as dear
Tears of laughter ran down my cheeks
As I worked my notice of four weeks
And I pondered on my next location
Thinking after this bollocks I need a very long vacation

So what was the reason for this mess?
Well, it wasn't completely EDS
It was mainly the business and the management team
Who make the decisions without knowing what they
mean
One decision they made was to use EDS again
I don't know why, as the result is always the same
Because mess after mess EDS presents
But remember, they do it with
Action, urgency, and excellence!

189

What a load of absolute bollocks.

Genius?

A number of people have previously told me that I am a genius. I'm quite obviously not. The first time this happened was in 1994 when I first studied computing at college.

In the first few weeks of the course, there was a question in an assignment asking to write a short computer program for one of the first-ever computers. It was a standard question that had been asked many times before, and it had a standard answer, but without having the Internet at the time, you couldn't just go and look up the answer unfortunately.

I looked at this question for hours on end and kept thinking that it can't be so difficult. I was even working as a computer programmer at the time, unlike many others on the course, so I thought it would be a bit embarrassing if I couldn't answer it correctly and the other students could. Finally, after many hours of working it out, I came up with an answer which was very complex, but which I knew was correct.

When I received my marked paper, I'd done really well, but there was a lot of red pen and crosses on one particular page – the page with the one question which I'd toiled over all night. I then noticed at the bottom of the page the tutor had put a small tick, next to which was the word "Ingenious!"

The question had initially been marked incorrect because I hadn't gotten the "right" answer. However, I did manage to come up with my own answer to the problem, a different answer than the one which even the tutor previously thought was the only way of answering the question.

I don't think this makes me a genius. Others might see this as genius, but I just think it makes me a bit thick for not seeing the simple fucking answer in the first place. It should have taken me less than five minutes to answer that question, but it took me about five hours.

This kind of thing happens quite regularly, not the genius part, but the part where I don't see something which might be quite obvious to someone else, such as your typical prostitute in Southeast

Asia who I think just wants to be my friend for the sake of it, and not for the wad in my trouser pocket.

I just can't see the wood for the trees sometimes, though I paradoxically can also be very perceptive and intuitive. I've no idea why this is. Maybe I'm just schizophrenic – like at least one of my ex-girlfriends.

Noughts & Ones

It started out as noughts and ones
Now take a look at what we've become
A bunch of lonely single bums
Our gadgets, our best friends
The code that hides inside of them
Was once quite cool to some of us men
But it's gone too far, and I can't recall when
On these things we didn't depend

Who do we have to thank for this?
Is it the crazy scientists?
No, I don't think it was their wish
For the way we are evolving
But information technology
Has since taken over you and me
Thank you, Mr. Berners-Lee
For a problem we have no way of solving

Just a few lines of hypertext
No one realised what would happen next
Who could predict the side effects?
And what we would become
I wish that we could just return
To the days before you went to CERN
Because I am just a little concerned
That our future is all but done

"This is for everyone," you said
At the beginning of the World Wide Web
But since how fast the virus has spread
Throughout our planet's nations
Typing those words, you couldn't foresee
What would become of you and me
How I just wish you had pressed DELETE
It might have saved our situation

But now here we are, no turning back

No algorithms or code to crack
Impossible, for us to go back
To save the human race
You may as well have dropped the bomb
And just got rid of everyone
Rebooted the world, and let it be done
It would beat the world in cyberspace

Chapter Seven

Back to Life

I'm trying hard not to make this book about ex-girlfriends, but as two of them brought out an artistic side of me that was dormant for years, and they have all played a massive part in my life, I've had no option but to bring them in. However, this will be the last one – hopefully.

In 2008, after over two years of being single, I met Abi – the polar opposite of Ling – in a pub one-and-a-half miles from home in Bolton. She was just seventeen years old, which was obviously an issue because I was thirty-six at the time. I know this does sound really bad, but bear with it. Don't judge me yet – although I definitely would judge if I was you.

I told myself over and over that this couldn't possibly happen, but it just did. She wasn't your typical seventeen-year-old though. She was older than me in many ways, which probably just means that I have never really grown up.

Before she had mentioned me to her family, Abi said that her mum would be fine with the situation. Not that this registered with me. I just assumed her mum would go mental if she found out, so I was reluctant to meet her at the time.

Then, one Saturday afternoon, as I walked through the door of my local pub, I heard a female voice say, "That's him."

It was Abi's mum, and I nearly died. Abi hadn't yet mentioned me to her, but someone must have had a word – and rightly so. She invited me over, and to my surprise she was great with me and fine with everything, though I didn't actually breathe out until she'd left the pub a couple of hours later. As Abi had told me, I had nothing to worry about.

Then, on Abi's eighteenth birthday, we even went out with my mum and dad to celebrate. Just imagine that. I'd done the same with my previous eighteen-year-old girlfriend almost eighteen years earlier, when Abi wasn't even one year old. Now that does sound terrible. This really is sounding worse the more I write.

But it wasn't terrible at all. It was accepted by everyone, and when I finally realised that all my friends and family loved Abi and thought we were great together, I started to accept it. It probably took me a couple of years to feel comfortable when we were out together though. Again, I think this was all down to me because to others we were just your everyday couple.

After two years together Abi moved in with me, and over the next two years she became my best friend of all time. This goes to show that age isn't always a barrier, and for someone so young Abi was so good for me, helping me rise from the depressing hole I'd found myself in and pushing me hard before the exams for my Computing degree. I doubt I would have even finished my studies without her, let alone achieved such excellent grades.

However, with her being so much younger than me, she hadn't really lived, and sadly, that was probably the only thing we didn't have in common.

After almost five years together, when she was out one night – let's say "living" – I sent her a message to say that I might have to ask her to leave if she carried on like she was. I didn't really expect her to then say, "OK. I'll move out on Thursday."

And she did move out, but five years on I still love her to bits and we are still good friends.

Those years we shared almost never happened though, and they only did happen due to Abi's maturity and the trust she showed me at the time. We had gotten off to a bit of a rocky start, and this was because I did the unthinkable, when after we'd been seeing each other for a couple of weeks I flew to Barcelona to see Ling – my ex-girlfriend.

I know most girls couldn't have handled this, but there really was nothing in it. Ling was dancing in Barcelona, and as friends we'd arranged this trip months earlier. I hadn't seen Ling since that awful day at the airport a couple of years earlier, but we'd kept in touch, so this was a chance to catch up while we were in the same continent.

I have to give Abi great credit here for understanding and trusting me to go. Then again, I've no idea if she trusted me at all, though she had no reason not to. It's sad to think that with the vast majority of girls the relationship would have ended there and then before it even began, but Abi showed so much maturity and common sense for her age that it was allowed to happen, and that is thanks to her.

Recently, Abi's maturity shone through when I asked her about Ling.

> I was nice about her for ages cos I didn't want you to think I was petty but I fucking hated it when you used to talk about her. Fucking tingling this ohhh tingaling that. Ohhh she was famous ohhh she had dogs ohhh everyone loves her 🙄 🙄 (all that said in a childish voice)...... Slag X

> Fucking cat eating raw squid eating saltanvinegar fake Chinese prick X

> Hahahahaha this is definitely in the book 😂 😂 😂 😂 😂

> Good! I want a motherfucking chapter! X

Abi's text message – brilliant.

Always a Woman

She's as strong as Geoff Capes
But she's not the same size
She knows right away
If you're telling her lies
She doesn't like losing
She's that much like me
She's only nineteen
But she's always a woman to me

She's quick with her mind
Even faster at shooting
She's good at most things
In that, there's no disputing
If you tell her she's wrong
Then she might disagree
She's stubborn as hell
But she's always a woman to me

Oh, she looks after myself
More than I ever could
I'm so happy she's mine
Oh and she never goes out
And we always stay in
It's my favourite time

She talks in her sleep
Every night when she's dreaming
She gets up to look
In the corner for demons
She gives me a fright
When I see her like this
She might be a freak
But she's always a woman to me

Everyone loves her
She's funny and straight
And people come over

To tell me she's great
I agree with them
But they don't see what I see
She's much more amazing
Than anyone knows
And she's always a woman to me.

Peace Be unto You

Abi was always entertaining, and she wasn't frightened to say what she felt. In 2008, we went on holiday to Egypt where we endured an excursion of hell to see the "wonderful" pyramids. This trip involved an overnight twelve-hour coach journey followed by another twelve hours of being mithered to death in the most horrendous place on earth – Cairo.

Also, those pyramids in Cairo look lovely in the pictures, but you don't see the dirty nappies flying around or the hundreds of annoying locals trying to sell you anything from camels to Cleopatra's preserved camel-toe juice.

At the start of our trip – which began at midnight – we waited for ages in the dark for our coach, but it never arrived. There was, however, another coach, which was meant for Russians, so we were asked to board this coach instead. We weren't really bothered at first because we just wanted to get going, but then we discovered our guide only spoke Arabic and Russian so we would have no idea what the fuck was going on throughout the whole trip.

We sat right behind the driver at first, but he immediately asked us to move because those seats were reserved for security personnel, so we found somewhere near the back instead. Then, after waiting another fucking hour to set off, the driver walked down towards us.

As he walked past, I was surprised to hear Abi say, "Wa alaikum salaam."

I had no idea at the time, but this phrase is Arabic for "Peace be unto you".

Smiling, the driver replied, "Wow! Where did you learn to speak Arabic?"

Straight-faced and tired, Abi replied, "The corner shop."

I couldn't stop laughing. I was amazed how blunt she was. It was just a pity no one else on the coach understood the joke.

The driver then sat down in front of Abi, only talking to her, and never once looking at me. It felt as though he was chatting her up – probably thinking she was my daughter – and I could see Abi slowly getting more and more irritated by him.

He must have been there for ten minutes before he surprisingly said we could now go and sit down at the front again if we wanted. This was because Mr. Security hadn't turned up. I suppose Egypt has always been a safe place to go anyway. Just look at the ten years or so after we visited in 2008 – nothing much happens there.

Abi was clearly pissed off by this point because she just wanted to get moving, though I found it amusing watching her slowly become more and more annoyed. She told the driver over and over again that we were now happy in our current seats, so could we please just set off. However, he wouldn't take no for an answer, until it even got to a stage that he was almost telling us to move back to the front so he could mither us for the whole trip, until finally, having had more than enough, Abi said forcefully, "Look, pal, just get back in your seat and drive us to fucking Cairo!"

Even the Russians were laughing now, and this was how things were for the next few years – Abi saying exactly what she felt, especially to those who needed telling. She obviously wasn't a shy girl. She didn't lack confidence.

Even though she was much younger than me, it was as though she was my voice for the time we were together. She didn't care what anyone thought. She'd just say it as it was, and that's what I liked most about her. However, I think this was also the part of her that I disliked the most too, because she'd often leave me cringing with some of the things she'd say, and I'd just want to disappear down a hole; maybe back into the same hole she'd helped me escape from.

Small Coincidences

I didn't meet Abi's mum and dad – apart from the pub incident – until we'd been seeing each other for about eighteen months. Not meeting them for so long was all down to the awkwardness we both felt with our ages – well, it was for me.

When I did finally meet her parents, it was at their house after me and Abi had been out for a few drinks.

Typically, Abi's mum dug out her wedding album to show me some photos of Abi as a young girl. The chap Abi called "dad" was her stepdad, Wayne, and Abi was six years old when he and her mum, Michelle, married.

I was smiling and pretending to be interested when one particular photo caught my eye. I thought I recognised someone.

I looked closer. It was only my fucking cousin, Dave.

And guess what. He just happened to be the bloody best man.

I couldn't get my head around this. Even worse, Dave was actually out with Wayne the night he met Abi's mum. My cousin Dave had actually been Abi's stepdad's best mate. Also, to shock me further, my uncle Jack even drove their fucking wedding car. What a small, ridiculous world.

Anyway, after almost five mainly great years together, it wasn't nice breaking up with Abi. Not only did I lose my best mate but I also lost my job at the same time. I felt lost again. Even more lost than before we met. I was even quite pathetic for a while afterward, hardly moving from my couch for the four months I was out of work. I would just lounge around, watch TV, and write poem after poem – all triggered by the break-up. The whole sorry situation, although quite depressing, really did seem to bring out this creative side of me again though, and ultimately it was the writing of these poems that prompted me to write this book, just going to show that good can always come from bad if you get up off your arse and do something about it.

I was writing many poems at that time, and I decided to share some of them for the first time in my life – first with my friend Ruby from the local pub, then with her mum, Jan, and after receiving such good feedback from the pair of them I had the confidence to share them to a wider audience – Facebook. I subsequently received more positive comments, and with my ego boosted further I wrote and shared more and more.

I slowly started to get it together, before hitting another low when Abi didn't want anything to do with me whatsoever. That seemed to hurt even more because I couldn't understand why, and it really wound me up. It made me angry because I still thought we were friends, and that's all I was bothered about – I missed my best mate.

A few months later having had no word from her at all, I was still feeling quite low. I know this is really pathetic. I know. You can't just lounge around and feel sorry for yourself. You need to get up off your arse and do something positive, otherwise you just get worse. Anyway, I wasn't at the time. I was still being a prick. Then, one day, something amazing happened to make me smile again.

I was working in Manchester by now in yet another shitty job, this time for Swinton Insurance. It's always the banks and insurance companies that are horrible places to work for me because I detest everything about their businesses.

This job for Swinton was even worse than the rest because I had an evil bitch as my manager – something I've never experienced before. She was the typical sort who had done nothing else in her life but work for the same company, and that company had become her life.

The way she talked to me made me feel like punching her in the fucking face sometimes, and she could get away with being like this because if I said anything back to her, she had the power to give me one week's notice on my contract – and I needed the money.

This particular day, I was feeling even more miserable than normal. However, I had a dental appointment in the afternoon so at least I was leaving work an hour early – doesn't it speak volumes that I was actually looking forward to a fucking dental appointment?

I left work to catch my usual train, which would take me to Bromley Cross – two stations after Bolton Central station. I was one hour earlier than normal, so I assumed my train to Bolton would still arrive on the same platform, just exactly one hour earlier. A train arrived at that time, so I boarded it. My plan was to take this train home and then collect my car before driving the few miles to the dentist.

However, when I was almost home, as the train was leaving the beautiful station that is Bolton Central, I noticed that it was on the wrong track, or more precisely, I was on the wrong fucking train. The train exactly one hour earlier than my usual train was a different train.

The next station on this line would now be Lostock, putting me about two miles from my dentist, and around five miles from home. I decided to get off the train at Lostock, and with it being such a lovely sunny day I would walk to the dentist from there.

I arrived at the dentist fifteen minutes late and covered in sweat. I was then made to wait another twenty minutes while I dried off.

When I was eventually in the chair being drilled for my filling, I remember thinking, "This is the best part of my day so far. How has it come to this?"

When the fun was over, however, things got even better. Not having my car with me, and with the sun still shining, I decided to walk home. I exited the front door and turned right onto Chorley Old Road, the main road, but then remembered there was a quicker route, so I turned back on myself – exactly like I did in Bali that time – only this time it was the logical decision. I then took a left turn onto Captain's Clough Road which cut through to bypass some of the unnecessary distance.

Seconds later, I noticed a lonely figure in the distance walking towards me. It was a girl with shades on.

When she was around fifty metres from me, she stopped, lifted her shades slightly so that she could peep underneath them, and gave me a look as if to say, "What the flying fuck?"

I'd never walked down that road in my life, and I was a few miles from home.

Abi was on her way to watch her friends play a game of rounders, and amazingly, although she only lived a couple of miles from there, she had just taken a wrong turn herself.

We both agreed that it was impossible how we met that day.

We hadn't seen or spoken to each other for over six months before this chance meeting, so we had a big hug and chatted for a few minutes, and we have been good friends again ever since.

That was the moment I stopped feeling low, and when I think of all the things that came together on that day, all the coincidences – the dental appointment, the wrong train, the sunshine, the delay in my treatment, my change of direction, the wrong turn Abi made, the rounders game being played that day, and even the shit job I had in Manchester, all leading to the two of us walking down that road at that particular moment in time, again – it was as if there was someone looking out for me, for us. It was fate.

I immediately stopped writing poems about break-ups, which were now becoming fucking tedious.

Kirby Grips

My ex she was a messy one
She didn't put things away
The kitchen was always a tip
The bedroom the same way
The bathroom had clothes on the floor
With knickers in the bath
And please don't mention Kirby grips
You're having a fucking laugh

Hair bobbles and Kirby grips
She left them everywhere
I found them in the strangest place
But never in her hair
And when she came to needing one
She had to buy some more
When all she really had to do
Was look down on the floor

She didn't know what polish was
She didn't have a clue
She couldn't switch the Hoover on
Hardly ever flushed the loo
She couldn't cook for toffee
And the washing was my job
As well as collecting Kirby grips
And cooking on the hob

Hair bobbles and Kirby grips
She left them everywhere
I found them in the strangest place
But never in her hair
And when she came to needing one
She had to buy some more
When all she really had to do
Was look down on the floor

She left me and it hurt me so

I didn't understand
I thought we'd last forever
And she'd wear my wedding band
Now when I'm sad and lonely
I just look down on the floor
I don't see any Kirby grips
And it hurts me even more

Hair bobbles and Kirby grips
Where have you all gone
I look for you almost every day
But I can't find just one
And though the place is spotless
It just doesn't feel the same
Without hair bobbles and Kirby grips
Driving me insane

3.14 (Three Point One Four)

I thought we were fine
I thought we would last
But there we were
Circumventing happiness
Sometimes it takes
To lose someone to make us
As when we divide
We can end up with a plus

3.14
3.14
Is that the answer?
You were looking for
It's pie in the sky
But if it makes you mine
It's 3.14
Every time

Fractions are small
We don't think of them at all
But add them and then
You start feeling mighty tall
Equating to this
A poem wrote when I was pissed
The brain cells are few
But they all still think of you

3.14
3.14
Is that the answer?
You were looking for
It's pie in the sky
But if it makes you mine
It's 3.14
Every time

One plus one is two

Or one, with some superglue
But it's not the same
Unless the other one is you
You're the denominator
In my life, there is no doubt
Take you from me
And I'm left with less than nowt

3.14
3.14
Is that the answer?
You were looking for
It's pie in the sky
But if it makes you mine
It's 3.14
Every time

We go round and round
In circles, we're lost, then found
We accumulate shit
That all ends up in the ground
We reach for the stars
But that is always too far
So stay close to me
We can be happy as we are

3.14
3.14
Is that the answer?
You were looking for
It's pie in the sky
But if it makes you mine
It's 3.14
Every time

Breaking Up Is Never Easy, I Know

Regarding break-ups in general, I've actually been quite lucky in comparison to many other people. I've not really had any hassle from my ex-girlfriends afterwards, mainly down to them either being at the other side of the world or just being nice human beings that wanted to put the past behind them and move on with their lives.

Some people put themselves and their ex-partners through a load of unnecessary shit, ruining their own lives in the process.

I've only had one bad experience. This was in the previous century (1999), and it's not worth mentioning. However, I feel that much of the bitterness that may exist in any of my poems stems from this one bad experience – the stupid bitch.

Valentine's Day Mascara

Valentine's Day mascara
All over her face
She still thinks she looks pretty
That's because her drinks were laced
This is the way it ends
Every single night
We start out to pretend
Then we end up in a fight

Valentine's Day mascara
All over her face
I once thought she was lovely
Now she's a disgrace
Is it time to leave her?
Save myself from this
She's been sat there being a dickhead
And now she wants a kiss

Valentine's Day mascara
All over her face
The tears have been turned on
To put me in my place
I was trying to be nice
Give the girl a treat
But it's like a competition
That always ends up in defeat

Valentine's Day mascara
All over her face
Just like the cum
From some lad that was round her place
She said she was confused
She said that she was mad
And I wouldn't be surprised
If she's been with his dad

Valentine's Day mascara

All over her face
Apparently, it was all my fault
I couldn't keep up the pace
She said I was a loser
She said I was a drip
I said my love comes from my heart
Not from between my hips!

Valentine's Day mascara
Now there is no trace
The tears have all dried up
From my smiling face
Happiness has returned
Now that she has gone
As I sit here grinning
Eating my Happy Meal for one

The Stupid Bitch

I can't do it. I just can't write this book without going back in time and writing about this experience. I will keep it short, though, because it's annoying to even think about, never mind write about in detail. Until now, this is something I've blocked out of my mind since the last millennia.

I was eighteen years old and Elaine was sixteen years old. She was about to leave school and go to college.

We met at an engagement party of a girl I worked with at British Gas. I actually had no intention of going to the party at first because I hardly knew the girl, and this particular evening I was collecting my new car – the shit black mini I'd bought from my cousin Dave was starting to fucking fall apart. Dave later went on to become a successful car dealer, with his own dealership, so I was probably his first customer – or first victim, depending on how you look at it.

Anyway, I was persuaded to drive to the party by my mate and colleague John. He was a part-time model at the time, though this was something he gave up due to the tough competition he met. He said he'd feel a million dollars going to an interview, but as soon as arrived and saw all these beautiful specimens – and was subsequently rejected – he felt anything but. It wasn't doing his ego and his confidence any good at all. Isn't it odd that we can go from feeling so full of ourselves to quite the opposite when we find ourselves in different company?

At the party, handsome John started talking to Elaine's friend, Adele, so I chatted to Elaine, who, funnily enough told me she was also doing some modelling at the time. We arranged a double date for the following weekend, and after that, John and Adele ended up going out with each other for about four weeks, while Elaine and I were still together nearly ten years later.

John – I've just realised this was your entire fucking fault.

Elaine's mum had left the family home when Elaine was just ten years old, and sadly Elaine hadn't heard a word from her since, although it later transpired that countless letters from her mum hadn't been passed on to Elaine by her lying father.

On the night her mother left, Elaine was crying in her bedroom when she heard her father at the top of the stairs saying, "Please don't

216

go, Joan. We love you." However, years later the truth came out that he was saying the opposite with a hand gesture. The words were just for show to get Elaine on his side.

When we met, Elaine's prick of a dad had a new love in his life and was soon to be remarried, with Elaine excited about being a bridesmaid.

All sounds fine up to now; a new start and all.

I went to the wedding and all still seemed great, but one week later, Elaine fell out with her dad's new wife, with the new wife deciding that she didn't want Elaine to live with them. Don't ask me why, but her dad then took the side of his new wife rather than that of his daughter – he also wanted her out.

Just a few weeks after the wedding, Elaine was in limbo. She had been staying at her aunt's house since the big argument, and I was there one night when Elaine's dad came around to discuss the situation with her aunt. Remember: Elaine was sixteen years old at this time.

I was with Elaine at the top of the stairs trying to eavesdrop when we heard Elaine's aunt ask her dad, "Do you want Elaine to live with you, Mike?"

Astonishingly, his reply was, "No."

Imagine. Just imagine how Elaine must have felt to hear those words from her father; her only parent around.

She just fell apart in my arms.

I was an eighteen-year-old boy doing his best to understand what his sixteen-year-old girlfriend was going through. What kind of dad can ever do such a thing? It's beyond my comprehension. Where was she supposed to go? She was fucking sixteen years old with no mum.

The following week, with Elaine still living at her aunt's house, to everyone's relief, and to my disbelief, her mum suddenly appeared on the scene again after a six-year absence. In that time, she'd married an Indian doctor called Lionel who was a really top bloke, and they were quite well off. Well, he was anyway.

They invited me and Elaine around to their home, and subsequently asked Elaine to live with them. After all the recent tears and heartbreak, this was like heavenly music to my ears, never mind Elaine's, but where else was she really supposed to go? Do parents not have a certain amount of responsibility?

This was obviously all such a relief to Elaine, and from this day she had eighteen quite settled months living with her mum and Lionel while she was at college. Then, sadly, the wonderful Doctor Lionel passed away, and things changed for the worse again.

This time, her mum actually fucking kicked her out.

Elaine wasn't a difficult girl. In fact, she was quiet and innocent back then, so I've no idea why her mum and dad both did what they did. I also don't know how they could live with themselves after what they'd done. It still beggars belief in my mind. They ruined their own little girl's life. I know this because I lived through it with her. They also ruined a few years of my fucking life too.

So there she was, seventeen years old with nowhere to go again. I felt useless at the time. I wasn't yet earning much money at British Gas, so it's not as if I could find a place for us both to live. I shouldn't have been put in that position anyway. I only had one option in my mind, and so did Elaine. I pleaded with my mum to let her stay with us.

My mum, being the wonderful person she is, said that she could stay with us just as long as we had separate rooms – which was perfectly fine. I was just happy for a break from the tears. We lived together with my mum and dad for over a year, but then I think it all just got to be too much.

We were so young. We didn't really have the money to get a place of our own, and we were together all the time, usually with my mum and dad. Everyone needs a break, a release, and I don't think either of us got that, never mind my poor mum and dad – though they always seemed perfectly happy with everything. Elaine was like a daughter to them.

Anyway, we eventually split up, so Elaine had to find somewhere else to live all over again. At least she was now a bit older and she was also working, so she was able to move in with a friend. I still felt terrible, though, because I wanted her to be settled for once, but now I felt as though I was the reason that she had to find somewhere else to live. I felt the guilt which I don't think her mum and dad ever felt. They couldn't have felt anything, otherwise they wouldn't have done what they did.

Months later, when things settled down and we had some space, we ended up getting back together. The following year, we even moved into our own little house. I paid for everything, but that didn't bother me in the slightest. I was just happy that we had our own place and Elaine was settled and happy – finally.

We had many really good times, and we finally got engaged eight years after we first met. Elaine then started to plan the wedding.

Out of the blue, she then sprung an almighty surprise on me – she wanted her mum to give her away. I suppose she did have some practice in this already, but really?

I couldn't believe it: the woman who had deserted her at ten years old and then again at seventeen years old, the woman who she had nothing but bad words to say about, was going to be giving Elaine away to me at our wedding. This left a bitter taste in my mouth, but I played along with it. However, after this I did often have doubts that this wedding was ever going to happen.

I think the signs were always there that it wouldn't happen, even on the first day of our engagement. We were having a party that evening to celebrate with friends and family, and in the afternoon, I drove to the pie shop to buy what I thought would be my final meal of freedom. On the way home, I drove through the estate near my parent's house – the one where the rocket was fired at me. I slowly started to make my way through an unmarked junction, but then I had the shock of my life.

Like another fucking rocket from my left-hand side came a fibreglass, light blue, disabled chariot. It smashed into the passenger wing of my little car, took off into the air, and appeared to land in two different places.

I assumed that the driver was dead with the speed he was going on impact because he didn't even brake.

The Thundersley Invicar model 70 – in one piece. You can stop fucking laughing now.

I clambered out of my car to see how the driver was. I was a bit shaken, almost choking on my meat-and-potato pie, but I thought he must be a lot worse off than me with his car in two pieces. The light blue shell of his car was thirty feet away from my car, and he was sitting in the remains of it a further thirty feet away from that.

I made my way over to him, not sure if I really wanted to look. I then saw an old man sitting there with legs outstretched, seemingly fine.

I tentatively asked, "Are you OK, pal?"

The instant and quite unbelievable reply that came at me was, "You made a fucking mess of that, didn't you!"

I might have been enjoying my meat-and-potato pie behind the wheel, but the accident was clearly his fault. I was hardly moving, looking left, and then right, when he came out of nowhere at what was probably his top speed.

Later, he even tried to blame it all on me to his insurance company – the lying bastard.

Needless to say, by some miracle he wasn't injured. He was a prick, though, and he could quite easily have killed someone. I was later told by a friend – though I can't verify this – that he often drank and drove, but with him being in a disabled car, he got away with it. There was no breath test taken at the time, but to come through that junction like he did, he was either pissed or a raving fucking lunatic.

I could have been killed, but at the party later that evening, everyone just laughed about it. Let's face it: there's only me who could get hit by one of those three-wheeled, light blue, fibreglass, disabled things.

Back to the real story: in the years we had together, I noticed that Elaine had grown to have a big problem with trust. I suppose this was down to her childhood, because if you can't trust your parents, then who can you trust?

The best example of this trust issue was the night her elder sister gave birth in Blackpool, with Elaine at her bedside. She later studied my credit card statement and saw that the very same Saturday night of the birth there was a debit for a hotel in nearby Lytham. She subsequently came to the conclusion that I'd taken a girl out in Lytham on that Saturday. Elaine proceeded to keep this from me but told all her friends that I was having an affair.

It was only after we broke up that she mentioned this to me. That's when I broke the news to her that she knew all about that night in Lytham. I worked in this place, and I'd stayed there on the Thursday night after a night out from work. It just happened that the date of debit on the statement appeared two days later, like it often does. Isn't it good to talk?

This trust problem came to a head one crazy Friday night when I came home from work a couple of hours late. We'd been arguing all week, and probably even that morning, so on my way home from work I stopped off at my local pub for my tea, two pints of lager, and a couple hours peace and quiet.

As I walked through the front door, arriving at the bottom of the stairs, she stood at the top, staring at me. She immediately began to question me about where I'd been, and what I'd been up to. When I told her to stop being a fucking psycho and that I'd just been to the pub, she attacked me. She wasn't drunk or anything: she was just naturally crazy, although I hadn't seen her anything like this in all the years I'd known her. She was wild, and I couldn't get her off me.

At one point I even locked myself in the bedroom, waiting for her to calm down. Then, thirty minutes later when I opened the door, she pounced on my back again, dug her long nails into my eyes and tried to scratch my eyes out.

Not knowing what else I could possibly do, with her behind me, I punched her in the stomach to get her off me.

She then cried out, "Why are you doing this to me?"

Why? Why indeed.

When she did eventually stop I told her that I was going to stay at my mum's, but even then she blocked the door and wouldn't let me out of the house for ages.

I finally escaped, ending up staying at my mum's for a while.

Not long after this, I obviously called the wedding off. We later talked, even becoming friends again, and we even came to an agreement between ourselves. I would continue to pay for everything while temporarily living at my mum's until she was ready to leave the house. I would also give her £10,000 – the wedding money I'd saved – if she left all the furniture in the house. I did this so she would have something to help her get her own place to live.

I didn't have to do half as much as I did, but I wanted to help her. With the little money Elaine was earning, she would have struggled to find somewhere decent to live, and as I was earning a great deal more by now, I felt that it was the right thing to do. Even after what she'd done, it was still devastating for me to see this happen to her again. After seeing her lose stability in her life over and over again, I almost felt sick for her, so I was trying my best to give her a little help.

Many people thought I'd gone too far to help her, that I'd given her too much, especially after what she'd done, but it made me feel better. I also thought the more I did, the easier it would be to separate – get her out of the house – and to stay friends afterward. It was all very amicable at the time, and I thought nothing of it while I was at my mum's. I'd already given her the £10,000, and I was just waiting for the call telling me she was leaving the house.

It took eight months, but she finally left the house.

I only found out she'd left because my mate Paddy called me at work to tell me he'd seen her and some others packing things into a van.

I immediately left work because I needed to see what was going on. I walked back into my house to find that she'd taken almost everything; even the light fittings.

She only left the fucking settee and my hi-fi cabinet, which thankfully contained the beautiful silver Denon hi-fi which I still use today – the only thing I still have.

I felt totally betrayed at what she'd done. How can someone be so deceitful; so calculated, especially after all I'd done for her?

I immediately called her, and I remember telling her to "watch her back". I just mentioned that some of my mates are a bit daft, and they might have a go at her for what she'd done. She then went straight to the police and made a report that I'd threatened her. She was obviously persuaded to do this by her unlikeable older sister, who was a policewoman that had lived away from the area for years.

It wasn't exactly a threat I'd made. It was no more than a very shocked man talking to his ex-girlfriend in complete and utter disbelief at what she'd done to him.

This is even fucking winding me up now – over seventeen years later.

Anyway, when I calmed down, I realised that my conscience was clear, so I left it there, deciding to get on with my life. I'd done everything I possibly could to keep the peace and to make things easier for us both, and I would still advise anyone to do the same, even after what she did to me.

This was one big thing that both Ling and I had in common. We'd done something similar at similar times in our lives. Rather than get involved in a petty fight over possessions, we'd just let them go, deciding instead that it was easier to move on.

What is the point in making things ugly when you break up with someone? What good does it do? Just get on with your own life and move forward, no matter how much the other person has hurt or betrayed you. There is just no point, so move on.

I still showed Elaine more trust after we split up than she had ever shown me in our ten years together, even after sticking by her through everything from such a young age and even though I'd never done anything to cause her to doubt me.

I dug my own grave, though, with one particular action, and this probably resulted in her being angry enough to steal all my furniture.

In the early weeks and months of our split, I couldn't get Elaine to make the break. She wouldn't let me go. This is when I told her my one and only lie. I told her that I'd cheated on her in the past, even though I hadn't.

It worked. It just worked a lot better than I ever imagined it would do, because she raped my fucking house, and to this day, amazingly, I have only seen her once in the seventeen years since our split. Oh! My little lie worked all right.

Having not seen her since, I've not had the chance to tell her that I was lying – lying for the greater good.

She kindly left me one thing.
Half of the photo from our engagement party.

Women Come from Mars

It hit me today
Like a bolt from the blue
I suddenly realised
Why I just don't get you
The reason we're different
Has nothing to do
With me being me
Or you being you

It can all be explained
In the blink of an eye
The reason we don't work
No matter how hard we try
Incompatibility
Is just in our genes
And I now understand
What all this shit means

Men come from women
Women come from Mars
And that's why our break-up
Left me with these scars
Us men are all grounded
You're up with the stars
That's why you like ironing
And I like fast cars

Interplanetary differences
Are ruling our hearts
And these must also govern
The smell of our farts
I like watching football
You bake cakes and jam tarts
And you just sit there knitting
While I'm watching the darts

You look like an angel

Floating with the clouds
But you open your mouth
And it's so fucking loud
I'm sure it's more peaceful
Up there on the moon
And the day I go there
Won't be a day too soon

Men come from women
Women come from Mars
And that's why our break-up
Left me with these scars
Us men are all grounded
You're up with the stars
That's why men are flat chested
And why women wear bras

Cooking and cleaning
Are clearly your traits
And what brought us together
Was nothing but fate
A stellar collision
In ten million BC
Is the only reason
That you came to meet me

It could have been different
You could have been green
Three heads, with tentacles
You know what I mean
But you look so much like us
It's difficult to tell
Until we live with each other
In unbearable hell

Men come from women
Women come from Mars
And that's why our break-up
Left me with these scars
Us men are all grounded

You're up with the stars
That's why I drink lager
And you drink Vladivar

You are a nutter
Of that there's no doubt
I'm Mr. Placid
You scream and you shout
But after all this
I'd change nothing between us
And baby if you go
I would follow you to Venus

Men come from women
Women come from Mars
And that's why our break-up
Left me with these scars
Us men are all grounded
You're up with the stars
But stick with me baby
I think we'll go far

Love Is…

Love is a blessing
That floats into our lives
When the bubble bursts
It takes heart to survive

Love is a feeling
Unlike no other
When it ceases to be
It takes time to recover

Love is a mystery
You just can't explain
It's the one beautiful thing
That eases our pain

Love is a toothache
That has just gone away
But the pain returns
The very next day

Love is a pizza
That hasn't arrived
The driver is lost
It's not materialised

Love is a board game
We used to play
But you lost like a fool
So you hid it away

Love is a letter
That's lost in the post
While you sit there waiting
Eating cheese on toast

Love is a cup game
That gets you gripped

But one bad decision
Can ruin the script

Love is the answer
I'm sure you'll agree
But the question is
When will it find me?

Chapter Eight

In Confidence

Like many people, I often lack confidence. I'm told all the time that there is no reason for me not to be confident, but, sometimes people are just how they are, so this is what makes me who I am.

I doubt myself quite a lot, but I mostly don't see this as a bad thing. I even believe it's the part of my make-up that has helped me progress in life. When I do something, I generally doubt that it is correct at first, so I go back and make sure I wasn't being a tit when I did it the first time. I might do this over and over until I'm happy, or at least until I'm happier. Therefore, generally, doubting myself ultimately ends up with me getting a better result.

However, lacking confidence can obviously have the opposite effect with many things, such as when I was fifteen years old and training with Blackburn Rovers Football Club. I'd been taken there by a scout who had obviously seen the talent in me which I'd been told I had for years. The fact that this bloke was a bit of a nutcase and was sacked two weeks after he took me to Blackburn shouldn't have affected me, but it did.

I say "nutcase" because while I was playing for Bradford Rovers as a teenager, he was the manager of a rival team, and one night he called my manager to ask if he could trade some of his players for me, something that just doesn't – or didn't – happen at that level of football.

I'm told that he actually offered my boss fourteen players in return for my services – three players more than a full fucking team. This is not normal behaviour because he probably only had about sixteen players at his club anyway, so he wasn't a full shilling. However, due to him being axed as soon as I'd arrived, I never really felt like I belonged at Blackburn.

I'd been training with them fortnightly for over a year, but I'd never been selected to play in a proper youth team match in all that time. It was as though they didn't know who I was. The other lads training with me all knew each other because they were teammates at all the best local clubs, but because I was alone and played for a team near the bottom of my league, I wasn't in the clique. I didn't know anyone else. In fact, I felt as though I was even looked down on by many of the others.

Even when one of the coaches praised me for some clever piece of skill or a fine pass, one of the lads would say something in my ear, telling me I wasn't good enough, or some other pathetic comment to put me down. This is the kind of thing that should have made me want to succeed more, to want to prove them wrong, but it didn't have that effect on me. For some reason, I would tend to believe the idiots rather than the coaches.

Throughout the years, my dad would always be there at every training session and every game, shouting from the side-lines; giving me advice and spurring me on, but my mum didn't come to watch too often after one particular game when I was thirteen years old.

Although quiet and lacking confidence off the pitch, I was the total opposite on it, probably because I knew I was better than most of the opposition. I was even cocky at times. Also, my emotions often got the best of me during a match, and this particular season I was booked fourteen times and sent off twice for bad behaviour – which was more verbal misbehaving than anything.

This is quite a bad disciplinary record at any level, but at such a young age when you are learning the game, it's quite embarrassing, especially for your mother to witness. In the final game my mum came to see that season I thought I was being unfairly treated by the referee, so I ran up to him, pointed my finger in his face, and shouted, "You're a fucking wanker, referee!"

He didn't even send me off. Quite unbelievably, he only cautioned me. However, my mum sent herself off immediately because she couldn't take any more of this nonsense from her usually quiet son. I understood completely. I was actually a bit of a dick on the pitch sometimes. I became someone else. I became a very cocky person that I didn't like afterward.

Returning to the other person; a good example of me being affected by confidence was when I was finally selected to play in a match against Blackburn's local rivals – Leyland. I was only picked for this game because my dad had a quiet word with the coach.

On the big day, three things contributed to making me feel like I didn't belong there, the first being that I was only there in the first place because my dad had asked the coach to give me a game. For some reason, I didn't feel as though I had earned my place.

We met up on Saturday morning at Ewood Park – Blackburn Rovers' ground – and as I entered the home changing room, there were two lads immediately to my right who both played for the top team in my local league. I overheard one of them say, "What the fuck is he doing here?" That was my teammate for the day, by the way, and this was the second thing to affect me.

I then walked to the far end of the changing room where some older blokes were getting changed. I only realised when I sat down that these were actually some of the professional first team players. I acknowledged them, and straight away the one with the big mouth said out loud, "Fuck me, lad, what are you doing with your fucking hair?"

My hair was at a youthful stage of growing from a short cut into something else, and it looked like it couldn't make its mind up where it was going next. It was also coated in Brylcreem, and I agree: it did look fucking ridiculous. However, the whole changing room laughed, and this was the third thing to affect me.

I hadn't even got fucking changed yet. In fact, I'd only just walked in, and everyone was either having a dig or taking the piss out of me. Being fifteen years old and quite shy, I just couldn't handle it.

With twenty or so lads in the changing room all laughing at me, I fell into my shell even further. This was obviously a problem because confidence has such a big part to play in all sports, and there I was feeling smaller than I'd ever felt in my whole life before the biggest game of my life.

This is the main reason I wasn't cut out to be a footballer. I knew I had the talent when I was young, but the older I became my game depended more on how confident I was feeling on the day, and I wasn't an overly confident person.

In the game against Leyland, I came on at half-time and set up the winner in a 3-2 win, but I was shite. Even my pass for the winner was another fucking miss-kick. As I left, I was paid £4 expenses, and thanked by the coach for turning up. I was never to return.

By that point, I'd already decided that I didn't belong in this environment. I'm not talking about the first teamer mentioning my hair, because that was just a bit of typical banter and nothing at all. It was the fact that some of my own teammates looked down on me before and even during the game. I imagined that a career in football would be like this quite often unless you were the star of the team, with bitching behind your back and people trying to put you down because they want your place or were jealous of you. It just didn't appeal to me, and I think that is why, ultimately, I failed – if you want to call it failure. My heart just wasn't in it after that.

I decided that I didn't want to go again, but a year or two later when I was working for British Gas, I was asked to go for a trial by Bolton Wanderers – my home team. The scouts from Bolton had been to watch me a couple of times in the past, but as I played for a team low in the league, we always got battered when they were there, and they always left early, missing some of the best goals I've ever scored.

The scouts from Bolton had only been reminded of me a couple of years later because I'd been selected to play for my county – Lancashire – at under-eighteens level, and one of the same scouts was watching. The trial at Bolton reminded me very much of the Blackburn experience though. It was full of cocky pricks.

Before the game, the coach was shouting out names in the changing room, and the players were responding with, "Yeah", "Yep", "Here", "Aye", and so on, all looking, sounding, and acting cocky.

It was embarrassing to see, and it seemed as though many of them thought they'd already made it as a professional footballer – just for being selected for this trial.

Then I looked up when I heard one lad reply, "Yes, sir."

The whole room laughed. I smiled.

The coach looked up, acknowledging this polite young man, and then he stared at the others until the laughing gradually faded out.

This lad's name was Alan Stubbs, and he became the only player of the whole group to make it through these trials, and ultimately to play for Bolton, Everton, Sunderland, Derby County, and Celtic, all at the highest level possible in England and Scotland.

He managed to ignore the room completely because he was focused on himself and his game. I was in awe of how he was completely unmoved by the laughter of the others. He showed the complete opposite emotions to what I had at Blackburn.

Unluckily for me, I was a striker, and Alan Stubbs was a centre half on the other team that day, tracking my every move, and snuffing me out whenever I had the ball. He didn't even have to wind me up verbally to beat me, either. In fact, he never said a word to me throughout the game. He didn't have to because he did his talking with the way he played.

A number of us were called back for another trial a couple of weeks later and, unluckily for me, he also marked me for the whole of that game too. On both occasions he made me look bad. Then again, did my lack of confidence make him look good?

The fact is, he was just better than the rest of those lads, and more importantly, he was polite, had the perfect attitude, and was confident in himself and his ability. He didn't come across as a confident lad, but he had something that enabled him to block out the idiots and the naysayers. He looked focused, as though nothing was going to get in his way.

This is why he succeeded, and well done to him.

From my limited experience of being on the fringes of professional football, before all the crazy money appeared, I know that not all footballers are pricks, but I can imagine that the vast majority really are massive ones. Even without the money, it was a painful environment with so many egos – I can't imagine what it's like nowadays with those egos boosted further by the daft amounts of cash being thrown at them.

Saying all that, pricks or no pricks, I'm sure the job would have eclipsed sitting behind a desk for the past thirty fucking years.

The Local Pub

My local pub has had a lot to do with how this book came into being. Most of those mentioned in the dedication, and the four named that have sadly died since I started writing the book are – or were – good friends that I made in that pub. Without the initial support and encouragement from these people, it just wouldn't have happened.

Apart from losing so many friends from the pub recently, and aside from the damage it's done to my liver, brain, bank balance, and many other vital organs, the pub really has affected my life in a great way. It's had its bad periods, though, especially a few years ago when there was often trouble brewing in many corners of it.

One of the previous pairs of owners were quite, let's say, dysfunctional. While they were serving food, you would often see their pet parrot lingering around, and on the odd occasion, I even witnessed the feathered freak shitting on tables and abusing gobsmacked diners.

On a quiet evening, three strangers stood up to leave the pub, and as each of them exited, amazingly, the parrot chirped, "Wanker! Wanker! Wanker!"

Also, the landlady – and chef – didn't like fish. One day, as she placed a plate of fish and chips in front of a ravenous customer, I heard her say, "There's your fucking sweaty fish!" It was unbelievable.

One memorable Saturday afternoon, the landlord found some cocaine on the back of his toilet cistern. He was going mental because he was, quite correctly, very anti-drugs, and he could lose his license if this was seen by the police. There weren't many people in the pub at the time so he dragged me, two friends – who wish to remain anonymous – and a further two other lads outside.

He then lined us up and shouted, "Who's been snorting cocaine off the toilet in my pub?"

We all looked at each other, each one of us trying to seem more innocent than the next. Then, one of my 'friends' ridiculously quipped, "Well, it wasn't us three. We're key men, us."

He was referring to the fact that if we snorted cocaine in his pub, then we wouldn't be so disgusting and uncouth to snort it from his toilet cistern; we would instead use our door keys to snort it straight from the bag – thanks for sticking up for us here, pal.

Now then, to me, whether this was true or not, it would still mean that you have been – or will be – snorting cocaine in his pub, and so he would obviously kick you out, wouldn't he? I therefore assumed that our 'mate' had dropped us all in it, even though we'd just walked through the bloody door. I thought we'd likely be leaving his pub, never to return.

But, no, that wasn't the case. The mental landlord let the three of us go back inside, while the other two lads were kicked out and barred from the place.

Even worse – and I don't know if this was a regular thing – but the landlady even sold cannabis to my mate Louie one day. She completed the transaction in the pub kitchen in-between cooking and serving her customers hot meals – and probably with that fucking parrot on her shoulder.

Not long after the deal was completed, Louie was sat at the bar quietly enjoying his pint when the landlady shouted, "I can smell weed! Someone's got weed in my pub!"

Louie, realising it was obviously the green bag in his inside pocket that he'd just purchased, popped his head over the bar, looked cautiously to his left and right, and through the side of his mouth quietly uttered, "It's me, you daft cunt. You've just sold it to me."

Incomprehensibly, she replied, "I don't want drugs in my pub. Get out!"

He tried to argue but there was no point.

The owners really weren't wired up right. They were even taken to court once for illegally showing football games in the pub from their personal Sky TV box. This would often result in a fine of up to £8000 if found guilty, so they gathered a few witnesses from the local clientele to support their case.

One of those witnesses included a good friend called Dave 'The Leg', who was often drinking in the pub in the afternoon. He was called to give evidence, and when asked, "What do you remember about what was on TV that Saturday afternoon?" he replied, "I don't know, Your Honour. I wasn't there."

They hadn't even bothered to ask if he was fucking there.

The pub was a mental institution at the time, and I was one of the few who hadn't been barred from the place. Thankfully, a few years ago it changed into much more of a peaceful institution, and this became another piece of the jigsaw that brought this book into being.

In my local pub recently, I have met people that have more than influenced this book. Alan (Mike) came up with the title of the book and that of some of the poems; Ruby and Jan – who currently own the place – were the first to read my poems and give me positive feedback, spurring me on to write more; Jan introduced me to Chris in the pub – the artist who has done all the amazing artwork for me; and I also met Dora, Tim, Mark, Rick – and I'm sure there are others – who all contributed by either giving me hints of what to write, by telling me how good – or bad – it was, or just by showing interest.

I know for certain that if my local pub was in another part of the world, another part of my country, or even another part of my home town, then I may well have been laughed at for writing my poems, and the book might not have got off the ground.

Life is all about the people you surround yourself with, and although most of these are brought into your life through luck and chance, and you can't choose your family, you can choose those friends who you wish to stay in your life, so choose the ones who bring love, happiness, positivity, intelligence, fun, and common sense. Leave the pricks, the naysayers, the drama queens, and those that hurt you, well behind.

Cigarette Butts

Cigarette butts
Dancing sluts
Drunken fools
Playing pool
Benefit cheats
Dirty sheets
Cocaine bags
Dirty slags
Yet again
There's people fighting
This is why
My fag needs lighting

Stolen gear
Living in fear
Cheating wives
Kids with knives
Dodgy schemes
Broken dreams
Got no money
Where's my honey?
She's out the door
That's why I'm writing
And this is why
My fag needs lighting

Morning aches
Fucking fakes
Angry pricks
With no dicks
Robbing cunts
Lost kid hunts
Dirty old man
Drives his van
Trawls the streets
For girls at night
And this is why

My fag needs a light!

Warring countries
Kids no lunches
Woman raped
Even taped
Chemical warhead
Millions dead
Another refugee
Thank god it's not me
The world is fucked
And I feel shite
This is why
My fag needs a light!

Children play
Beautiful day
Happy times
Wedding chimes
Birds are tweeting
Baby's teething
No more nappies
Everyone happy
I really don't know
Why I'm smoking
I'm putting mine out
And I'm not joking!

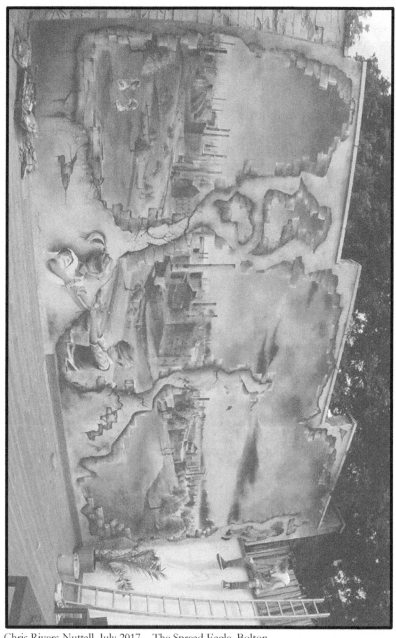

Chris Rivers-Nuttall, July 2017 – The Spread Eagle, Bolton.
The artist admiring his work at the back of my local pub.

Handbags

Stolen handbags
Tattooed slags
Dirty mouths
And a floor full of fags
Jealous stares
Unlikely pairs
A sly remark
For the clothes that she wears
Rowdy groups
Toilet toots
Those you hope
Will never reproduce
Another potbelly
The next obituary?
Fuck it
Tonight I'm staying in watching the telly.

Chapter Nine

It's Not Just Cricket

Just a few weeks after I started to write this book, one Friday afternoon at work in Newcastle, I was trying to think of somewhere to go on holiday for a couple of weeks over Christmas. I couldn't decide, but my workmate Jim suggested I go watching England play cricket in Cape Town. This sounded fantastic, and although I'm not really a big cricket fan, I booked an expensive trip, and left for South Africa the day after Boxing Day.

I quickly discovered that Cape Town must be the best place in the world to watch cricket. With Table Mountain as the backdrop to the cricket ground, the sun smiling down, and cold beer from the Castle brewery around the corner, you just can't beat it.

You almost forget about the cricket. It's as though you're having a day out and there just happens to be something going on in the middle. If you don't like the game, you would still love a day at the cricket at Newlands Stadium in Cape Town.

On the first morning of the test match between South Africa and England, I had a quiet moment thinking of my grandad Ken, and how he would have been completely in his element sitting there with his beer and cigar, a big smile on his face. There was certainly a big smile on my face.

Watching cricket anywhere can be relaxed and chilled, but watching it in Cape Town was just something else, like no sports venue I've ever experienced.

Newlands cricket ground, Cape Town.

On the second day of the test match, I was sitting on the grass behind the wicket, which wasn't my allocated part of the ground. Some parts of the ground were a free-for-all, so I made the most of

246

this and found my perfect spot. It was going to be a long day, so it had to be perfect – and it was.

Late on in the afternoon, I spotted someone who I thought I recognised. He slowly started to saunter my way, and then hit me. It was Scott.

Almost thirty years previous, I'd been a ball boy for Bolton Wanderers at the old Burnden Park stadium, and so had Scott. When I had moved on, being too old to carry out the role at sixteen years of age, Scott took my place in the empty Embankment End behind the goal, which I had all to myself for a year or two in my early teens.

Being the only person in one whole end of a famous old football stadium watching the game, with the other three ends of the ground bustling with supporters of each team was amazing. I was basically left in sole charge of one-quarter of the ground. It was great. I just sat there on my own and watched the match, sometimes even forgetting I was there to do a job.

When Scott took my place, however, he took the experience to another level. Like myself, he'd sit there in sole charge of the Embankment End watching the game go by, but he actually did it while smoking a joint. He would have been either fourteen or fifteen years old at the time.

I hadn't seen Scott for about ten years, so it was amazing to bump into him in Cape Town of all places. He hadn't been sitting in his allocated stand either, so it seemed like another of those strange coincidences had occurred, and this meeting was just meant to happen.

Scott was on holiday with his mate Liam. They'd been planning this trip for almost a year, and were staying in South Africa for three weeks, whereas I'd only booked ten nights.

The day we were reunited, I'd tasted my first pint at around 10.30 a.m., which is quite normal for a hot summer's day at the cricket. After the game, which ended early in the evening, we then shared a few more drinks and decided to explore some of the city's night life with Liam and a couple of other lads, Richard and Paul. These two were staying at the same hostel as Scott and Liam.

About 3:00 a.m., when we were all obviously a little bit worse for the wear, it happened.

We were walking through Main Street when we got chatting to what we thought were a few locals. I was a few feet behind Scott, Liam, and Paul, when I stopped to talk to four lads for some daft drunken reason. They'd been walking alongside us for a few minutes, asking us daft questions. As I stopped, those three, intelligently continued walking in front. I think Richard had gone to get some food at the time and was a bit behind us.

One of the "local" lads then strangely put his arm around me, and then did something even more odd, saying "The girls in Cape Town, when they talk to you, they always do this."

At that moment, he bent down and pulled the denim of my jeans below the knee, making me bend down.

If that wasn't bizarre enough, he did it again.

I was obviously quite disoriented at the time, so I don't know how this even came into my head, but I just thought, "That was odd. Was he or one or his cronies doing something else to me when he tugged at my jeans? Was this all a distraction for something else?"

I then patted my back pocket to check for my iPhone. It wasn't there.

I obviously thought the bastard had nicked my phone.

Then I thought, "I'm leathered, so maybe I just left it in the last pub. Maybe I lost it hours ago? Who knows? I'm fucking leathered. It could be anywhere."

I honestly didn't have a clue.

I visualised these and a dozen other scenarios in a split second, but my head quickly returned to scenario number one, assuming that this prick or one of his assailants had nicked my phone.

Then I did one of the most amazing things I've ever done in my life.

Without him noticing, I managed to slip my left hand into his right-hand back pocket, and snatched something with my fingertips.

I'd only gone and found my fucking phone.

I then stuck the phone right in front of his face and said, "You thieving bastard!" He laughed.

I then had to double-check that it was actually my phone, because for a split second I even thought I'd nicked *his* phone. I was just a little bemused with everything, not quite believing the whole situation.

I tapped my four-digit code into the phone, and was almost surprised to see it unlock. Even then I was still confused, and that prick was still laughing.

I'm not surprised he was laughing. The shit bag had pickpocketed me, and I had somehow managed to pickpocket him straight back, and all when I was drunk and didn't really know what the hell was going on, and was even surrounded by four lads.

Amidst the laughter, his face changed to a picture of utter bemusement too. He seemed as surprised and confused as I was at the whole thing.

So I'd been pickpocketed by a pickpocket, and then I pickpocketed the pickpocket. The most amazing part of all this was seeing him actually check his back pocket after I put the phone to his face. He didn't even feel me take it back from him. Unbelievable!

I turned to walk away, leaving him and the others looking rather stupid, while I was actually shaking. I couldn't quite believe what had just happened.

Richard then appeared behind me. He managed to catch the latter stages of it all – where I grabbed my phone and shoved it in the thief's face; otherwise I don't think the others – or anyone – would have believed me.

We were later told by someone in the bar that the pickpockets weren't locals. They were Nigerian immigrants, apparently.

Go on then. Blame it on the immigrants.

Road Trip

I was due to go home in two days' time, while Scott and Liam were lucky enough to still have another two weeks of their holiday left. They were hiring a car and driving all the way to Johannesburg for the next test match, stopping off at a few places on the way. I joked that I might join them, without really thinking about it. However, the next day they said they'd love it if I joined them, so I didn't think twice. All of a sudden, I was going on a road trip through South Africa with a couple of great lads. How lucky was I?

I emailed work, just to ask if it was okay to stay off work longer, but no one responded. I'd forgotten that it was the Christmas holidays and everyone was at home. Nevertheless, I still booked a flight home from Johannesburg for two weeks' time and prepared for the road trip of a lifetime. Work later replied to me to say it was fine, but I was already well on my way by then. I'd taken the chance of going along, and it was definitely worth it.

On the big day, Liam and I went to collect the car from the rental place. Liam was the only one of us to bring his driving licence with him – so only he could drive – legally anyway.

However, Liam hadn't driven much since passing his test, and he really didn't want to drive. In his own words, he was a "nervous driver", so me and Scott were going to share the driving – legally or not.

Those two idiots didn't have real credit cards with them; just having these "travel" credit cards instead. These are cards which you add money to and you just have that amount to spend. They are not credit cards, and don't come with all the protection you get with a credit card. To rent the car we actually needed a real credit card. Months of planning from Scott and Liam, and without me and my credit card they wouldn't have been able to even rent a fucking car. Was it fate that we met? I don't know about that, but it was definitely good for the three of us in different ways.

We collected the car, and Liam was to do his one and only stint of driving for the whole trip. As he was the one with the licence, he at least had to drive us out of the rental place. That experience was enough for me. He was exactly as he'd described – a "nervous driver".

We didn't have a map with us, or even a SATNAV. We were to be going on a real adventure, and doing it "old school". However, the night before, we did have a quick look at a map online, and it looked to be quite a straightforward journey. We just needed to follow the coastal road north. What could possibly go wrong?

This was probably the main reason we didn't buy a map, ask the rental place for a SATNAV, or buy data for our phones. We just thought we'd be able to drive up the coastal road and follow road signs to the places where Scott and Liam had booked their hotels. It all looked so simple.

As I was driving the first leg, Scott would be in the passenger seat, and he would therefore be our navigator for the day. Our navigator, that is, without a fucking map.

We made just one rule before setting off, that none of us could drink alcohol in the car, as this would be unfair to the driver. I thought it would be best anyway if we all stayed sober. We had no idea in what kind of places or situations we could end up. No drinking was therefore the sensible approach.

However, Scott, who had himself suggested this non-alcohol rule, never once mentioned making a rule about not smoking the odd bit of "Children in Need". Maybe this was because Scott was the only one of us smoking the drug. He would therefore be allowed to smoke as much as he wanted, obviously only while he wasn't driving.

We set off North along the East coast from Cape Town, and the scenery was absolutely stunning. I had the endless blue ocean to my right and the impressive mountains to my left – through the navigator's thick grey smoke. It was heaven, and we all enjoyed the beauty so much that we probably paid a bit less attention than we should have to where we were actually heading.

I know that I was driving, and therefore I need to share some of the blame for this, but after experiencing a wonderfully relaxing *two* hours of the most beautiful scenery we will ever see, we managed to end up in the wrong place. Unbelievably, we came to a halt in almost the exact same fucking place we'd started – Cape Town.

No, I'm not making this up. Maybe Scott's weed – purchased in Cape Town – was a lot stronger than he'd thought. Also, maybe we were all off our tits – not just our navigator.

The road signs in South Africa really are shit, but they were nowhere near as shit as the driver-navigator combination of Scott and me.

The two of us shared the blame equally. Liam did absolutely fuck all, so we couldn't really blame him for anything. What he did do, though, was join us in laughing uncontrollably for about five minutes afterwards.

We then began our second attempt, which was much more successful and we finally arrived in sleepy Mossel Bay several hours later than expected.

Those two had booked their hotel here months earlier, in a lovely little place by the coast, but there was no room at the inn for me. I was therefore put up in one of their sister hotels. Those two pricks were staying near the beach, while my hotel was situated a few minutes away between two local businesses. These businesses each offered the same kind of service. "What might that be?" I hear you ask.

Well, the services they both offered were fucking funeral services.

The hotel was more like a big house than a hotel, but what a place to live – never mind spend a night on holiday. It was basic and weird, but I was happy to find anywhere to rest and relax. It was only about £20 per night too, so I couldn't complain. Even if I wanted to complain, I couldn't be arsed anyway. I was just too knackered.

Later that night, after we'd eaten the most amazing steaks costing us next to nothing in the wonderful Route 57 restaurant, we ended up in the Sundowner's bar.

After a few beverages it was getting quite late, and Liam left us. I think he wanted to Skype his girlfriend or something.

Scott and I decided to stay and have a few more drinks because it was just getting interesting. Scott was winding up a few of the locals, and having a bit of a laugh with them.

It was busy by now and everyone in there seemed to know each other. They were also aware that Scott and I weren't local to their sleepy little town. One of them even shouted, "You're Barmy Army!"

He was referring to the English cricket fans which have a group of supporters calling themselves the "Barmy Army".

Scott immediately disagreed with him. He said that just because we are England cricket supporters, it didn't mean we were included in the group that was the "Barmy Army". I agreed totally, because I'd initially travelled to South Africa with the Barmy Army Travel Company, and it was clear that I wasn't one of them.

The Barmy Army was a bit of a clique. I don't know who came up with the name for them, but certain individuals created a travel company of the same name, and they make lots of money by arranging travel for the group. I know they make lots because I paid a lot for my ten-day trip to South Africa, but then realised when I arrived that the amount they were charging was ridiculous, when I considered the cost of arranging the trip myself – especially on match tickets. The Barmy Army was charging over forty times the price of tickets purchased at the ground.

This no doubt enables the owners of the company to follow the England Cricket Team around the world. Good luck to them, but I will definitely sort my own trip out next time I follow England abroad. Just like Scott, I certainly wasn't part of the Barmy Army. We were just two Englishmen who happened to be there, supporting England at cricket.

This continued on and on. "You're Barmy Army! You're Barmy Army!" Then at about 2:00 a.m., Scott tried his best to explain why he wasn't part of the Barmy Army, and he came up with a comparison to aid his argument.

He said, "If I'm Barmy Army just because I'm English, then if you are South African, that means you must be a nigger."

Yes, he actually said that, out loud, in a pub full of people, in South Africa.

Somehow, this one bizarre statement ended up with around twenty locals, who were all white, at each other's throats in total disagreement about the political situation in their country. It doesn't even really make sense, but I know why he said it; to shut the idiots up. There were one or two blokes that kept going on and on about the bloody Barmy Army, so he thought he'd end it.

However, half of the pub, for some strange reason, totally agreed with Scott, and the other half totally disagreed with him. None of them took it out on Scott, though. They all took it out on each other. It was as though Scott had started a fire which had lay dormant for many years, and then sat back to watch it burn.

After a while, with the drunken argument – about what I don't know – in full flow, and with nobody even trying to calm the situation down, we decided that we should try to leave quietly. However, as we were trying to do this, everyone actually stopped their arguments and moved away from each other's throats, just so they could shake our hands and say goodbye to us.

It was all very odd. Maybe they weren't arguing at all. Maybe this was just a typical drunken discussion in South Africa and they shake each other's hands at the end of the night, just like at the end of a hotly contested sporting contest.

As we exited the place, Scott then turned left towards his lovely little hotel by the sea, while I turned right to my shithole near the undertakers. We walked a few feet and then both looked back at each other and laughed. No sooner had we left the building, than the argument started again.

I don't quite know how he'd managed it, but I doubt that bar will ever be the same again – and from what? I think the only answer I have is: "Scott." He had created it all from nothing and then disappeared into the salty night air.

Later that night, in my death-encased hotel, I lay in bed, thinking, "I could die here." Then I thought, "Maybe people do die here? That's why there's an undertaker on either side of me. Maybe people actually come here just to die? Maybe it's the South African equivalent of the pie shop next to the barbers in Sweeney Todd?"

I was obviously a little drunk. I was also so scared that I even locked my door and put a set of drawers behind it, just in case. Why was I so paranoid? Maybe it was through inhaling Scott's fucking weed for eight hours on the drive from Cape Town. I can't think of any other reason.

Anyway, I didn't wake up dead. I woke up with a smile on my face because our navigator from the previous day was driving today, and I couldn't wait to get back on that heavenly coastal road.

Dickheads

After Mossel Bay, we spent two days in Port Elizabeth, and not surprisingly our drive to Port Elizabeth was also a bit of a nightmare. We got lost in some dangerous looking neighbourhoods, and this was just after, between the three of us, we failed to spot the cityscape of Port Elizabeth. We were driving for miles before we spotted it. It turned out to be directly fucking behind us.

After spotting the city in the distance, and making our way in the right direction, we even then ended up going to the police station to ask for directions. We let Scott go in to ask while Liam and I looked after – or locked ourselves in – the car.

All this was nothing compared to the next part of our road trip, though.

On leaving Port Elizabeth, we really had meant to plan our route properly, but we still didn't have a map. We didn't think we'd need one if we just studied the digital route properly before we left. All the places we were going seemed to be on the way to major cities anyway, which are generally well signposted in most countries, so we thought it would be quite simple. We agreed that we would study the map properly beforehand this time, though, just in case.

Not long after we set off, Mr. Navigator told me that he hadn't looked at the map because he wasn't driving. He thought I would have looked at the map. However, I hadn't looked at the map because I wasn't fucking navigating.

You really couldn't make this up. What a pair of complete and utter fuckwits.

As we were now away from our hotels, we had no Wi-Fi and therefore were stuffed.

The previous night in Port Elizabeth we'd found a small bar, which, quite unbelievably, was showing on TV the FA Cup third round tie between Eastleigh and my team, Bolton Wanderers. This was a match that I was supposed to be going to – I'd even paid for a match ticket and flight ticket to get there. My extended stay in South Africa, however, meant that I would miss it.

The fact that this was actually being shown in the pub we were in was a minor miracle. It would almost certainly have been the only place in Port Elizabeth where it was being shown.

While watching the game, seeing the shivering people at home on TV, from this quaint bar with iron bars on the windows, we met some lovely people. One particular couple had told us that we should take a scenic route on the way to our next stop – our next stop being what we'd been told was a beautiful beach at Chinsta.

We had also considered the possibility of continuing to Durban, our destination for the day after, but we thought we'd just see how the day panned out first before deciding on this.

When it came to the vital point where we had to decide which route to take – the scenic route or the main road – we were in three minds, and it really was a split-second decision.

I was driving along the road that we all knew would almost certainly take us to our destination. The slip road to the scenic route was then quickly upon us. The other two idiots said that the decision was up to me, and at the very, very last moment, I took the fucking "scenic" route.

The scenic route was not very scenic.

After driving on this one boring road for one hour, we saw a big sign in a field to the left which read, "Thou shall have no other gods before Me."

Please note the small "g" in gods and the capital "M" in prick.

Then, just as I was digesting that bollocks, we drove passed another similar sign.

This one read, "Thou shall not make idols."

I was just wondering what kind of farming freak owned this field when the next one was immediately upon us.

"Thou shall not take the name of the LORD your God in vain."

Scott then said, "Fuck me. It's like *Deliverance* this."

Deliverance is an absolutely terrifying film where a camping trip goes wrong and a load of rednecks make the men "squeal like pigs". The thought of it actually made me shiver.

256

Next was "Remember the Sabbath day, keep it holy."

We didn't catch the rest because I just put my fucking foot down. However, I do remember the final one, which I didn't even know was an actual bible commandment until I saw it. I obviously wasn't a very good Catholic.

The sign read, "Thou shall not covet."

Thou shall not covet? In other words, "Thou shall not yearn to possess something, especially that belonging to another".

Why then do all religions ask not only for the money of their followers, but for the one thing they possess which is of most value? The one thing that is precious to them – their lives. It's because they are using these people for their own benefit, just like the Bible-bashing arsehole-bashing rednecks from the film *Deliverance*. I see that there is no commandment for raping a child, woman, or man. It's as though, just as long as you're not married, then that's perfectly fine.

We didn't actually speak until we came to stop in a small town later on. We all sighed with relief on arrival, however. We had actually been shitting ourselves for a while, so this twenty-minute break was good for us.

On setting off again, we couldn't figure out where to go now. We were actually back on the coast again, which was obviously where we wanted to be, but finding the road North was ridiculous. We drove up and down the same road four or five times, before thinking "fuck it", it must be this road.

We drove in a straight line for one hour or so. Then we got lost. We got very lost. We'd been driving for about four hours when Scott said those fateful words, "I'm sure that is fucking Lesotho to our right."

I didn't even know what he meant at the time, thinking he was joking, but it was confirmed soon after when we saw a sign for Bloemfontein. This place is far West, when we were meant to be going up the East fucking coast.

We had somehow managed to drive almost *four hours* in the *wrong* direction, and Scott had been totally right about Lesotho.

"How?" I can hear you shout. "How can this happen?"

Yes, we are idiots for not having a map or SATNAV, but the road signs are almost non-existent and useless in South Africa. Try it, if you don't believe me. There was also nowhere that we thought we could stop to ask. We passed several towns, but they were all so busy with people in the road everywhere, and we didn't want to get out of the car – we didn't feel safe and just wanted to get through it as soon as we could.

Scott later mentioned that it seemed like they'd built a motorway straight through all the little towns – the towns being the motorway with buildings either side of it – so we'd go from travelling at 80 mph to being stuck behind a load of people walking in the road. It was a bit mad really.

We were so pissed off that we genuinely considered carrying on driving another few hours to Bloemfontein, dropping the car off there and flying direct to Johannesburg. This would have meant missing out on Durban completely, and I couldn't have done that, not after all we had been through.

Instead, we decided to turn around and drive back along the same road. We did this for over three hours, finally ending up in a shithole called East London – how ironic that we were in South Africa, driving for hours on end, and we only managed to end up in East fucking London, which was a mirror image of its twin back home in England – dark and dirty.

It was around 10 p.m. by now, we were in complete and utter darkness, and we had nowhere to stay. We were frightened, and we were all exhausted after ten hours of aimless driving. Then, to make things worse, in all the confusion I drove straight through a red light, just as a police car passed us.

I immediately looked in my mirror, and was horrified to see the police car's blue lights flash. I watched it drive forward, before it found a spot to begin a U-turn. The copper was obviously coming back for me, so I quickly and sneakily pulled into the side of the road, parked quickly in-between two cars, and turned my lights off.

The police car sped straight past us. I am a genius at times, I agree.

We then made a collective decision to get the hell out of this shithole and keep driving North. We wanted to be anywhere but here.

Luck or Fate?

It was dark, and we had no idea where we were going.

We almost decided to just carry on towards Durban, which we should have been doing seven hours earlier. I'd suggested driving through the night to get there, and we were all seriously considering this.

Then, amazingly, after eleven, long, hard hours on the road, we were shocked, but over the moon, to see a sign for Chinsta. We then drove down some ridiculously narrow, pitch-black roads before eventually finding the most amazing place by the beach.

It was a big hotel, and the bar was closing shortly, so we quickly checked in, ignored the fact that we hadn't eaten since setting off, and bought loads of beer and rum to take away with us.

We then took our drinks to the beach and sat there looking at the stars. What we experienced that night on the beach was probably the most amazing spectacle any of us had ever witnessed. It was pitch black, and there was no light pollution whatsoever, so we could see everything clearly in the sky. The three of us were completely blown away by it. It was incredible to witness.

We've all seen stars in the sky, but this was something else. We were all mesmerised. Everything that happened that day had led us to this beautiful moment which we were meant to share with each other; a moment we will never forget. If we hadn't been lost, we would have probably just carried on straight to Durban, therefore not experiencing this spectacular event. It was so perfect, it's impossible to put into words.

However amazing the day turned out in the end, we later decided to plan our route properly from then on. It was the sensible thing to do.

The three of us had seen the complete "Sagittarius, The Archer" constellation in the sky, which I didn't think was even possible with the naked eye, then those two nob-heads decided to create their own sign to the rest of the universe.

It was a ridiculous end to a ridiculous day; an amazing day.

Liam and Scott proud of their MCFC (Manchester City Football Club) message.

Back Door? Exit!

As we'd agreed, we meticulously planned our journey to Durban, and arrived after eight hours without any drama whatsoever. It was safe and efficient, but quite boring in the scheme of things. I suppose we did need a day or two like this, though.

The following evening, we enjoyed another beautiful steak and a few drinks on the town to wash it down. Then we met two Canadian women who were in Durban on business. I don't quite remember how this came about, but we all ended up going back to their hotel for a drink when the bars shut. We had a couple more drinks in their room before Scott and Liam both walked back to our hotel.

For some reason I stayed with the Canadian girls. I really don't know why I stayed because I didn't fancy either of them. I was also pretty drunk, and one of them was already tucked up in bed.

Miss Canada No.1 – the one not in bed – and I then went downstairs to have a cigarette, while Miss Canada No.2 lay in bed, apparently trying to sleep. We chatted for a bit, while looking out to sea. I was just enjoying listening to the waves beneath her Canadian mumbo jumbo when she suddenly kissed me.

This came as a bit of a shock really because she hadn't shown any signs of affection to me at all before that. In fact, when we all met in the pub I'd asked her if she was married, and immediately she snapped, "No, and I'm not interested, thank you very much."

I told her not to worry because I was gay anyway. Maybe that was it; she saw me as a challenge, the freak. I really can't remember if I told her the truth later or not: that I wasn't gay.

We went back upstairs and sat on her bed. This was right next to the bed in which Miss Canada No.2 was trying to sleep, but who I could see was clearly still wide awake.

Miss Canada No.1 then whispered in my ear, "What would you like?"

Now then, I'm usually a bit slow in these situations, but I was very switched on this particular evening so I gathered she was asking what I would like to do "sexually".

In my own typical way, I whispered, "I'm not really bothered."

She must have been completely seduced by my words.

Nevertheless, I really wasn't expecting her response.

She actually then said, "I'd like anal."

"What? We've just met. You freak," I gasped.

Just also remember that her friend is still wide awake in the next bed all this time.

She then told me that she was "going on the toilet" before handing me a condom, which for some reason turned out to be half the size of your typical condom. I won't go into detail about that. However, I've recently considered the reasons for the quite ridiculous size of this condom.

One theory was that this was your typical everyday Canadian condom? However, there was another possible reason for all this, and it originates in my hometown of Bolton and, more accurately, with my close friend Alan – also known to some as Mike for some unknown reason – the person who actually came up with the title for this very book.

Every now and again, Alan (Mike) would come up with a title for a poem that he thought I should write. This is how most of my poems have originated. I started with just a title, and I took them from there.

One evening in mid-2016, Alan (Mike) and I had a night out with three other friends. After a few too many drinks, Alan (Mike) was somehow left all alone, wandering around looking for the rest us. I'd actually gone home by this point, and I remember telling him I was going, but he was rather pissed and obviously completely ignored what I said.

The next morning, I received a text message from him giving me the title *Lost in the Crowd* and saying that he thought it was a good title for a poem. I suppose it just summed up his situation at the time really – lost, wandering around people he didn't know while all his mates had gone home.

I have to add that in the ten years or so I've known Alan (Mike), this is the one and only time this has happened – us getting split up on a night out – and it happened when I was looking for a title for my book.

Alan (Mike) is a businessman. In his own mind, he's a bit of an entrepreneur. He's done quite a lot of business in China over the years, and in the 1990s, he had an idea for developing some inexpensive condoms. He developed and tested these condoms in China, and he was confident of making a tidy profit from them.

He explained the condom-testing process to me, and it all seemed to be done by machine. They were stretched this way and that and blown up to quite unimaginable sizes, though he didn't commit when I asked if they were actually tested by a human. He gave me a dirty look when I suggested maybe he was the only human to test them.

Anyway, he manufactured 1.5 million of these little buggers, and he actually shipped a container of one million of them to no other than – wait for it – Africa.

I am no condom expert, but my old friend and ex-colleague Usman had often told me about the world men "size" league table, saying there were four positions in this league table. Way out in front at the top were African and Caribbean men and so on, second were Caucasians, third were Indian and Pakistani men and the like, while at the bottom were the Chinese.

Therefore, Alan (Mike) had his condoms made in China, probably using the specifications for Chinese men, and he then tried to sell those same condoms in fucking Africa of all places. They turned out to be too small, and he ended up selling that batch on the cheap while the rest ended up in the Catholic country of Ireland – where contraception was actually illegal until 1980 – after he sold them to two Irishmen who were paving his driveway.

Forgetting Ireland, could that condom I was given that night in South Africa actually have been one of his from all those years ago? If only I'd been sober and aware enough to look at the packet. Then again, that really would have freaked me out if it had been.

I even knew the name of them – they were called "ModCons".

Anyway, to continue with the story, it all finished by me telling Miss Canada No.1, "I'm sorry, but I'm not going to put my penis up your bum, especially with a condom that doesn't fit, and especially not with your mate wide awake in the next fucking bed."

Really? Is it me? I've no idea why I apologised to her.

Not long after this, I fell asleep. Not long after that, she fucking woke me up.

She then asked me what her name was. My first confident guess was "Candice", which unfortunately just happened to be the name of her mate in the next bed. I knew I'd heard the name recently, but how unlucky was that? Anyway, that didn't go down too well at all.

My second guess was also wrong, but I saved the best until last.

I said, "Is it Craig Forrest?"

Craig Forrest is a football goalkeeper who played for Ipswich Town in England, and also for the Canadian national team. He was the only Canadian person I could think of at the time.

On hearing this pathetic answer, she asked me to leave. I left.

When I arrived back at our hotel, Scott told me that she'd had her hand on his arse for a time while we were sitting in the room. It therefore looks like I wasn't even first fucking choice, though I'm guessing anyone would have done for her that night – anyone with a small cock and no morals, that is.

It might have only been a small condom, but it was an extra-large blessing.

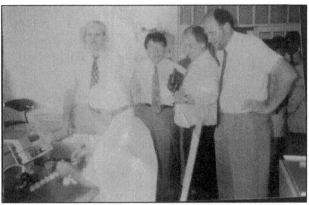

My mate Alan (Mike) – left – with project developers at a *Modcon* testing lab, Guangzhou Province, China – 1994 – Testing condoms!

Johannesburg

We did well to get to the outskirts of Johannesburg, again with no drama. However, it was just about to go dark, and although we were in and around Johannesburg, we had no idea where our hotel was. I'd heard that this city was one of the most dangerous in the world, so it's probably not the place to get lost at night time. However, we did exactly that.

We came off a slip road into the city centre, and things quickly took a turn for the worse, putting us in a very bad situation where we genuinely feared the worst. We ended up in what I think was either Soweto or a township just outside. It was so full of people wandering around, with these fucking annoying white vans, being driven by lunatics, constantly beeping their horns. The fact that Scott managed to drive us through it without hitting anything was a miracle. It was awful. We were all frightened to death, and though we got out, and eventually found our hotel, we didn't stop shaking until the morning after; it was that bad.

However, as Liam pointed out later, no matter how scared we were in this, and all the other situations we'd been in around South Africa, we'd never been threatened by anyone anywhere. I'd had my phone nicked, but that's all, and that can happen in any city.

Were we scared because we had these preconceptions about the place due to what we were told about carjackings and shootings, or what we read in the media over the years about the high crime rate? I'm not sure, but it looked like a right fucking shithole, and we were the only three white people who just happened to be driving through with a car full of our belongings, silly hats and all.

What probably didn't help us feel at ease was that on many of the highways, as we approached cities, there were often extremely large shanty towns which looked awful. On the highways before these towns, there were often flashing signs reading, "DANGER – NO STOPPING AREA".

This is where we saw a number of abandoned cars burnt out with nothing left in them. The sign was there for a reason. If you broke down in that area, that would probably be your car in the morning. As for you in the morning, it's not worth thinking about.

On our first full day in Johannesburg, still shaking from our experience the night before, we went to the Wanderers Stadium to watch the second Test match. It cost us about £1.40 to get in. Now, compare this to the £50, £60, and £70, I was charged by the Barmy Army for different days of the Test match in Cape Town, and you will realise that they are a bunch of robbing bastards, like I said previously.

Late in the day, the rain started pissing down, so the cricket finished a little early. We therefore jumped in a taxi outside the ground to take us to a nice little area called Parkhurst. This taxi wasn't your typical Johannesburg taxi, though, which was usually falling apart and looked like it'd had twenty different violent owners in the past week. This was a posh car, clean, and with a driver who seemed really nice. He talked to us, and was interested about our travels, so we had a good chat with him the whole time we were in the taxi.

Not long after he dropped us off, I was gutted to realise that I didn't have my phone with me. I remembered having it in the taxi, and we'd literally just jumped out of the cab and into the pub, so I was sure I hadn't been pickpocketed again – surely not. I just assumed that it must still be in the taxi, that the driver would notice it and then bring it to the place where he'd just dropped us off. He seemed like a really nice bloke, so I thought this would definitely happen. It didn't.

The day after, I discovered that my service provider would require a police report if they were going to replace it, so I would need to visit the police station.

I flagged a taxi down in the city centre near our hotel. This was typically a wrecker. I couldn't even open the passenger door from the outside; the driver had to kick it open from the inside. It was quite comical really. He told me that he'd been carjacked the previous week by three armed men, therefore confirming what we'd already heard about Johannesburg. They took his car and his two mobile phones, so he was trying to get by driving this shit-heap.

Now, just try to picture the Central Johannesburg Police Station. There was a poster on the wall which read, "PLEASE STOP POLICE KILLINGS". I'm sure since I left Johannesburg, this poster is the sole reason for the amazing drop in police murders over the past year, because they were asking rather nicely.

It was an awful place, and this sign just about summed it up. I also couldn't get any sense out of the police. They said they wanted a cancellation number from my service provider before I could report it lost, but my service provider told me they didn't do that, so after two visits to the police station and numerous calls to EE, I gave up trying to report it. It seemed hopeless.

My driver had kindly waited for me outside the station, but when he took me back to my hotel for the second time, he also ripped me off, charging almost five times what it should have cost. I couldn't be bothered arguing the toss with him, almost feeling sorry for his recent carjacking experience, which must have been quite traumatic. I gave him what I had in my pocket.

I'd been back in my hotel room for five minutes when Scott knocked on my door.

He said, "Give me a kiss."

I said, "Fuck off, you weirdo."

He said, "Just give me a kiss on my cheek!"

Reluctantly, I did. He then told me to go to reception because the taxi driver was there waiting with my phone. It turned out that we were his last customers of the day, and when he got in the car the next morning, he saw my phone on the floor below the front seat. I'd made numerous calls to my phone from Scott's phone, so he'd seen the name Scott, and that's why he asked for him at the hotel reception. How did he know which hotel we were staying in? He'd asked us when we were all chatting on the way home from the cricket.

I always thought he seemed like a nice man, but everything about this was lucky because no other taxi driver we met would even speak to us, other than the one who took me to the police station, though he was only telling me his sob story so I'd feel sorry for him and give him some more money.

A few other things happened that I could mention, such as the taxi on the way back to our hotel one night. The driver got lost and ended up reversing one hundred metres the wrong way down a three-lane one-way system and even through a red light. This was because Scott spotted the hotel behind us, so the driver decided that going backwards was the best way to get there rather than to make his way around the one-way system.

The place is mad.

On my final day, I was up at 5 a.m. to go to the airport. I was on a different flight home than Scott and Liam – leaving a couple of hours before them. Just a few minutes into my journey to the airport, as if anything else could really happen on this trip, my "safe" Uber taxi was involved in a four-vehicle pile-up. We were hit both front and back.

It was funny in a way, because I think it was actually my fault. I was excited about getting home, and I was having a right good chat with the driver. He was actually looking at me at the time, while I was looking straight ahead, so I saw the need to break before the driver did, and I did break only there were no fucking pedals on my side. I'm a nervous passenger, so I do this a lot.

Anyway, his taxi was now fucked. We even had to force the boot open to get my suitcase out, and then I had to walk back to my hotel with all my belongings to get another taxi that I could trust.

So, now I'm walking through this dangerous city – the carjacking capital of the fucking world – with everything I own, at 5.45 a.m., in the dark.

I just wanted to go home now. After safely finding my way back to the hotel and ordering another taxi, we then drove past the scene of the accident, seeing that nothing had moved. Twenty minutes later, my new driver told me that the accident was on the radio news because it was causing havoc in the city centre. So you could say that me leaving the country was actually on the news.

At least I wasn't part of the chaos any longer.

Even when you have an amazing holiday, it's still a great feeling to be going home, but on this occasion, getting home was all about feeling safe.

It was an amazing trip, but I was so glad it was now all over.

Thick as Fuck

Most South Africans are thick as fuck. Maybe that's a bit strong. It's probably just that the majority are not educated. Make your own mind up after you've read this, but as you already know, even the pickpockets are shit.

Certain people in South Africa just seem to tell you what you want to hear rather than tell you the actual truth. Nothing explains this more than the first night in our Johannesburg hotel when I was trying to find the bar.

There was a sign in the hotel, saying that there was a bar on the third floor, so I walked up to the third floor where the main reception was also located. I couldn't find the bar, so I asked at reception. I was then told that the bar was on the ground floor, so I walked down to the ground floor. I couldn't find a bar on the ground floor either.

There was another reception desk on the ground floor, so I asked them.

They told me, "The bar is on the third floor."

What was that all about? There was no actual fucking bar in the hotel, anywhere.

The same night, the three of us were in a bar in Johannesburg with the time coming up to 11 p.m. We asked the owner if there were any more bars nearby, and he told us that there were a couple open just up the road. He also told us that his bar was open all night, so we thought we'd have a wander first, and if the other bars were no good, then we'd just come back here.

We walked around for an hour in what didn't look or feel like the safest place in the world, but we didn't find any life anywhere, so we headed back to the same bar. We were all a little confused. We'd been sent on a wild goose chase because there were no bars nearby either open or closed.

When we arrived back at the other bar, guess what? It was fucking shut.

The owner had told us his place never closed. Why?

We decided to go back to the hotel, and on the way, we stopped off for supper. We had the national dish of South Africa, which is actually KFC. KFC is absolutely everywhere in South Africa; believe me. I ordered a Zinger Burger and a Chicken Burger with fries, but I ended up with two Chicken Burgers and no fries.

Over and over again, these things kept happening, but not everyone is incompetent or stupid. There are two types of people in South Africa: those who can and those who can't. It's just that the ones who can't are definitely in the majority, and most of the time it's probably not their fault because of where they have come from. There is still so much poverty in South Africa, and it seems that the transition from apartheid – which clearly had to happen – has happened too quick – before many of the poor people had been educated to the standard required to do many of the jobs. It will no doubt take many more years to sort out many of the existing problems, but after witnessing so many poverty-stricken areas all across South Africa, it looks like many problems are there to stay for the foreseeable future.

However, I love South Africa, and I would return tomorrow if I could. It's a beautiful place, if just a little crazy.

IN THE MIDDLE OF
DIFFICULTY
LIES
OPPORTUNITY

ALBERT EINSTEIN

272

Chapter Ten

Too Many Pricks

You've no doubt noticed that I often get myself into some daft situations, and I can also be quite accident-prone. Many of these accidents have occurred since I departed Taiwan, so in a strange twist of fate, I wonder if the stupid Chinese name I was given has something to do with this.

My Chinese name is Shen Shao-bai (沈少白), and it was given to me by Ling in 2003. The Shen part was picked because – to Ling – it sounded similar to the beginning of my surname "San". The meaning of Shao-bai is "less white", so Ling's thinking was that I was becoming less white, and therefore becoming more yellow, or more Chinese.

I used this Chinese name for a while to fool Ling's students on an Internet forum. It was a good way for me to practice typing and reading Chinese, and the forum format gave me as much time as I needed to work out my replies. Nobody had any idea it was me for weeks, or even that Shen Shao-bai was a foreigner, so I was quite rightly proud of myself for a while. That was until Ling gave it away and I became a laughing stock.

I remember that day clearly, because when she told her students that Shen Shao-bai was me, one of them made a remark and everyone started laughing out loud. Then Ling started laughing too. The reason for this laughter was down to someone realising *Shen Shao-bai* was a character in many old Chinese comedy films, and strangely enough, he just happened to be a big, clumsy, fucking idiot. I suppose you could say he was the Chinese Mr. Bean.

So there you have it. By complete chance, even my Chinese name says that I am an idiot. This will all become clear as you read on, though it's generally not my fault what happens to me. I just seem to attract it.

How Is Your Nose?

Even after I have an accident, and get myself to hospital, there is still the potential for more to go wrong.

When I was thirteen years old, I chipped a bone in my ankle playing football. Funnily enough, the lad who did this to me was the first bloke to take Elaine out after we split up fifteen years later. His name was Glen, and he was also one of the people who started working me at British Gas as a sixteen-year-old, becoming both a colleague and fellow student.

Elaine had no idea who he was, having never met him until after we'd split up, so this was an extreme coincidence which she only found out about on the one occasion we spoke in the past seventeen years.

Anyway, the injury caused by Glen's 'legal' tackle happened one minute before half-time and left me in agony. However, I decided to play on because we had no substitutes.

The team we were playing – Christ Church – were always the top team in the league, and the week before they'd beaten us 8-3. One week later, after initially trailing 2-0, we surprisingly went into half-time leading 3-2.

I was the captain, and though I could hardly walk back onto the pitch for the second half, I had to play on – but the fact that my manager and my dad let me continue is a mystery because they could both see I was crying.

I somehow managed to play the remaining forty minutes, even clearing a certain goal off the line near the end, and amazingly we ended up winning the game 3-2 – by far our best ever moment as a team at the time, so the pain had been worth it.

Being in agony hours later with an ankle looking like a pineapple, my dad eventually took me to A & E, where my leg was put in plaster for the next six weeks.

However, the best part was after I'd had the X-ray and we were waiting for news of my injury. The serious-looking consultant walked into the room with a large brown envelope, took out an X-ray, and held it up to the light, at which point I thought, "That looks a bit weird".

Then, he asked, "So, how is your nose?"

I actually touched my nose at the time, and while looking at my dad, I said, "Fine, I think!"

How did someone else's nose X-ray end up in an envelope with my name on it?

Luckily, my real X-ray was also there, so I was given the bad news and plastered up, but what about the nose guy? The poor soul probably had to spend hours going through the whole X-ray process all over again.

Then again, it was probably some prick from Farnworth who went looking for trouble in the first place.

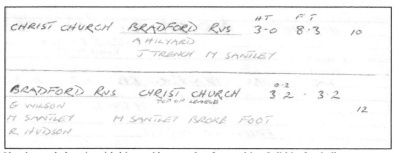

Here's my dad again with his weekly records of everything I did in football.

13 years old, December 1984.
I broke my leg.

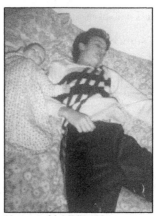

13 years old. NYE 1984.
I got drunk for the first time.

Thriller

In 1992, I surprised Elaine with tickets to see Michael Jackson at Wembley Stadium. He wasn't exactly my cup of tea, but he was Elaine's idol.

We were at the stadium very early, and managed to get a spot near the front of the stage. This seemed like a good idea at the time. Then it filled up and there were kids passing out next to us being dragged away crying. It was horrendous.

It was, however, a wonderful occasion, apart from the moment just before Michael Jackson came on stage.

Being a hot day, people were throwing water around, and the empty plastic bottles were also constantly being thrown into the air. Then, someone threw a large plastic bottle which still had some water in it. But they didn't throw it up into the air. They threw it sideways.

I was six feet tall, towering above the hundreds of kids around us, so when the bottle happened to come my way like a guided missile, flying inches above all the heads in its path, my head was the first thing to stop it.

From the thousands of people in the stadium, it therefore managed to find yours truly, hitting me right between the fucking eyes and knocking me out – *head trauma #2!*

I was helped to my feet by some of the kids around me, all of whom were quite rightly pissing their sides with laughter, along with Elaine.

A few years later, the ever-so-loving Elaine suggested that we should get a kitten. Like men often do, I went along with this just to keep the peace, and after a visit to the animal shelter, she came back with an adorable little furry thing around six weeks old.

He was called Tab. He was cute, and I loved him, especially after I'd saved him three times from the clutches of death. The final time being when we moved into our new house and he went missing for two days.

Those two dreadful days I would stand at my front door for hours on end shouting his name, hoping to hear a whimper from somewhere. I'd almost given up hope, but around midnight on the second night, I heard a faint cry from next door – which was an unfinished, semi-detached house. I made my way into the half-built shell and crept upstairs – which was yet to have a ceiling fitted – and I could hear his feeble moan coming from behind a wall. It was Tab, and he was stuck inside the wall cavity.

I rushed back downstairs, borrowed some ladders from a sleeping neighbour, and quickly returned. When I looked down the cavity I could see his eyes shining back at me, but he was halfway down the wall and just wouldn't – or couldn't – come out. It was heart-breaking seeing him there looking paralysed and scared to death.

I nipped back home again to get a tin of cat food to see if this would coax him out, but even that didn't work. He didn't move, so I stayed there for hours, pleading with him, reaching lower and lower with the food, slowly tempting him closer, until I eventually had him close enough to get my hand on his head to drag him out, though the little bastard still fought and scratched me all the way.

Something must have chased him there because he was almost too petrified to move, and seeing the fear in him at the time I thought he would never be the same again afterward.

I was wrong about the little bastard.

He soon recovered and started to go out again at night, returning home at dawn most days. When he'd want to come back into the house, he would climb on the front door handle, hold himself up with one paw, and stick his other paw through the letterbox, cleverly flicking the inner metal plate to make a racket and wake us up.

Early one Monday morning, I could hear him at the door again. I got out of bed completely naked, and with my eyes barely open made my way to the top of the stairs. Then I fucking slipped.

My right foot swung outward and kicked a wooden spindle on the bannister, and as I tumbled down the stairs, my little toe was forced the other way as it hit the spindle. I subsequently ended up at the foot of the stairs.

The loving words I heard from the bedroom were, "I hope you've not got blood on my carpet." Her fucking carpet?

Anyway, I later went to work, but as I couldn't walk properly and was in agony, I had to go to A & E again. My little toe wasn't

278

broken, but the doctor decided that I needed stitches, so they actually put stitches in the crease behind my little toe.

As I've had quite a few by now, I know that stitches don't usually hurt after the area is numbed, and the injection to numb the wound doesn't usually hurt much either. It just stings a bit. However, lying on my front with my foot in the air, that initial injection in the back crease of my little toe is the most painful thing I have ever felt in my entire life, and I'm quite sure it wasn't necessary at all. A plaster would have done the fucking job. I just think the doctor was a sadistic bastard. In fact, it was probably one of Elaine's mates.

Can you see what you've done? Before this, I hadn't thought about Elaine for over seventeen years, but now, having written that story about her in a previous chapter, I can't get her out of my fucking head.

A Tale of Two Heads

My mate James and I used to go drinking together almost every Saturday. Having had enough of each other over the years, in 2007 we decided to go on holiday without the other one in tow.

James went "partying" in Ibiza with a group of animals, while my trip was a little more sedate. I spent ten days alone in a villa in Marbella. I was studying for a BSc (honours) degree in computing at the time, and with my full-time job and social nonsense getting in the way of my studies, I was behind schedule on two important assignments. My plan was to spend time in the sun studying and complete both pieces of work. I did just that, and I subsequently ended up getting excellent grades in both, so everything went to plan – almost.

I didn't actually drink much alcohol while I was away. I studied, walked, jogged, studied more, and then had the odd beer or two later in the evening.

However, one morning around 2.30 a.m. when I was tucked up in bed, I received a terrifying phone call from Kyle, a friend of both James and me. James had fallen in Ibiza and hit his face on the concrete floor, and Kyle was shouting and screaming down the phone, asking me what he should do. It was horrible and it seemed that James was in a very bad way.

I was hundreds of miles away, so I've no idea why he phoned me or what I was supposed to do, but I was sober so I tried my best to talk him through it. I asked, "Is he breathing? Can you see where the blood is coming from? Has anyone phoned an ambulance?"

A garbled conversation continued for a few minutes because I wasn't getting any sense from Kyle, but then he suddenly said, "We're at the hospital now, bye!"

When I answered the call he'd given me the impression it was just the two of them in a dark street, and that he was watching my best mate James slowly die. I don't know where that came from, but I was obviously overjoyed to be told they were at the hospital. Ten minutes earlier, I'd really thought James had been dying.

The next day, Kyle called back to say that James had thirty-eight stitches in his face, mostly inside his mouth, but otherwise he was fine

– that's if you can actually be fine after having thirty-eight stitches. I was so relieved for James, but I was also relieved for myself that I hadn't gone with them on this trip of madness to Ibiza, and that I was in the relative serenity of Marbella.

The following day, almost laughing about James and his messed-up face, I spent ten hours studying, and then had a walk early in the evening. I walked for miles but stopped twice to have a beer. I then stopped for a third time, at a bar near my apartment.

I finished one final beer, having just the three bottles in total all day, and then the owners of the bar gave me a *free* extremely large brandy. I only remember having one sip of this when I started to feel very light-headed. I quickly tried to make my way to the downstairs toilets to sort myself out, but as I got to the top of the fifteen or so marble steps, I passed out.

I remember trying to reach for the bannister while falling into the wall, only to realise that the only bannister was on the other fucking wall. That was the last thing I remember before I ended up at the bottom of the stairs – *head trauma #3!*

I woke up in the toilets, groggy, with three people around me. I'd fallen around twenty feet, landing head first on a solid marble floor. I could quite easily have died. The owners had heard the thud from inside the bar and luckily were at my side within seconds.

There were just those three people in the pub at the time; the two owners and their friend, who later drove me home. I remember them asking if I'd taken any drugs that night. Well, if I did take drugs, then they were in that large glass of brandy which they gave me. They never mentioned taking me to hospital to be checked; I wonder why. Only now, ten years later, I am even wondering why they dragged me into the toilet out of the way, rather than try to wake me up where they found me.

I'd never collapsed before, and I never have since, so these people were obviously trying some drug out on me. How frightening is that? That is twice I've been spiked while away on holiday alone, and those people could have done anything to me – anything. That is why, when I woke up in the toilets, I first checked my pockets and then my backside, both of which seemed to be intact.

What was also frightening was that in Ibiza, James had just fallen from his natural height and hit the floor, but he needed thirty-eight stitches in his face and mouth. He still has no feeling in part of his mouth.

I had fallen around twenty feet onto a marble floor but had just a few 'comedy' cuts around my eyes and forehead. I was so lucky; it was as if I must have slid down the steps slowly after passing out.

It was actually quite funny when we arrived home. We'd been away on holiday separately, but James and I both walked into our local pub together the following Saturday with our faces smashed to pieces.

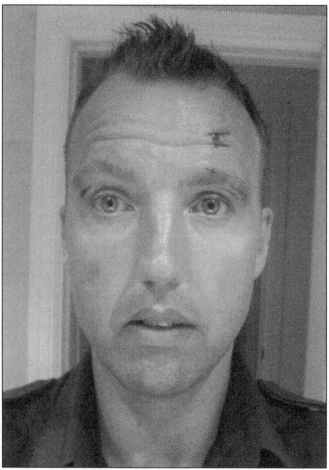

Me in Marbella, just after the kind gentleman took me home.

Fucking Tourists

While playing in a friendly football match in Taiwan, I was accidentally head-butted by the tallest Japanese lad I have ever set eyes on. We'd jumped up for a header, and while I headed the ball, he just nutted my left eye, and blood started to pour out – *head trauma #4!*

I walked off the pitch, hearing everyone saying that I needed to go to hospital, but I didn't have a clue what to do. I felt completely lost in this foreign place, so I hung around waiting to go back on the pitch. Where was the hospital? How do I get there? Where do I go when I get there? What do I say? Is it free? Everything was in Chinese so I just stood around watching the game wondering what to do.

Then my teammate Sunil from New Zealand, who had lived in Taiwan for ten years, reluctantly said he would take me. He spoke the local language and knew where I needed to go. He also took the photo below, and when he took it the doctor was saying something in Chinese. Sunil told me later that the doctor's words during the photo were, "Fucking tourists."

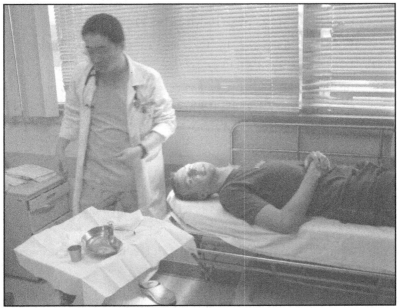

Stitched up in Taiwan.

283

Marathon Matt

On the Saturday morning that Abi texted to say she was moving out, I decided to go for a long run. I had entered the Manchester Marathon which was in two weeks' time, and though I'd been training for it for over three months I really hadn't done enough. On this day, I therefore decided to run fourteen miles, which would have been the furthest I'd ever run.

I was on my final mile, struggling slowly along when I started to think about Abi moving out. Although I was the one who'd suggested it, I wasn't really sure I wanted her to move out at all. She was my best mate and I was going to miss her loads. Then, at that precise moment, my other best mate James drove past in his white transit van full of beer kegs, beeping his horn while giving me a V-sign.

As it was Saturday, he was working, delivering beer and spirits to the pubs in the locality. He would be finished by 1:00 p.m., and by 2:00 p.m. he'd walk the fifty feet or so to my apartment where we'd regularly have a couple of swift drinks before spending the day in the pub. This was no different than any other Saturday that year. Abi used to work until late on Saturdays so what else was there to do?

Just after James drove by, I received a text from him which read, "I can walk faster than that, you dickhead."

Just before this, I had actually been considering walking the final mile or so home, but after reading his message, I decided to put a bit of a spurt on for one final push. My legs were really tired by now, and I was finding it difficult to lift them, so the inevitable happened.

I only needed to lift my foot off the ground around 10 cm to make it over the curb, but my foot clipped the top of it and I lost my balance. With this happening so quickly and my hands slow to react, my face then hit the gravel and concrete before anything else – *head trauma #5!*

I landed on my right eye and then slid on my face in the gravel and stones.

Seeing what had happened, a kind couple pulled over in their car to see if I was OK. They kindly took me home, where I said I would check the wound before deciding whether or not to go to hospital.

The gash was full of stones and gravel, and as I was picking them out one by one I realised I needed medical help, so again, I drove myself to A & E.

There, the nurse kindly used a wire brush to scrape out all the stones before stitching me up again. I then returned home, and ten minutes later, Jimmy turned up laughing his fucking head off.

Two weeks later, I completed the Manchester Marathon. Abi was there to watch because she'd always said she would be. Just before the start, I decided that if and when I crossed the finishing line and Abi was there to greet me, then at that moment I was going to propose to her. Even though she'd just left me, I still had this thought in my head for some reason. I thought that proposing might bring us back together.

When the moment came, first my left leg cramped up, then my right leg cramped up, and then I did too. I just couldn't do it. Months later when I told her about my failed plan, she said there was no way she could have possibly refused at the time. It would have all been complete bollocks, though, and we both realise that now. At least I can blame that ridiculous idea on the bang to the head.

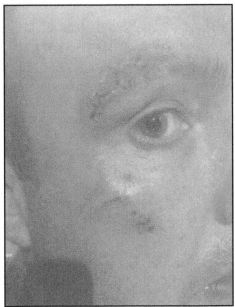

Me, again.

Prestatyn

Where did it all go wrong?

In the summer of 2016, on the weekend my friend Aidan from the pub was going into hospital for a mystery operation, me and five friends from my local pub had a weekend break in Prestatyn, North Wales. I had my reservations about this, mainly because the six of us were only really friends in the pub, and we were going to stay in a caravan on some shit Welsh holiday park. At some stage during a Sunday of drinking in my local pub, I'd agreed to join the trip, so I stayed true to my word.

It was everything I expected – and worse.

The kids. Oh, the kids.

It was obviously a place where parents go to have their own "well-deserved" holiday while they let their sprogs run riot, leaving some other poor fucker to deal with them. It was kid fucking carnage.

You might have noticed that the expletives have just increased a tad. I will try my utmost to only use them when necessary from now on. I will try.

Prestatyn Fucking Sands Holiday Park doesn't exactly sound like the place I would normally frequent, and now I know exactly why.

The people with me, Alan (Mike), Alan, Pete, Sally, and Jackie, are all lovely people whose company I enjoy, and if it had been just the six of us on a secluded island it might have been fine. However, in places like this caravan park, you have no choice but to mingle with the crowd, and the crowd was not my kind of crowd. It was just hundreds of annoying little shits all high on sweets and sugar-laced drinks, running around causing fucking havoc.

Alan, Pete, Jackie, and Sally with that bloody caravan.

I mostly just sat there watching them with my mouth wide open, wondering what the fuck I was doing there.

They had an "adults" bar, but strangely this was also full of kids, so there really was no escape. We were all in similar states of disbelief about this, so we just drank more and more alcohol to deal with the situation. We didn't know what else to do.

Maybe this was the whole idea behind the business model? Let the kids cause so much havoc that punters have little option but to drink more to ease the pain.

On the Saturday lunchtime, following our first night, me, Alan (Mike), and Alan went for a walk because we needed a break from the mayhem. After fighting our way through the kids and caravans, we managed to find the park exit, and then immediately started to relax.

Stumbling on a few nearby pubs, we thought we might as well stop, but momentarily we panicked when we first heard and then saw kids meandering. For a few seconds, we were in two minds what to do. Then god gave us a sign.

We immediately turned into raging bulls, fighting to be the first one through the door.

I never thought heaven and hell existed in the same space, but they do, and although we were just around the corner, for a couple of hours we were safe.

Later that Saturday, our good friends Greg and Lesley arrived, and they were equally gobsmacked at what they saw. This particular night, the entertainment in the "family" bar was a football presentation – a private function.

This was the reason that the "adult" bar was even more rammed that night, because it was now catering for every kid in the whole fucking place, plus everyone else.

We endured it for a while, but I had to get out. Alan(Mike) and I therefore decided to go for a cigarette, making our way to the exit by fighting our way through countless overturned chairs and screaming kids. Before going for a cigarette, I nipped to the toilet, and then as I was making my way outside something very typical happened.

Double doors with long metal handles were the norm in this place, and I encountered two of them. Being right-handed, I chose to open the door on the right, giving it a forceful tug. However, some stupid prick had locked the right-hand door, so I ended up just pulling the fucking iron bar out of its hinge.

Only the top hinge came out, so the solid iron bar then came down at me at just the perfect angle to twat me on my forehead – *head trauma #6!*

It fucking knocked me out. I'd actually knocked myself out by hitting myself over the head with a fucking iron bar.

This topped off an extra "special" weekend.

I was helped up by a couple of staff, completed an accident form, and was then offered a free week at the park for my "inconvenience".

I didn't accept it. I would rather hit myself over the head a million more times.

To this day, I've not had any more head traumas. This trait now seems to have been adopted by my brother though – as you will soon discover.

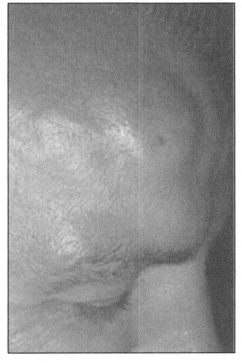

And again.

Aidan and the Caravan

He joked that he was going
For a six-inch cock reduction
When we all assumed
It was for liposuction
Then somebody quipped
"It was to halt his reproduction"
But these were all just guesses
And his punter's wrong deductions

The surgeon didn't arrive
He made him wait and wait
There wasn't a free day
On which to operate
So Aidan carried on
Pretended to be a brave man
While an "odd" group from his pub
Stayed in a Prestatyn caravan

While we were living strangely
In that place not far away
We often thought of Aidan
And his continuing delay
But we soon forgot his troubles
We had some of our own
And after just ten minutes
I wanted to drive the fuck back home

As we entered the park
We could see it was chaotic
So me and Alan had no choice
But to become alcoholic
We went inside the boozer
Thinking we'd escaped
But before we could scream for help
We were both fucking mind raped

The dirty little bastards

They were just everywhere
As I wandered aimlessly
Picking up strewn chairs
The drink just wasn't helping
The evil force too strong
While on the stage some Welsh tramp
Belted out yet another shit song

It didn't get much better
The second and final day
I just sat with cotton wool in my ears
Wishing the time away
But then it got quite lively
And all because of me
I banged my head on a faulty door handle
And they said I could have one week free

I did politely decline
Because I'd had enough
In fact, I'm really lying
I told them to fuck off
The place was just not me
In fact, it was a dump
And when I looked in the mirror
You should have seen my fucking lump

Now all this very time
Aidan awaited his operation
The six of us shared extremely basic
Shit accommodation
And if he feels unlucky
About his situation
He should go down to Prestatyn
For his very next vacation

As I drove home and pondered
On those days of discontent
I remembered my father's words
He'd said, before I went
"I spent one year in Prestatyn,

On a Sunday afternoon."
And will I be going back there?
Not anytime fucking soon

YOU'RE A SAINT, MATH

GEORGE SANTLEY

Chapter Eleven

Belgrade

The opening scene fades out with Matt shouting his brother's name.

MATT (Shouting, screaming, almost crying)

   Chris! Chris! Chris!

FORTY-EIGHT HOURS EARLIER

OPENING CREDITS BEGIN

A SONG PLAYS

SID VICIOUS - MY WAY

INTERNAL. GOVERNMENT OFFICE BUILDING, LYTHAM ST. ANNES. 4pm.

Ugly, dated, mostly-empty office complex. The place is filled with decade-old Personal Computers and large beige-coloured ICL (International Computers Limited) mainframe computers dating back to the nineteen-seventies.

As the song intro starts we see Matt sitting at his desk with his earphones plugged in. He looks bored, even desperate. He just doesn't want to be there. He's had so many more interesting days than this in his life that his colleagues know nothing about.

He looks to his left at one colleague – a small ageing gentleman with a balding head, but with long curly hair dropping from the back and sides, as though this bloke is hanging onto his past 'rocker' days. Matt focuses on the man's little finger nail. For some reason, unlike the rest, this nail is almost two inches long and painted purple.

Matt shakes his head slowly.

He looks as though he is mouthing the words, "What the fuck?"

Matt logs-out and closes his laptop. He gets up to leave as the music speeds up.

MATT

I'm off. I'll see you all tomorrow.

Three people sitting nearby don't move their eyes from their computer screens.

Mumbles of goodbye can be heard as Matt exits the office.

EXTERNAL. OFFICE CAR PARK. LYTHAM. 4:02pm

Matt climbs into his car. We don't see what make of car it is.

He drives home as the song plays to the end, the expression on Matt's face not changing all the way, as if not to match the loutish music that he's playing. He seems bored with life, and especially with his slow drive home from work which he's done countless times over the past twenty years.

INTERNAL. UNDERGROUND CAR PARK. OLD MILL APARTMENT COMPLEX. BOLTON. 4:50pm

Matt arrives home, parking his car as the song finishes.

In silence, he slowly walks up the steps to his plush apartment on the second floor.

INTERNAL. MATT'S APARTMENT. 4:52pm

Matt is extremely tired. He collapses on the sofa, ready to fall asleep any minute.

He has been craving this moment for most of his miserable day.

He seems annoyed when his phone makes a noise.

It's a text message from Deb – his brother's ex-wife.

Matt throws his head back and looks upwards.

MATT

Oh, for fuck sake.

Do Not Try This at Home

I'd thought my days of travel chaos were over. I was wrong.

It was early one summer evening in 2016, and I'd finally arrived home from work. It had been an early start and a torrid day, and I was so knackered I'd even been falling asleep at the wheel driving home. The one-hour journey from Lytham St. Annes had become too much after doing it for over twenty fucking years.

I couldn't wait to just collapse on the couch and fall asleep, a regular occurrence at the time. I opened the front door, took my shoes off and did exactly that. Then, as soon as my head hit the cushion – before I'd even closed my eyes – I received a text message. It was from Deb, my brother's ex-wife.

It read, "Can you speak later?"

I immediately threw my head back, closed my eyes and said out loud, "Oh for fuck sake."

I knew this message was about my brother, who was by now quite a messed-up alcoholic. He'd been travelling with his son around the Balkans a year earlier – a trip Chris had arranged for Sam's twenty-first birthday – and he'd decided to do a similar trip on his own this year.

Chris was self-employed, selling gas and electric plans from home – something he'd done for far too long. I actually blamed this for the start of his downfall due to him being alone all day, and I'd mentioned it to him on countless occasions, saying that it wasn't healthy spending so much time alone. He really needed to do something else and get out more during the day.

However, at least his situation enabled him to go on holiday whenever he wanted, though he left on this lone trip at a time when he really shouldn't have. He needed looking after at the time. He was a danger to himself, drinking far too much, and it had started to become a real problem.

My parents and I optimistically thought he might somehow sort himself out on this trip, though, by slowly weaning himself off it. That was actually his plan – or what he'd told us – but the opposite was true. In the six weeks he'd been in the Balkans alone, he'd gotten much worse. He'd had half a dozen bad falls – possibly seizures – and been to hospital six to eight times. During that period, he'd had more stitches in his head and face than a fucking woolly glove.

In the space of just a few weeks, he'd somehow managed to beat my lifetime record of head traumas. I never mentioned this to him, but if I had done, the way his mind was working at the time, it would have no doubt been something for him to feel proud of.

His falls were much more serious than what happened to me, though. He made my injuries look quite comical in comparison, which they were really.

Some locals in Macedonia and Serbia had even called my mum because they were worried about him, saying that he really needed help. One even actually complained that he couldn't get Chris out of his house at one point, and also said that he had caused some damaged to his home. This person even told my mum to send him money to pay for the damage. All this obviously added to my mum and dad's worry.

After this, an elderly woman from Macedonia even took him into her home and looked after him for a while. It was all becoming quite ridiculous and more worrying each day. He'd been lucky to have these complete strangers take care of him, though it was becoming obvious that many had now had enough of him.

When I mentioned to Chris in a text message that we were all really worried, suggesting that he should come home immediately – echoing what my mum and dad had already been telling him – he just said that we were drama queens and that he had no intention of cutting his trip short.

This meant that we'd have to cope with another few of weeks of this at the very least. It was getting so bad, though, that it was difficult to see how he would survive that long, and then how he would make his own way home. He didn't even have a return flight ticket.

I was beginning to think he must have some real mental issues. It wasn't just alcohol now. It didn't compute to me. How could he not realise the damage he was doing to himself each day he was away from home in these foreign places, not forgetting the damage he was doing to the rest of us, who it seemed he never thought of for a minute?

My mum was going off her head by this point. My dad too, but he would never show it. I knew deep down that I had to do something, but I really couldn't bring myself to. In my mind, he didn't deserve my help. This was all his own doing, and what could I possibly do anyway?

I'd had enough of him by now. I'd had enough of the pain he'd caused my mum and dad, his kids, Deb, and me. I didn't have the energy to care for someone who didn't seem to listen, didn't seem to help himself, and more importantly, didn't seem to care for those whose lives he was slowly destroying. I just thought, "Fuck him."

My reply to Deb's text was, "Yeah, I can speak, just as long as it doesn't involve my brother."

Moments later, I spoke to Deb. Of course it was about my fucking brother.

Deb was worried about him. My mum and dad were at the end of the road with worry, and they all wanted to find a way of getting him back home. But what could they do if he didn't want to come home? He wasn't just around the corner. He was in fucking Serbia.

My mum and dad hadn't told me much about their dilemma over the previous weeks. They know that things like this affect me greatly. They would only bother me if completely necessary, and maybe when my mum had called in the past I hadn't been so helpful anyway. I didn't know what to do or say.

My mind just tells me not to get involved or even think about something that I cannot help with. This is why I'd started to ignore my brother. I knew I couldn't help him in any way. He could only help himself, and after I'd speak to or see him in his recent state, the vision would affect me for weeks, even months afterward. I just thought, "What is the point in destroying two lives? You can destroy your own life but you're certainly not destroying mine too." Is that selfish? Or is that sensible?

At first I told Deb that we should just leave him to it. He'd survived this far and we'd been asking – pleading – with him to come home for five weeks already. What else could any of us do?

Later that evening, after I'd had a few cans of Boddingtons Bitter – which is quite low in alcohol, for the record – Deb called again. It quickly became apparent that there was no way Chris could get home by himself, even if he wanted to. He didn't even know where he was most of the time. He really did need help, so I finally thought I'd try to do my bit.

I discovered that there were no direct flights to Manchester from Belgrade, so even finding a way to get him to the airport in Belgrade wouldn't work. He'd need a connecting flight to somewhere first, and there was no way he'd be able to manage that in his state. He'd definitely get lost or hospitalised again on the way.

His mental state was all over the place. He'd even managed to lose six or seven phones in the space of one month, while also losing his debit card – his only source of cash. You get the picture. Just imagine him trying to catch a connecting flight in some foreign airport. There was no chance.

Also, the way he looked in the pictures I'd seen on Facebook, even before all the visits to hospital, together with his constant drinking, meant that he probably wouldn't be let on a plane in any case. He would have frightened all the other passengers.

That is what I derived from the situation anyway. All this, and not knowing if he would actually still have his passport with him meant that even one of us flying out to collect him seemed out of the question. It was hopeless. What could we do?

Then, in a later call from Deb, she told me the heart-breaking state my mum and dad were in. They were on holiday at the time in Cornwall, Southern England. My mum had called Deb, and had been screaming down the phone at one point. I can only gather that this was down to the utter worry and frustration of it all. It had all built up inside, probably over a lot longer than the previous few weeks. My dad had even run off to get away from my mum after they'd fallen out. This whole situation was destroying them.

I knew I had to do something this time. Doing nothing was now no longer an option. This had to end and it had to end soon. Reluctantly, I made the logical decision. I decided that the best chance he had of getting out of there alive was if I drove to Serbia to pick him up. What other option was there?

Why on earth should I have to do this for anyone? Never mind my elder brother. He was forty-seven years old, for fuck sake. Would anyone else have attempted this? Would you? It would be a three-thousand-mile round trip – three thousand fucking miles to get somebody out of a self-inflicted mess. I was annoyed. I was fuming, but thoughts of my mum and dad persuaded me to do it.

I called my mum to tell her what I was doing. She kept telling me that I didn't have to do it, and that it wasn't fair on me. But I did have to do it.

I booked a ferry from Dover to Calais, which would leave at 6.40 a.m. the following morning, and packed a few bits, including a thermos flask containing twenty shots of extra-strong espresso. I'd only had the coffee delivered the previous week, and I didn't even drink espresso. I don't like it. I was just giving it a try to see if it would help keep me awake at work – something I needed at the time.

Since arriving home from work, craving sleep, I hadn't managed to close my eyes once, and now I had to go on a fucking three-thousand-mile drive of mystery. It was absolutely ridiculous.

For courage, I had one more can of Boddingtons – probably putting me over the drink-driving limit. At the time I didn't care about this in the slightest. It was the least of my worries.

I prepared to leave at 10.45 p.m. I was feeling determined, emotional, stupid, and worried. I kept telling myself that it had to be done. There was no other way this situation could end well. It could actually end a lot worse with me going on this journey, because I would now be in danger as well. However, I had to put myself at risk and take the chance.

I departed alone, nervous, apprehensive, and still very tired, though the adrenaline – and not forgetting the coffee I'd necked while filling the flask – had started to kick in, so I also felt a little hyper. For some reason, I'd also become a little excited.

I drove the first slow mile down the dark and typically wet Blackburn Road, the road otherwise known as the A666. Yes, hell is actually a place on earth – it starts in Bolton and ends up in Blackburn, Lancashire. As I arrived at the place where the A666 meets St. Peter's Way – the road linking me to the motorway network of the UK – I really was in hell because the road was fucking shut.

I'd just set off on a three-thousand-odd mile drive to Serbia and back, and after just three minutes this happens. As I waited at the temporary red lights, I stared at the orange traffic cones, my mind immediately flashing back to one particular day I experienced in Taiwan.

A random local woman had stopped me in the street in Taipei. Strangely, she asked if I could help her make sense of some English technical documents she had on the manufacturing specifications for UK traffic cones. She even offered to treat me to lunch in return for my help, which I obviously agreed to. During our two-hour meeting, I think she said she'd wanted to manufacture them herself, but then again, I could hardly understand a fucking word she said. However, maybe it was all a ploy? Was it me she was interested in all along? Was I being slow again with a woman's advances? She was actually very attractive too.

Anyway, I just thought, "What a bizarre situation that was."

My mind came back in a split second. What a fucking bizarre situation this was.

From here, believe it or not, I had to endure a twenty-minute detour through fucking Farnworth. I had to laugh at this, but only because I was half-pissed.

From here, things were OK for a while, and I landed in Dover six hours later. I was surprisingly quite lively, though I guess this was the last dregs of my adrenaline and coffee buzz. I boarded the ferry with time to spare, and watched the white cliffs in the distance as the sun began to rise above them. I thought, "What the fuck am I doing?"

The ferry to Calais was much quicker than I'd expected, so even before I'd had time to relax, we'd arrived. It then hit me. I now had to drive all the way from Calais to Belgrade. Even at this point, I really needed to sleep. I'd already been up for over twenty-four hours. How on earth was I going to manage the rest of this journey? I hadn't really thought about it until now.

I input the city of Belgrade into my car's SATNAV, shook my head at the thought of the twelve-hundred miles I had to drive there, and began to follow the female instructions. Unfortunately, Miss SATNAV sounded like a very boring Canadian woman. On top of everything else, I now realised that I would have to endure her for the next couple of days too.

I had another flashback – this time to South Africa.

I was in a hotel room with two Canadian women, one asleep, and the other one asking me to pleasure her in the wrong place. My mind added a vision of Meatloaf in the background. He was singing, "I would do anything for love, but I won't do that!" I then wondered if I'd finally cracked the mystery of the words in this song. All these years I'd wondered what the fuck Meatloaf was singing about, but my tired mind had finally solved this mystery. I laughed. What else could I do? My mind would need to create many more entertaining moments like this if I was going to stay awake and survive this journey.

Back with my eyes on the road ahead, I was thinking that I'd never driven in mainland Europe before, so this was all completely new to me. Not knowing where I was going, on unknown roads, on which I would be driving on the opposite side I was used to, and all without any sleep. Surely this was the perfect recipe for a huge disaster. I'd actually driven on the opposite side of the crazy roads in Taipei, so I suppose that part didn't really bother me. It was everything else about the journey.

As I was leaving Calais, the sun came out. I put my foot down and opened the window, feeling a heavenly refreshing breeze on my face. It was lovely. Then something hard hit me plush in the throat.

It felt like a stone, but when I looked down there was a paralysed bee on my lap. I brushed it off and panicked for a while, almost crashing my fucking car before I was able to pull over.

When I was ten years old, playing hide-and-seek with my friends, I ran into a bush where my brother was hiding, and inadvertently disturbed a wasp hive. I was stung approximately seventy times by those wasps – they left my brother alone – and ever since then I've never been fond of black and yellow things, so I panicked.

It was bizarre how hard the bee felt when it hit my throat, though; and what a way for the poor thing to die; like I really gave a shit.

To both my surprise and delight, when I escaped the busy roads of Calais, the drive was pretty amazing at times. Due to an accident quite early on, my SATNAV took me on a short detour through Holland and into a couple of beautiful little Dutch villages. I stopped there for a short break and to have a look around.

I've no idea what these places were called, and I doubt that I could ever find them again if I tried. However, this short break from the madness seemed to calm me down and spur me on a little. I was able to take stock for the first time.

It was midmorning. I'd only been driving in Europe for around one hour but I needed this. I tried not to think about the next twenty hours or so I still needed to drive to reach Belgrade. The return trip never even crossed my mind. That really didn't bear thinking about. I could only focus on this first half of the journey for now, and even that was hard to comprehend.

Other than this short detour, the roads through Belgium, Germany, Austria, Slovenia, Croatia, and finally Serbia, were mainly all like motorways. This was great in one respect because I was able to drive extremely fast most of the time. However, imagine driving on lifeless roads for more than a day, trying to stay awake when you haven't slept for a day and a half beforehand. It really was pretty grim and dangerous.

I couldn't complain, though. After leaving England, I'd only had one delay on the roads, this being a long jam in Germany.

I'd found conflict with the irritating Canadian SATNAV slag because she was asking me to turn around. Funnily enough, the previous time I'd spoken to a Canadian female, this was something I'd asked her to do for me in bed, just before I fell asleep.

I wasn't going to turn around.

I could see that the road behind was gridlocked, so I felt I had no option but to trust myself and disagree with her, and carry on along the same route.

I later regretted this decision because I ended up not moving for three fucking hours. I muted my SATNAV at this point, not wanting to hear the words "I told you so" from the annoying bitch. This delay was to be quite a pivotal moment in the trip. I'd previously thought I could stay in a hotel somewhere overnight, calculating that I could still arrive in Serbia late morning or early afternoon, my thinking being that Chris might not be quite as pissed early in the day, and therefore he'd be more manageable at that time.

This plan obviously went tits up there and then in that traffic jam, so when I got going again and the roads started to clear, I decided to drive through the night and get this journey out of the way as quickly as possible.

I figured that I could always have a sleep when I arrived in Belgrade to recharge for the journey home. Of course you could, Matthew.

I should mention here that in 2010 I stupidly purchased a silly car, a Porsche Cayman S. This has a 3.4-litre engine and a top speed of 172 mph.

I was partly persuaded to buy this by my girlfriend at the time – Abi. I didn't need much persuasion, though. I was almost forty years old and obviously having some kind of midlife crisis. I already had the young girlfriend so the next obvious thing was the sports car, though I doubt I'd have bought it if it hadn't been for Abi. She said that it suited me and that I deserved it. That was enough for me. I can be easily persuaded.

The year after I bought the car, however, I came to regret the decision to buy it. Our break-up and the subsequent loss of my job put me in a position of wanting – almost needing – to sell it. I did love it though, and I managed to keep hold of it. Selling the thing would have meant losing shitloads of money in the process, so I was overjoyed that I'd managed to keep hold of it; even more so at this particular moment in my life.

It's strange how things happen, and as I set off on this trip I wondered whether the sole reason for me buying this car four years earlier had been all for this very trip. In reality, if I'd just had a run-of-the-mill car I don't think I would have attempted this mental journey, because it would have added hours to my trip. With this car, there was also something quite exciting about driving all this way, especially on the Autobahns in Germany which have no speed limit. It was as if the car had been built for those roads. Well, it was actually built in that country after all.

Admittedly, I drove like bit of a fucking lunatic, and I enjoyed it immensely. The trip wasn't all bad. I loved it at times. I'd never done anything like it before, and although it was quite stupid in parts, it was also extremely exciting. On some roads I even felt like I was playing the best computer car racing game I could ever imagine.

I was driving at speeds of 100–140 mph for hours on end in Germany. Even faster at times. I also did this on roads where there was a speed limit, almost not realising what I was doing.

I told myself that driving like a careful nutcase was a good way of staying awake. I was concentrating so much, driving at such crazy speeds in darkness on foreign roads and on the "wrong" side, that there was no way I was going to fall asleep. The intensity of it would keep me awake. I was right too, but that can't work forever.

Concentrating so hard for so long does take a lot out of you. It drains you. There was also a big difference between my situation and the computer game I'd imagined. There would be no extra life waiting for me, or more importantly anyone else if I crashed and burned. It would be game over.

I Don't Understand

In the early hours of Friday morning around thirty hours after setting off, I stopped at a petrol station on a mountain somewhere in Austria. The roads for miles before this had been totally empty and looked new. They were also pitch black.

I could just about make out the mountains through the blackness, wondering what beauty was out there, but this remote black place started to scare me. I wondered what the hell I'd do if I had a problem with my car, if I fell asleep at the wheel and had an accident. Being alone outside on this almost-deserted black foreign road would be terrifying.

I finally saw some lights and decided to pull over for a short break. I'd done nothing but drive like a dick, drink coffee, and smoke my tits off for hours. I needed a rest. I filled up with petrol – again – and then had a few moments pondering, with yet another coffee and yet another cigarette.

I started to think about Chris. How had he got himself into this situation? How had his life suddenly turned like this? I had visions of him looking the mess that he had recently, but these then turned to visions of him as my real brother – the real Chris, as a happy kid.

I saw us playing football together in the snow. I saw us both celebrating Bolton Wanderers scoring a goal at Burnden Park. I saw us on holiday in St. Ives, sitting in an inflatable dingy, my dad pushing us into the choppy Cornish sea. Then I saw the three of us playing football on the beach, my mum watching, drinking a cup of coffee from a flask.

My mind switched back to the task at hand. I had another couple of extra-strong coffee shots from my own flask and sped off again. I'd had my well-deserved rest, but the job was a long way from being complete. I put away my feelings and emotions for a while and thought, "Here we go again."

I put my foot down again, the clear roads ahead almost begging me to go faster. Then, from nowhere, I was suddenly hit by thousands of bright lights. It was just what I didn't want – fucking roadworks. These weren't just any roadworks, though. They continued for ages. The worst part of it was that there were speed cameras everywhere, so this stretch added over an hour to my journey, and this very slow, very bright stage of the drive was the first time I really started to struggle.

I was so tired now. I didn't feel I had anything left and I still had such a long way to go. I was slipping in and out of sleep, the bright lights of the road coming in and out of focus, and I was still probably five hundred miles away from Belgrade at this point. How was I going to manage this?

I kept going, somehow, finally hitting the Slovenian border a few hours later. This was heaven to my eyes, even if I hadn't realised I would actually be going into Slovenia beforehand. For a while I even questioned whether I was going the right way. The monotony of the Austrian roadworks was broken though, so I just followed the further SATNAV monotony of the Canadian slag's voice and tried to smile. She was becoming my friend now. She was my only friend. She'd also guided me this far and hadn't asked me to bum her yet, so maybe she was all right after all.

I only seemed to be in Slovenia a matter of minutes before I hit Croatia. Thankfully, I was suddenly transported back to clear empty roads. This was fantastic, and my car responded by flying again. I can't remember much about the next few hours, only that I was back in the Grand Prix and I hardly saw any cars, before I finally saw natural light on the horizon. The sun was rising, and I suddenly realised that I'd now been awake for over forty-eight hours, most of it driving. How, I really don't know.

I drove until it was light. I was now in touching-distance of the Serbian border, probably around thirty miles away when the time hit 7 a.m. I decided that I should now get my head down for an hour. I was more than ready for it. I could then drive the final hour or two, and hopefully arrive at the hostel around 9 a.m. This would be a perfect time to catch Chris.

After finding my way to the hostel, I thought maybe I could have a rest, and then getting him home would be the only thing I'd have to worry about – or would it?

Belgrade: The Screenplay – Scene Eleven

EXTERNAL. COUNTRY ROAD. GERMANY. LOOKS MORE LIKE HOLLAND. DAY. TRAFFIC IS QUEUEING FOR MILES.

The scene fades in to reveal Matt standing beside his car. There is a noticeable heightened state of urgency and worry in his demeanour. He has been awake for almost forty hours and on the road for sixteen hours but he is still over one thousand miles from his destination. The return journey can't enter his mind yet. He is wondering what to do, even questioning his decision to make the trip. What the fuck is he doing?

A SONG PLAYS FROM MATT'S CAR

SOLAR STONE - SEVEN CITIES

(V-ONE'S 'LIVING CITIES' REMIX)

Matt starts to narrate the scene over the music

MATT (NARRATING)

By this point I'd turned my car into a fucking one-man rave. What else could I do?

I was trying anything to help me stay awake, keep myself going, and help me through this ridiculous thing I was attempting.

I was constantly searching for adrenaline but I was running on low now.

I'd actually had some lovely moments so far, but after being awake for thirty-six hours and stuck in a fucking traffic jam for three hours looking at poppies and fucking windmills – when I'm sure I was in Germany – I'd just had enough.

I didn't know what to do.

Should I find a place to rest? Should I give up and turn back? Should I stop at that Burger King that's been to my right for the past two fucking hours? Should I just start crying?

I thought, "I can't carry on like this or I'll never make it. I need to get this thing over with. I need to get moving. I need to get there before that prick does anything else to himself. I need to finish this quickly for my mum and dad. I need to get home. I need help. I need fucking sleep."

I pondered on all those thoughts for a while.

Then, as the traffic started to clear and I managed to put my foot down for the first time in fucking hours, I remembered that I was in a country where some roads didn't even have speed limits and I was driving the perfect car for the job. It suddenly all started to make sense.

After a few seconds of tired contemplation, it was like a bomb went off in my mind, changing my whole perspective of my immediate world. My eyes slowly motioned towards the heavens with a "God fucking help me, you prick!" look, then returned to stare at the long dull road ahead, only now the road looked different; it looked clean and inviting. I don't know why, but something inside me had suddenly changed. I could clearly feel it and it was intense. It was as though I honestly didn't give an actual fuck about anything anymore, other than completing my mission. Then, like the inflatable auto-pilot from the film Airplane, I smiled ridiculously, turned up the volume of my rave to full-blast, pressed the barely-used "Sport" button on my dashboard, and just said, "FUCK IT!"

The song starts to speed up with Matt as he puts his foot down

EXTERNAL. AUTOBAHN. GERMANY. 7PM. STILL LIGHT.

MATT IS DRIVING AT SPEEDS OF UP TO 150MPH

For the next minute we see Matt driving to the pace of the music, speeding past everything in his path. He even overtakes a Police car at 140MPH at one point but laughs out loud when he remembers there is no speed limit on the road. He is driving like an extremely careful maniac. The concentration on his face is intense as the names of foreign towns and cities flash by, while a timer on screen showing the hours he's been awake goes up and up; 39 hours…40 hours…41 hours….

After one minute the music slows and quiets slightly as we see Matt flying along completely deserted, new-looking roads in Austria. He is now heading for the mountains. It is pitch black.

His car window is open. He is starting to look worn out and has cold air blasting in from outside to keep him awake. As the music slows further, we see Matt at a lonely petrol station on the mountain with nothing around for miles.

Matt is filling his car up with more fuel; drinking more coffee; then smoking another cigarette.

The music takes a 'dreamy' turn as Matt looks up to the sky and blows smoke up into the cold night air. Through the smoke we can see Matt below getting further and further away. The smoke slowly transitions into images of his childhood as it rises up further into the black sky.

The images are of him and his brother as kids; playing football on the beach; fighting; laughing etc. The images of childhood slowly disappear as we see a kind of Google Maps scene of Matt's location – Bolton far to the left; Belgrade far to the right; Matt's flashing location directly below. We realise how far away Matt still is from the end of even the first half of this journey. He really is in a desperate lonely place, but he now has no choice in the matter.

As the music speeds up again, we drop back down to Earth in a similar fashion to the bomb from the memorable scene in the film Pearl Harbour. Matt speeds off into the dark again. What else can he do?

Soon after this we see a sign for Slovenia; then we see a sign for Croatia. As the music slows again Matt speeds down a single dark road in Croatia and we gradually see the sun start to rise in the distance. It was daylight when Matt was in Germany and he decided to drive like a madman. He's hardly stopped for a rest since then and it is now becoming light again.

Matt has somehow just driven almost one thousand miles in twelve hours.

Finally, he sees a sign for Serbia which is now only around thirty miles away.

He pulls over into a petrol station. It is 7am. He now hopes to close his eyes for the first time in almost fifty hours.

Oh Brother, Where the Fuck Are You?

After setting off from Bolton at 10.40 p.m. on Wednesday, I arrived in Belgrade at 9 a.m. on Friday.

Serbia is one hour in front of England, so this was thirty-three hours and twenty minutes after leaving home. During that time, I'd had just one hour of sleep, and that was in my car at the petrol station in Croatia. I'd therefore slept just one hour of the previous fifty. I was fucked. I was totally fucked.

I think my main reason for not stopping to sleep was that I just wanted to get this thing over with, though I still don't completely know why I drove straight through. Something just told me that I needed to carry on. It was probably nothing but instinct. Whatever it was, I now know I was right to do it, though I still don't know how I managed it. Most of it is now just a blank space in my mind.

Relieved, I finally found my way to the place where Chris was staying, the City Zen Hostel. I thought I'd walk in, give Chris a big hug, put him in the car, and then drive us both home. However, I soon discovered this was not going to happen. Things were actually going to get a whole lot worse.

I walked in, and to my shock, horror, and utter fucking disbelief, I was told there was a problem. Chris was missing. He'd only gone and left the hostel at 3 p.m. the day before and not been seen since. As if he'd really done that!

Just before I'd left home I'd called the hostel and even spoke to Chris. I told him not to move, and though he'd sounded not quite with it, he had actually agreed, even sounding excited at the prospect of coming home. When we spoke, he'd just heard that his son would be home this weekend. Sam had been in the United States for a few months teaching and coaching football, and was coming home earlier than expected. This was nothing to do with his dad's situation, but it was all seeming to work out just before I'd set off.

I also told the staff at the hostel to keep him there, and they were all in agreement. I therefore assumed I only had two things to worry about; getting me to his hostel and getting us both back home. This was the reason I didn't even think of trying to contact Chris or the hostel after leaving home. In fact, if I had done and heard that he was missing, I've no idea if I'd have even carried on. It would certainly have changed things. As it was, I was completely oblivious until I arrived.

Just try to imagine how I felt at that moment.

I'd been up for over fifty hours and driven fifteen hundred miles to rescue my brother from this ridiculously perilous situation he'd got himself into, and he wasn't even fucking there. He'd been missing for eighteen hours.

I can't tell you my full range of emotions, but it was a similar lost and helpless feeling to what I'd experienced twice previously, first in the office on that dreadful day in Lytham, and then at the airport when I was leaving Taiwan, the difference being that this didn't end here. There was maybe something I could still do to help; but I was exhausted, and Chris not being there was almost too much to take. I was so alone in this alien city, miles from home. I thought, "What the hell can I do now?" I had no one. I was on my last legs, and I wanted to fucking kill him, if he wasn't already dead, that was.

The people at the hostel were great – calling hospitals in the city for me, albeit with no luck. They mentioned that he'd actually disappeared overnight in the past, so he might just turn up at some point. This gave me some hope, though I still feared the worst.

They also told me that in the week or so Chris had been staying with them, he would go to buy shoes and shades every day. This was because he would wake up without his previous day's purchases, having lost them somewhere on his drunken wobbles around the city.

When I heard this, it brought home to me what state his mind must be in, and I just assumed he would be in a ditch. If he wasn't in hospital, then he must have fallen somewhere and not been found. That was the only outcome I could think of.

I walked around Belgrade alone for a couple of hours looking for him, but after a while, I just felt lost in the crowd of unnerving foreignness that surrounded me, so I decided I needed to stop. I sat down outside a café overlooking a main road not far from the hostel. I ordered a nice, cool, well-deserved beer, and then scanned the road, thinking and going over the options I had available to me.

I didn't even think about ordering any food. Since setting off I'd only eaten a ridiculous Bratwurst sausage thing at a petrol station somewhere in Germany, and that had really put me off eating altogether. I think I was numb to many of my senses for most of this time – even hunger.

After twenty minutes, the only thing I could come up with was that I really needed another beer. I didn't really know where I was at that moment. I could have even been on holiday with the sun on the back of my neck as I sipped a cold beer. It definitely wasn't a holiday, though, and it didn't take long for me to come back to reality.

I decided I would be staying in Belgrade that night. My plan of action would be to go on a pub-crawl around Belgrade and hopefully trace Chris's steps. What a great idea. What else could I possibly do?

When the waiter came over with my second beer, I thought I might as well start my detective work there and then, so I asked, "Have you by any chance seen an Englishman with cuts, bruises, stitches in his face, and a black eye?"

The waiter replied, "Oh, Chris? He was here yesterday evening."

Unbelievable; I'd asked just one person in Belgrade about Chris, and he'd already started to fill in the pieces. After two hours of wandering around aimlessly, I stopped just once – in the right place. Was that a coincidence? No, it was great detective work. I'd returned to the nearest place to his hostel that served alcohol, so they would obviously know him. Then again, he was probably already well known throughout every drinking establishment in the city, even in the short time he'd been there.

That was it. I suddenly thought I was Sherlock Holmes. I figured I would find him easily on my tour of Belgrade's drinking haunts. However, I then also had a vision of me ending up in the same state as him, getting drunk, lost, and hurt in this strange city. This is quite usual for me. When I have a positive thought, my mind often quickly plays out all the negative possibilities to counteract it.

At that moment, as I was finishing my second pint of strong, rather nice lager, and considering all the possible terrible outcomes, Sherlock Holmes and the negatives could be put to bed.

I received a phone call from the hostel.

The owner had called the central police station in Belgrade, and Chris happened to be there for some reason. The judge of the police station was going to call the hostel back to give more details. That's all I was told at the time.

The words "the judge" sounded serious to me, even quite scary. Why would the judge be calling? Why not just a police officer?

I quickly made my way back to the hostel. On the way back, I wondered what crime he could have committed. Chris wasn't violent, so he must have either exposed himself while drunk, been disorderly in some other way, or stolen a bottle of vodka, not that he'd ever done any of those things in the past. It must have been something really daft, though. What else could it be? My mind gave up trying to figure it out. I was too tired and confused to care, though it was obviously important because his crime could be the difference between us getting home or not.

I arrived back at the hostel just as the helpful owner was on the phone to the judge. He was explaining to her that I'd driven all this way and was ready go to the police station to talk to her. The judge was apparently very happy I was there because she just wanted the prick out of her country after the night she'd had. She summoned me to go to the police station immediately.

So, what was his crime?

I didn't have it anywhere near daft enough. He'd only gone and climbed into the fucking Canadian embassy. What is it with me and Canada?

I actually laughed at hearing this. I was so worried what it might be, but there was something quite comical about this crime, though in some countries I'm sure you could be seriously punished for what he did.

The hostel owner booked a taxi for me and gave the driver directions to the police station. The judge would be there waiting for me. My lack of sleep for two days, the ridiculous drive, and the two pints I'd just had then started to hit me. I thought, "Shit! When I get to the police station the judge is going to take one look at me and think that I'm just as fucked up as my brother."

I couldn't have been more wrong.

Judge Dread?

When I arrived at the police station I was told to go through to another building. As I opened the door to this building, my brother was there, sitting directly in front of me but behind a locked iron gate. I was so happy that he was there; but in many ways he wasn't there at all. This wasn't my brother. It looked like an old man on his last legs. He was a bit messed up the previous time I'd seen him, but he was nothing like this.

The state of him came as a massive, massive shock, and compared to him I must have looked like an angel. When he saw me, his ugly black eyes lit up as he said the single word, "Math!" This is the name only he and my dad call me.

At the same time, he did a very tame, pathetic, but touching jump into the air. It was as though he was celebrating a goal for Bolton Wanderers away at Manchester United, only to immediately realise he was sitting in the wrong end with the wrong supporters, so he'd cut his celebrations short.

He was a mess. His right eye was purple and completely closed. He had new open scars and large healed scars that weren't there when he left Bolton. He also walked like a one-hundred-year-old man, having become partly disabled due to his drunken actions of the past weeks.

He looked as if he'd been living with a pack of dogs for six weeks, not friendly dogs, but the kind that kick the fuck out of you every night. It hurt me to see him like this. I was over the moon to see him, and he was obviously more than pleased to see me, but it hurt me, and I'm sure it embarrassed him for me to see him in this pathetic state.

Then again, I don't know if he had enough working brain cells to get embarrassed. He was a feeble effigy of himself, and I immediately thought he wouldn't last another week by himself if he had to stay here in this condition. I've never seen anyone in such a terrible state – and that includes heroin addicts I've seen on the streets. That is how bad he was.

To me, he looked like the living dead. I saw no future for my brother, just a living hell for him and my mum and dad. I was there to help him, but was there any chance he would take that help on board? I hoped he would, but I wasn't very optimistic.

The judge welcomed me. She was lovely. It could have been so much worse. It was actually like having my mum as the judge. She had to abide by the law, but she was so nice it was ridiculous. She explained that she'd been trying to rehydrate Chris by making him drink lots of water, and also increasing his sugar levels by feeding him biscuits. She told me that I must do the same on our journey home. She was there to help him, even if he didn't realise it.

After this, we both had to go into her office, which was actually a mini court. Then we sat court. This felt like a dream even then, never mind now looking back.

It was almost forty hours since I left Bolton and almost sixty hours since sleeping, then after spending a few hours wandering around trying to find Chris on the alien streets of Belgrade, and even having a couple of pints, I'm now sitting in fucking court with him.

Quite unbelievably, while the judge was trying her utmost to help Chris during the court proceedings, he still wanted to disagree with her. He just wouldn't admit his crime, saying he hadn't done anything wrong. Should I believe him or the Serbian police? It was a no-brainer.

I had to intervene a number of times, explaining to Chris that she was helping him out by almost letting him off. I just kept apologising to the judge for my brother's nonsense over again.

His crime usually had a minimum fine of around £350, or twenty-eight days in prison if he didn't pay the fine, but she was actually only charging him around £70, which I was fucking paying anyway. Whether he'd committed the crime or not didn't matter. There was only one option here, but he still couldn't see it.

Brain-dead, that sums him up at that moment. In fact, that just sums him up full stop.

When I'd greeted Chris at the station, I put my shades on him. The first thing he'd said to me was that he needed to buy some shoes and shades. I almost laughed when he said this after what I'd been told at the hostel. He'd gone and fucking lost them again somehow.

He wanted the shades because they did slightly help to cover his wounded eyes – as though that was the most important thing right now? In a few minutes' time, he could be sent to a Serbian prison, yet he was more bothered about how he looked.

Something about him wearing my shades in court seemed to tickle me, though. Every time I was trying to say something to the judge I'd look at him and start to piss myself with laughter. I couldn't help it. It just seemed so ridiculous to see my fucked-up brother answering charges to a judge in a Serbian court with no shoes and my shades on. Maybe the lack of sleep also had something to do with it, because I was quite delirious by now.

I eventually got through to him and his shades about admitting his crime, and he finally shut up. The judge then let me pay the fine, and we both walked out of the station, free men.

Chris gave the judge a big hug. I think this was because he was so surprised, even shocked that this was happening. He had no idea what was going on in the court. He wasn't drunk in the slightest. He just seemed to be on another planet.

So there we were outside the police station. He was barefoot with my shades on. I was shagged and looked dog-rough from the past two days. Together, we must have looked a right pair, him especially, but we could now go home, couldn't we?

No, we couldn't. Not just yet.

Come on Now. Who Put That Chair There?

Stage one complete, we now just had to get back to my car and begin stage two of this nightmare.

Having left my car in the security of the car park behind the hostel, we now needed to get back there, which was only ten minutes in a taxi. I'd been told by the judge that we could get a taxi from the main road, so we walked, arriving there after a couple of minutes. Everything seemed fine, and we were both just looking forward to driving home.

However, it wasn't going to be so straightforward. After ten minutes trying to flag a taxi without any luck, something strange and worrying happened to Chris. He became nervous, panicked, and started to shake. It then got worse when he tried to run away from me.

He'd been right behind me, but as I was messing about trying to sort a taxi out, I'd taken my eye off him for just a few moments. I turned around and he was no longer there. At first I thought he'd vanished into thin air, but then I saw him in the distance, scuttling along in a pathetic attempt to escape.

I was in bits. I'd driven over fifteen hundred miles, not slept for over two days, found him, saved him from twenty-eight days in a Belgrade prison, and the bastard tried to run off.

I chased him, and grabbed him, and we then began to tussle at the side of the road. This obviously made it a little harder to flag a taxi down. What taxi driver was going to stop for two foreign, odd-looking lads fighting with each other at the side of the fucking road?

I just couldn't understand what was happening. With tears in my eyes, I shouted, "Why the fuck are you doing this, Chris? Why?"

I was in shock. I couldn't grasp the situation. I wasn't used to dealing with anything like this. Who is?

Right there and then I thought, "How the fuck can I get him home in this state all by myself?"

I didn't think I had any chance at the time. I'd have to hold him down just to try to get him into a taxi. How could I drive all the way home with him in this condition? I was already totally exhausted, and I couldn't rest because I had to look after him. I would also have no option again but to just try to drive non-stop all the way home. I had to get him to my car first, though, somehow.

I really needed some help.

While we were grappling with each other at the side of the road and I was wondering what to do, I happened to notice a random chair. It was a red plastic garden chair. I don't think I'd ever seen a chair like that in this particular colour, but there it was, just sitting there a metre away from us at the side of this busy main road. Why? It just didn't belong there. There were no other chairs or people anywhere to be seen.

However, this chair kind of saved me really. After noticing it, I managed to guide Chris over to it, sit him down in it, and then hold him there while I finally flagged down a taxi. Thank you again, Serbian Chair God.

I was so relieved to finally get him in a taxi, although the driver looked a bit wary when he noticed the state of Chris.

Then, just as the driver, seemingly quite reluctantly started to drive, Chris became a whole lot worse. He became even weirder. He plucked all his cash out of his pocket, which wasn't much and was obviously the last of what he had to survive on. I immediately took this off him, as he slowly became like a zombie. He was just feeling around for things, spaced out. He didn't seem to have any idea where he was or what the hell he was doing.

This frightened me. All this time I could also see the driver looking on in the rear-view mirror. He seemed as bemused as me. I was just hoping he wasn't going to stop and kick us out. I could tell he didn't trust us.

I didn't know what it was. I'd never seen anyone like this before. He was obviously in a much worse mental state than any of us had previously thought.

Did I sympathise with him? No. He's a prick. He did all this to himself. Yes, he was ill, but he was a prick long before this, and the fact that he was ill was a consequence of him being a prick.

In fact, at the time I didn't know why I'd done this journey for him, because he was such a prick. I couldn't remember him doing anything for me apart from annoy me in recent years, though he would never understand what he'd done to annoy anyone.

He was clueless. He never actually listened to anyone, even when people were trying to give him some good advice. In his own mind, he always knew best.

He didn't deserve this help, but my mum and dad did. They were the only reason I did this, I think. Maybe not; maybe I did it for him too, but he's still a prick.

Fancy a Drive, Brother?

We arrived at the hostel and Chris's bizarre episode in the taxi had ended. He'd gradually improved during the drive. I've still no idea what caused it and why it went away.

I gave him a minute or two to say his goodbyes and collect any possessions. He had nothing – no clothes, just the dirty, ripped shorts and Serbian football T-shirt he was wearing at the time, nothing else.

However, thankfully, he did have the one important thing: his passport. The reason for this is that he needed to hand this over to the hostels when he checked in, and they would only return it when he checked out.

We were in my car within minutes and finally on our way home in a daze.

Just a little frustratingly, it then took us over one hour to move about five miles because we were now in the bastard Belgradian rush hour. At least we were on our way, though, and albeit slightly agitated by the traffic wankers, I felt as though I'd got the hardest part of the job done.

At police central station de Belgrade, Chris had not only said he needed to buy shoes and shades, but he also needed to buy some vodka before we left. At the time I had told him to fuck off. Maybe that is why he initially ran off: the thought of not having any alcohol for such a long time possibly freaked him out.

He'd calmed down and was in a much better state when we arrived at the Serbian border with Croatia about ninety minutes after setting off.

We'd stopped at a service station just before this. Up to then, I'd managed to fend off Chris's calls to stop, but it was obvious that he would need alcohol on the way home. There was no point in me trying to fix him over the next day or so. There was plenty of time for that after we arrived home when the professionals had a chance to look at him.

The last thing I needed on the way home was any more episodes of him freaking out due to alcohol withdrawals. It was going to be hard enough as it was. I therefore bought him a couple of mini vodkas and a few beers, plus one beer for me.

I was waiting until we'd left Serbian road space before opening mine, and I was ready for it by then.

At the Serbia-Croatia border, Chris's passport had flagged-up his crime, and even though I had the paperwork showing that I'd paid his fine, they still wanted to double-check this with the judge. I'm sure she was probably crying when she received the call. I could just imagine her saying, "Please just push them over the fucking border!"

We finally got the nod after thirty minutes. I put my foot down and drove us the hell out of there.

We then had a celebratory beer each because we'd escaped Serbia. I felt as though we were finally on our way now. It was time to put my foot down and get us home.

Then about ten minutes into Croatian airspace, literally seconds after finishing my beer, Croatian police brought us back down to earth with a big fucking bang. I'd been doing 180 kph (111 mph) when the speed limit was only 130 kph (80 mph).

I didn't know. I didn't really know what day it was. I'd seemed to have completely forgotten about speed limits by now. I was just driving at my own pace – my own pace being "get me there as soon as fucking possible".

This policy had worked quite well for the previous fifty hours or so until this rather worrying moment.

The police guided me off the highway and onto a slip road. One of the officers then walked over to my side of the car and started to question me. I showed him my driving license and passport, but he also wanted to see the registration document for my car to prove it was actually mine.

I just assumed this document was in the glovebox of my car. It always had been previously. However, it wasn't there. I opened up the boot to have a look, and was shocked to see two spare number plates which didn't match my car registration. When I'd bought the car, I'd put my own number plates onto it, and then put the old plates in the boot. These other plates would have looked ultra-suspicious to the police, so I quickly closed it and said it wasn't there. I had my insurance renewal quote with me showing the car registration, but this was not enough by law in Croatia.

Robocop said that I must have had to show my registration document when I entered the country, otherwise they wouldn't have let me in. I explained to him that I'd actually been in nine countries in the previous two days, and I'd crossed approximately ten borders by this point. Not one of them had asked for this document.

He started to laugh out loud. "That is not possible. I don't believe you," he said.

I replied, also laughing, but almost crying, "Believe me. Look at the state of my brother. I've driven all the way from England to Serbia overnight to rescue him because he is ill. He needs help. I didn't have time to think about packing my fucking car registration. I just left, and not one person has asked me for it on any country border."

There we were, we'd just escaped the police in Serbia, and now it looked like we were stuck in Croatia. This really couldn't be happening.

The most worrying part for me was that I was probably over the drink-drive limit in every country in the world, so I tried to keep my distance from his pig-like nostrils.

I continued to smile and laugh along with the policeman, even playing slightly dumb and innocent, which can come quite natural to me. I kept pointing to Chris, explaining that I had to get him home to see a doctor. The policeman must have also seen that he was a mess.

I was then asked to follow him over to his mate who took out some documentation to show me. It was in English, and it explained the speeding fine system operating in Mother Croatia.

In the old slag's own words, it stated that I must pay a fine of around €150 in the currency of the Croatians. I would also be subjected to a twelve-month driving ban in the motherland. Fine; and not for the first time that day I just thought, "Where do I fucking sign?"

Cop-of-the-year, aka Robocop, then suggested that I probably didn't have any Croatian currency, and I replied, "Correct officer. I'm just passing through your beautiful country after rescuing my brother from a Serbian prison, and I didn't think I would have any need for it."

Looking slightly blank, Robocop's sidekick then showed me a completely different charge. This was all very confusing, because this offence was speeding at a different speed on a completely different road, but this fine could actually be paid in euros, unlike the other charge.

It was a bit like being caught doing 100 mph on the motorway in England with a 70-mph limit and then being given the opportunity to take a much lesser charge of 70mph in a 50mph zone, but also allowing you to pay in a currency that wasn't the country's own. This fine was €72.50.

Why was this fine payable in euros but the other fine wasn't? And why was he giving me the opportunity to accept this lesser charge? I didn't care in the slightest.

I didn't argue. I had only €80 in my pocket. I gave him €75, told him to keep the change and thought that was the end of it. He then gave me a ticket. However, the ticket came with a condition: quite bizarrely, having just given it to me, he said that I must rip this ticket up.

He explained that as I didn't have my registration document with me, he couldn't put these details on the ticket, which he had to by the law of the land. He therefore needed the details from this document before he could even give me a ticket legally. If I was caught speeding again in Croatia, and another copper saw this ticket, then cop-of-the-year might be in trouble because he had broken the law.

It all sounds rather dodgy, doesn't it, and it was. But I think he was trying to help me out really. He said at one point that if he followed the letter of the law then he should impound my car. Just imagine if that had happened. I don't think either of us could have coped with that.

I told them not to worry. I would dispose of the ticket immediately, and then I just thought, "Let's get the fuck out of here!"

The kind officers, now each with an equal share of €75 inflating their pockets, had offered to guide us back onto the "Croatian supersonic highway", so I duly followed them.

After following them for a very long thirty seconds, the police maniac, aka cop-of-the-year, aka Robocop, slammed his brakes on. I followed his lead, but I almost hit the prick because my reactions were dwindling by the minute.

He then walked over to my car and started swinging his arms around, shouting that I had missed the turning he was trying to guide me to. Croatian Super Fucking Robocop seemed like he was having bit of a malfunction. I sympathised completely. I was also broken inside.

Rather embarrassingly, I then did the exact same thing again. I followed, I missed the turn, he slammed the brakes on, and he walked over, shouting the same things, only this time, a bit louder.

Look, I'd been up for over sixty-five hours with no real sleep and with all this shit going on. I was obviously going to be a little confused.

Also, I have to slip this in here. My brother, however fucked he was at the time, had just done something brilliant which probably helped the situation we now found ourselves in.

Only minutes earlier we had stopped at a service station in Croatia because Chris needed the toilet. As he fell out of the car, he started shaking and limping awkwardly towards the toilets. However, within seconds, he turned around to head back to the car. He'd somehow realised he was wearing a Serbian football shirt and decided he must change it, so I gave him a top I had in my car

The Serbians and Croatians are not the best of friends. In fact, many still hate each other since the war not too long ago, and even in that state, Chris realised this.

This probably helped us out five minutes later when we were stopped by the police. If he had still been wearing that Serbia shirt, they might have taken us to a field and put a fucking bullet in our heads.

That's probably very much of an over-exaggeration, but it might not have turned out as well as it did. Put it this way, they might well have impounded the car.

After the two failed attempts at guiding us back onto the highway, Croatian Chips then took us right to the junction and stopped there. Cop-of-the-year walked over again. He came right up to my window. He then shouted at me to give him the speeding ticket, which I did, and he ripped it up right in front my eyes.

Half laughing, half crying, he said, "I don't trust you. You are going to give me trouble. They should write a book about you!"

I started to tell him that I was actually writing a book about myself, though I think this fell on deaf foreign ears, and he shouted, "The speed limit is 130 kph. You can do 160 kph all the way out of Croatia. No one will stop you. Please just get out of Croatia!"

And we did.

But I was tired. I was more than tired.

The Darkness

It was quite nice for the next few hours. The sun was just going down. Chris had his fix and become quite normal. It almost seemed like we were on a road trip for the fun of it and not for the real reason.

Chris said that he couldn't believe I'd driven all this way to get him home, and that it was the best thing I'd ever done. I had my doubts, but I did feel a sense of pride which brought a tear to my eye. He also said that this part of his holiday, driving home with me, sipping a beer, while watching the sun go down on the Croatian countryside was the best part of his whole holiday.

It was nice for a moment, but I knew what was in store for us over the next twenty-plus hours so I couldn't really enjoy it. However, the stress of being stopped by the police had given me an injection of adrenaline which kept me steady for the next few hours. It was almost as if I'd seen a menu and thought, "Now then, what can I have for €80 to keep me going for a while? Oh, look, they do a 'police stop & speeding ticket' for €75, I'll take one of those please."

Yes, I was going slightly mad.

I'd been quite looking forward to driving over the mountains in Austria during daylight. I missed them on the way there, having to endure hours of complete darkness on that stretch. That was the place where things started to take a turn for the worst previously. I'd felt quite alone and worried during the pitch darkness then, but I thought it would be different on the way back. Previously, I could just about make out the outlines of mountains, so I thought it could be a beautiful sight.

That thought was scuppered, because it was already dark before we were at the Croatian border with Slovenia. I knew that now we'd have eight to ten hours of darkness on the worst stretch through Slovenia, Austria, and southern Germany.

I was annoyed that it was dark. I think the drive through the final part of Croatia, then Slovenia and Austria, would have also been amazing.

As it was, I knew that hell was waiting for us.

I also still hadn't slept a wink since I was previously here, so hell would probably be a whole lot worse this time.

Now then, Austria might be a beautiful place, but I only saw tunnels, speed restrictions, and more tunnels. I found out about the speed cameras in quite a comical moment on the drive down. I mentioned that I was driving like a lunatic through Germany, seemingly with no one batting an eyelid. However, Austria is a very different place, different that is, apart from the language, which looks the same as German to me.

Also, due to the wondrous European Union and freedom of travel given to EU members, there are no border controls. Sometimes I didn't even see a sign to inform me that I was crossing into a different country, which was bizarre. I mean, there's even a sign when you cross from Bolton into fucking Farnworth, so why no sign between Germany and Austria? There must have been one, surely?

Anyway, I previously had no idea that I'd crossed the border into Austria from Germany. I didn't see a sign in any language, and as both countries have place names looking like they could belong in either country, I hadn't even realised.

I only found out I was in Austria when the bright flash of a speed camera hit me smack in the face from the side of the road, prompting me to shout, "Fuck off!" while giving the camera a tired two-fingered salute.

I hadn't been looking forward to Austria in the dark again with the numerous tunnels and speed controls. However, something happened to make it a whole lot worse. Something I never accounted for: sleep deprivation!

You've probably heard stories about what sleep deprivation can do to you, and I am just the same; I've heard the stories. The stories are true – hallucinations.

I was driving towards the opening of a tunnel in Austria, and to enter it I had to drive under a hippopotamus. Why a hippopotamus, I just don't know, but that's what I saw.

Then, from two cars directly in front of me, four red lights turned into ice skaters, all in matching costumes, and all skating backwards in a beautifully synchronized motion towards me, while appearing to stare me down in a very camp way.

I was actually enjoying this, even smiling through it, but how dangerous was driving in this state on these roads at night?

Every road sign I looked at turned into a face. However, it was always a smiling face, so I just smiled back. Yes, I smiled back. What the fuck?

There were countless stretches of roadworks for miles, and this meant thousands of lights making the situation a million times worse. The lights formed strange shapes and patterns, which were often beautiful, but obviously distracting. I have no idea how, but they still managed to guide me through.

These ridiculous visions drove me to stop twice. I had to catch an hour or two of sleep, otherwise anything could have happened. The short breaks did help me a lot, but the hallucinations slowly came back when we got going again.

It's quite terrifying thinking about this now, because I realise the precarious state I was in at the time. I was driving fast on foreign roads in the dark while falling asleep and seeing things because I'd been up for seventy hours, and all this time I was trying to keep one eye on my brother. How I'm still here writing this book, I don't know.

I also don't know where we were when it started to get light; Austria, maybe Germany, but with the sun rising, I woke up on a mission, after another broken nap.

I remember thinking that this is the last leg now, but when I thought a bit more about that, there were still around twelve hours to go before we even reached Calais, never mind sunny Bolton. This thought really felt like simultaneously being kicked in the balls and punched in the cock. It wasn't quite the last leg; it was anything but.

Chris had been rather quiet, even sleeping a while, which was heaven, though he'd soon let me know when his withdrawals started. At one service station he walked with me to buy some alcohol, but his leg just gave way, and he almost had another head wound to worry about. There was obviously something seriously wrong with him. He didn't trip. His leg just gave way.

Also, at certain non-EU borders we had to stop to show our passports, and with my car being right-hand drive, I often asked Chris to pass our documents over to the guard through the passenger window. However, he couldn't even lift his hands enough to do this simple task. He really was that bad.

We'd reached the Slovenian border with Austria around midnight, when Chris was asleep. I walked our passports over to the guard. He took one look at the documents, took another look at me, and then switched his eyes to the mess in the passenger seat that was Chris.

The guard's expressionless gaze returned to me as he matter-of-factly asked, "Is he dead?"

With much effort, I turned my neck to glance at Chris, and then turned it back to the guard.

Without an ounce of emotion and with no expression at all, I just replied, "Probably."

Then, similarly, with an understanding gaze and half a smile, the guard gave me the passports back, and said, "Thank you."

I then drove through the border with a smile on my face.

Sometimes it's the small things that cheer us up. That little moment between me and the Slovenian guard was priceless – it was as though we both knew what the other was thinking. It also reminded me how similar I am to my dad, because that expression and reply I gave the guard were him in a nutshell; though I think I was so tired by now that even showing emotion was really hard work.

It became even harder on this "last leg". It was a real struggle. In fact, I was actually on my last fucking legs. Then again, I think I had been for some time now.

I kept telling myself that I could do it, that I had to do it. While driving, I was constantly moving around in my seat, opening the window, and even chain-smoking to stay awake; that worked by the way. But all this was only going to work for a certain amount of time. I mean, you can only go so long without sleep, or you'll no doubt just die, and you'll no doubt die a lot sooner if you're driving like a dick on foreign roads at the time, in such an emotional and stressful situation.

In the early morning, we stopped in France because we both needed to use the bathroom. However, every single one of these shitty little service stations in Europe seemed to charge seventy cents for the convenience, and between us we now had zero euros or cents left. We'd drunk and pissed them all down the grid.

We were both quite desperate so I drove on and found a narrow country lane just past the service station. I pulled in. We both jumped out and immediately started to unbutton ourselves. At that precise moment I saw another police car turn into the road.

I shouted, "Chris, put your cock away." He was fine, because he was still struggling with it.

We both then tried and failed to look innocent as the police pulled up next to us.

One of them shouted, "No stopping here!" and that was it.

We climbed straight back in the car and drove off. If they'd arrived three seconds later, or if Chris wasn't half paralysed and had actually been able to get his cock out on his own, we would probably have been charged with pissing on French France or something. However, we got away with it. It was another lucky escape.

So between us we've now had scrapes with the police in Serbia, Croatia, and France. Not to mention the speeding fine from Austria heading my way. Nothing happened in Germany, though I suppose you could say I'd already ticked that one off my list in Munich, 2007. So it seems like we almost had an EU police full house now.

I must add that neither of us had ever been in trouble with any police before. We were generally perfectly decent, respectable, and law-abiding individuals.

I was paranoid by now. I kept thinking that we were actually being followed. Also, I couldn't work out how the French police knew we were English? It's only now, writing two weeks later, that it was obviously the Union Jack on my fucking number plate, the number plate that I'd had in a drawer for five years, but just in case I had to drive on foreign roads I'd put on my car just a few hours before I left home.

To explain the number plate to those who might not be aware, when driving on the continent there is a requirement to have a sticker on your car denoting where your car is registered, either that or an EU sticker if your country is in the EU. I had neither, so I would probably have been fined everywhere if I'd driven without putting this number plate on beforehand. I don't even know why I ordered it all those years ago because I'd never even driven in Europe before. I had it, though, just for this very journey.

I hope this rubber-stamps my previous comments concerning me being an upstanding citizen who normally goes out of his way to abide by the law. It was only after I set off on this trip that I went a bit daft.

Now deciding to abide by the French pissing laws, we eventually stopped at one of those lorry break areas. We pulled up and saw a single dubious-looking portable toilet. I was going to just do the business outside, ignoring what we'd just decided, but as there were people around and I was convinced we were now constantly being watched, I cautiously ventured in.

It was the most disgusting toilet I'd seen since the film *Trainspotting* in 1996, but this excuse for a toilet had flies, which must live longer on the continent due to their healthier diet; there were too many to mention.

I reluctantly stayed in the cubicle of shit and disgust for a whole thirty seconds. I finished, opened the door, and I immediately put my hand in my pocket for help.

When I'd bought Chris his mini vodkas, I also secretly bought one mini whiskey, just in case he had another turn, or in case I had to get some courage from somewhere. This was now for me.

I could actually taste piss, and shit, and flies – and French – so I immediately opened the bottle and had a sip. I should have necked it but I was driving, and I was now being responsible.

Anyway, that little sip was enough to get rid of the taste, a taste at the time I had named "French mouth".

Over seventy-five hours I'd now been up, with only three hours sleep. Fifty-nine hours since I'd set off on my drive. Much of the next ten hours is a blur. I was just struggling on with tears in my eyes, just like I am at this moment trying to write about it.

We finally arrived in Calais at 2.50 p.m. on Saturday.

We drove through passport control, first the French window, then the English window, but at the third window, where we were to show our ferry tickets, we were told that we had to go right to the back of the queue.

In Dover, you can buy your tickets at the kiosk as you drive through. I discovered this because on the way there, my online booking had disappeared when I arrived in Dover, so I had to buy one there and then. Not in Calais, though; it was different.

I had to drive to a different nearby place and then come back, queue up all over again, then go through three checkpoints, again. Oh, what fun we had.

We now had to take the later ferry at 5.30 p.m. But we'd made it. I paid them whatever and we eventually boarded the ferry.

The "last leg" came into my mind again – but no, it wasn't. We still had to drive from Dover to fucking Bolton after this.

Tears and Rain

Find a place to lie down; that was my only thought.

To manage this we would have to run onto the ferry, which was difficult with Chris. He could hardly walk, but we somehow managed it and found somewhere we could probably have had a nap.

However, when he needed to go to the toilet after five minutes, I had to go with him, and we lost those seats almost as quickly as we'd found them.

After wandering around each deck trying to find somewhere to sit on this people-infested floater, I bought us both a pint and Chris a hot dog. I carried the pints as Chris held onto his sausage. The ferry was so busy, and there was nowhere for us to sit. I wanted to sit out of the way of everyone else, but there was nothing.

Chris then sat on a seat surrounded by families and started to eat his hot dog. It was killing me watching him. He had mustard and ketchup all over his face, and he was just creating a mess in his hands. Everyone was looking at him, wondering what the hell was wrong with him. This wasn't withdrawals. It was something in the brain. What else could it be?

Whatever it was, I couldn't cope with it. I persuaded him that we had to get away from these people as it wasn't fair on them seeing this. I took the hot dog from him and said he needed go to the toilet to wash his hands and face. He did this, and I then found us a quiet spot on the floor, next to a door which kept opening and closing, making the most annoying noise you can imagine every thirty fucking seconds. At least this was away from everyone else; I could cope with this a lot easier.

I'd shouted at Chris when he was eating the hot dog, telling him that it was like looking after my "fucking mongy brother"! I know that sounds bad, but if I am anything I am honest, and that is what came out. This was the only time I'd shouted at Chris since I'd found him, apart from the roadside grapple in Belgrade anyway. I'd obviously had enough by now. What I'd said hurt him, though, because he knew I was right; he was a complete mess.

Minutes later, we were both sitting on the cold, hard floor in what was basically a corridor. I looked at him to my left, and underneath my shades – that he was still wearing – a single lonely tear trickled down.

It was obvious that he didn't want to be this person he'd become, no matter what he'd done and no matter what I'd previously thought. I put my arm around his shoulder. He is my brother. What could I do? I've no idea what I said, if anything at all. I think we both just knew what each other were thinking.

We had a nice chat soon after that, another normal moment, a lovely moment.

What was the answer? I didn't know, but he needed to start helping himself at some point, otherwise the end was definitely around the corner. This kind of behaviour had become normal for him over recent years; he always wanted to stay out longer than everybody else, always wanted to have a few more drinks. The difference I'd noticed now, though, was that previously he'd known what he was doing. He had no idea what he was doing now. He would have made his own way home after the first week if he did.

We'd been talking for an hour just before we were finally allowed off the disgusting ferry. Chris actually seemed fine by now. He wanted to eat something sweet, and luckily I found loads of biscuits in the boot of my car from when I had been working in Newcastle twelve months earlier. The hotels used to put biscuits in my room every day, and I would usually put them in my bag to save for a rainy day. This turned out to be a very rainy day.

Now then, even on a normal day, the M25 around Greater London really is the cunt of all motorways. However, when it's absolutely pissing down, and you're on the real last leg of a three-day drive from hell, it's a tad worse. It took us at least an hour and a half to get off it, and after that, the heavy rain still continued to batter us.

The day before, I'd told my mum that we expected to be home for 8 p.m., Saturday. This kept changing, and as it transpired we were still on the M25 at 9 p.m.

As we finally moved away from the M25, my mind started to go crazy again. Eighty-seven hours, I'd been up now, with just three hours sleep. Over fifty hours of that, I'd actually been driving. It's just not normal. In fact, I'm thinking of writing to David Blaine to ask him to try what I did, see how he fucking gets on. Maybe he and his

English younger brother Dynamo can do half each to make it easier, though I'm not sure Dynamo can drive yet.

When I think about that last stretch I can't help but cry because that is what I wanted to do at the time. But I couldn't, I had to carry on. I just had to. I really was in bits, and I didn't know what was still keeping me together. What I did know, however, was that it wasn't going to hold much longer.

I suddenly heard beeping noises and saw strange bright lights directly in front of me. I looked up and realised I was doing just 20Mph. I was in the middle lane of the M6 motorway.

This happened more than once. I was nodding off all the time now. I was a danger to us both and to everyone else. In fact, Chris had even woken me up a number of times when I'd been veering off one way or the other. I just told him I was okay and would carry on. Luckily, he was wide awake all the way home from Dover due to eating all those fucking biscuits. What a stroke of luck having those was, because they seemed to help prevent his other cravings and crazy episodes at the right time to help me.

On reading this story, you might be wondering why I did this and why I did that. Why I had the odd drink when I was driving? Why I didn't stop off more to rest? Why I didn't plan my trip more? Maybe you think I was a bit reckless, a touch irresponsible? I totally agree. I was all of the above.

My honest answer is just that I wasn't thinking for three days about anything else. I dropped everything at the spur of the moment. I had a mission: to get my brother home as soon as physically possible and I was going to do it.

I don't know what was driving me, and thinking about it now I could no doubt have made things much easier for myself, and much safer for everyone else. But I didn't. I coped with the situation in the only way I could see at the time. I did what I did; what I thought I had to do, and if I'd done things differently then maybe it would have been better – maybe it would have been worse. But sometimes you just have to go with your heart; go with your gut; trust yourself.

I did trust myself, so much so that I was doing things without even knowing it, and it worked out in the end. I only saved Chris from prison by a matter of hours. If I hadn't arrived when I had, he would have been sentenced because he had no money to pay his fine. Therefore, it was obviously the right thing to do at the time, wasn't it?

You might also be thinking that I must have taken drugs on my journey to stay awake so long. I'm so honest that I will tell you the absolute truth. Before I left, I asked someone "in the know" if they had anything for me. This person happened to completely ignore my question because he was more concerned about me driving to Serbia on my own than anything else.

Even the drug dealer was worried about me.

I didn't ask again, but I would have had whatever I'd been offered at the time if I thought it would have assisted me.

Due to this, the extra-strong espressos, Red Bull, beer, and fags were all I had – the diet of heroes.

Home at Last

We arrived back in Bolton at around 1 a.m. I took Chris straight to my mum and dad's where he freaked out again just as soon as we arrived. He started shaking and couldn't get himself out of the car, as if to say, "I need a drink."

I wasn't convinced about "the shakes" he kept telling me about, because they only seemed to come on when he mentioned it. To me, it was as though he wanted to make you aware that he needed a drink. He hadn't had one drink for eight hours after eating those biscuits, so why did this happen at this exact moment, the moment I parked up and he saw my dad?

I went in for a bit, but I just had to get home. I could only keep myself together a little longer and I didn't want to fall apart in front of my mum and dad.

I've no idea what was said by anyone before I left. I just remember as I exited the car my dad saying, "You're a saint, Math."

The previous time I'd heard that name in the Serbian police station seemed such a long time ago now. This was a much better feeling than hearing it then.

Around 2 a.m. on Sunday morning, I arrived home. From getting up for work ninety-two hours earlier, I'd had just three hours broken sleep in my car. I'd driven from Bolton to Belgrade and back in seventy-five hours. During this time, I'd been in nine different countries, driven through sixteen country borders and travelled over three thousand miles. From Northwest England through France, the Netherlands, Belgium, Germany, Austria, Slovenia, Croatia, and finally Serbia, then back in one go. I really can't get my head around it now. I was a physical mess.

However, I was a much bigger emotional mess, and I collapsed on the rug on my floor in a blubbering heap. I cried my eyes out. I think this was for all sorts of reasons: tiredness, pride, exhaustion, shock, worry, and most of all, relief. It was a release that had been building up the whole time.

I'd managed to complete the hardest thing I'd ever had to do; something that took so much out of me and will stay with me for years. Only I will ever know what I really went through.

It mentally, physically, and emotionally destroyed me.

But I did it. I fucking did it!

I just hope it was worth it.

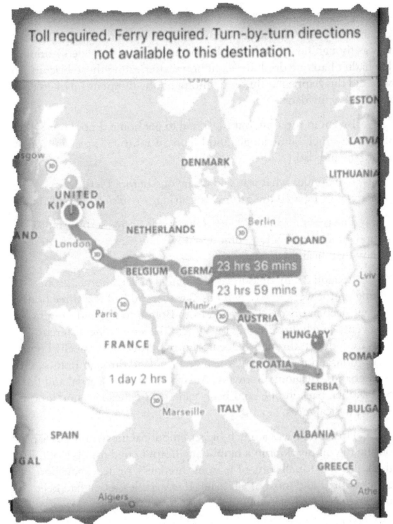

Please do not try this at home.

Hello,

I just want to thank you all for what you did for Chris while he was in Belgrade.

He would not have survived without people like you. Thank you so much.

I'm sure you were so glad to get rid of him but you still looked after him nevertheless.

He is now home safe staying with my mum and dad, and he looks and feels so much better already. The recovery has started thanks to you.

One day I hope to return to Belgrade with the 'real' Chris so we can both thank you all again in person

Please don't have a heart attack if you see us outside 😁

Thanks again.
Forever in your debt.
Matt

My thank-you text to the hostel

You are welcome, I can say that even though he was not the best guest we had ;), I am also glad that he survived the Balkans. Salute Chris from all of us and don't wary, we won't have heart attack, we will be glad to see you in shape again on our door :).
Adem, Anja, Nikola and Miguel

The wonderful people from the CityZen hostel, Belgrade, Serbia.

Just Say No

"Just say no," that's what they said
And that fixed firmly in my head
Until it happened that fateful day
When "no" was a word I just couldn't say
Just a couple of dabs of that white powder
Seemed to make me louder and louder
And in the end, "Oh what a night"
I didn't sleep until I saw daylight
And when I awoke, the morning after
I remembered the night and all the laughter
It was something that I could not miss
There was nothing in the world that could beat this
And so it continued for a while
Me and my everlasting smile
But more and more powder was required
And I was becoming forever tired
So I decided that it was time
To move on from Amphetamine
I really had to get a grip
Either that, or try a trip
So I decided on the latter
Leaving my mind even more in tatters
I didn't even know the day
Or whether I was straight or gay
And I decided this had to end
The feeling I could not comprehend
So what did I do? I tried an "E"
Then I went back for another three
So there I was, completely off my head
Just lucky that I wasn't dead
My mate though did not share my luck
And he had a fraction of what I took
In the club that night he passed away
Never to see another day
And people say it's down to me
Because I gave him the deadly "E"
So here I spend my days inside

Sometimes wishing that I had died
At least I would not feel this guilt
About the problem that I had built
My mate would still have his life
And his widow would still be his wife
But it didn't end there for me at least
Because prison was just one big drugs feast
I needed something to ease my pain
And so I turned to crack cocaine
This was the start of something bad
Whatever there was to take I had
I was trapped with no way out
No family or friends to hear my shouts
A vicious circle had begun to turn
When one drug wore off the next I would yearn
And it all began from something so small
Something I never really needed at all
I was happy before all this you see
All my family and friends were there for me
But now what I've done has drove us apart
And on the way broken so many hearts
So all I do now is suffer alone
Hoping that one day, I might just get home
But the chances of that are so slim indeed
I doubt that I will ever be freed
It's gone too far and there's no way back
I can just lie here and crave on my back
My body has aged at a staggering rate
So much so that I fear it's too late
If the doctors are right, I'm too sick to save
And it won't be long until I see my grave
So all I will say is "I'm sorry, so sorry"
For all the grief and all the worry
But maybe from this just one person might gain
And realise the high is just not worth the pain!

Belgrade: The Screenplay – Final Scene

A SONG PLAYS

WHERE IS MY MIND – MAXENCE CYRIN

EXTERNAL. APARTMENT COMPLEX. BOLTON 1:50am

Matt leaves Chris with his parents. There is no sound as he climbs back into his car, apart from the quiet background music.

He drives the short distance home. Both windows are open so he can feel the cold wind on his face.

There are tears in his eyes. He looks as though he is ready to fall apart at any moment. He doesn't. He holds it in.

INTERNAL. UNDERGROUND CAR PARK. OLD MILL APARTMENT COMPLEX. BOLTON. 1:55am

Matt arrives home, parking his car in the usual spot.

He slowly walks towards the elevator. It is out of order. Matt gives it a vacant "fuck off" stare before making his way up the steps to the second floor.

INTERNAL. MATT'S APARTMENT. 1:58am

Matt closes the door. He slips his shoes off.

He staggers into his living room and immediately collapses on the floor with his face in his hands. He is finally broken and his emotions start to pour out. It is finally over.

Though you don't see his face, it is obvious the tears are flowing. He cries until the song finishes.

In silence, he gets up and slowly walks over to the fridge. He takes out a can of Stella Artois lager. He walks over to the sofa and collapses in the same position in which he was trying to sleep over eighty hours earlier. He has finally made it back there and his sense of relief is overwhelming.

He opens the can of lager and takes a small deserving sip.
He holds the can up and smiles directly into the camera.

MATT

I fucking did it.

FINAL CREDITS BEGIN

A SONG PLAYS

**BILLY PRESTON - THAT'S THE WAY GOD
PLANNED IT**

"Jesus said to Moses, "Come forth." He came fifth and won a bag of peanuts."

GEORGE SANTLEY

Chapter Twelve

Let Us Pray

On second thoughts, let's not pray. I'd had enough of all that bollocks before I'd even left primary school.

Up to the age of eleven years, I attended St. Williams School, where I was treated to a Roman Catholic upbringing. It was, in hindsight, a pretty ridiculous environment in which to begin my education, though it ended up, like most things in my life, being a wrong thing that would still point me in the right direction.

I somehow managed to escape becoming one of the walking indoctrinated. This was, funnily enough, thanks to a slight by the Catholic Church when I was a kid. I was an altar boy, and with the church being next to an old folk's home, I had the pleasure of enduring dozens of fucking morbid funerals and other black services before I was even ten years old; and all this after being told regularly that if I didn't pray to the almighty, then I would probably go to *hell*.

I have no problem with people putting their faith in something to help them through life. In fact, I almost admire the dedication. I just believe we should all be left to make up our own minds without being pushed or swayed by our teachers or parents, which is how almost everyone becomes associated to a particular religion – it's just passed down through the family. This is basically the same as how most of us decide which football team to support. Just reading that bit should tell everyone all they need to know about religion.

How can a young child possibly be labelled as a Christian or a Muslim or anything else before they've even had their eyes open to what that means? This brainwashing of kids before they are capable of knowing better is just wrong. It narrows their possibilities in life and inhibits them – though I suppose that is the fundamental point of any religion. If you want your child to be the best they can possibly be, then you need to leave their minds open so they themselves can explore and ultimately make their own minds up about religion without prejudice.

If only these people would wake up, open their minds, and realise that religion is just another fairy tale. Humans didn't just appear on the earth one day. There was no Adam and Eve. The first human was born gradually, through evolution. I find it so bizarre and even sad that people still want to believe the uneducated ancient made-up stories rather than the findings of some amazing scientists from recent centuries. Given time, I'm sure education and common sense will change things, unless the mobile brain-dead world we currently live in continues on the same worrying blinkered path, that is.

Some religions are worse than others, as we are currently experiencing with the almost weekly terrorist attacks, which, no matter what you hear on the news, are almost all down to one set of particular warped religious beliefs. These terrorist attacks are in the name of jihad – the murdering jihadist believing that if he kills at least one infidel – a man not believing in Islam – then he will go to his version of paradise, a place up in the sky with a load of young virgins. I mean, really?

Islam is particularly poisonous and oppressive, believing that it is the "only" and "final" religion, and at the time of writing it is extremely threatening to the way most of us live our free lives, though you could say the same about most other religions in centuries past. It's just that it's now the turn of Islam with many other religions slowly dying out over recent years.

I drive down the main road near my home and see countless women covered from head to toe in black. How are these women to integrate without a face? Without a voice? Without a smile? They are being controlled because their free thoughts are a threat to the whole sad way of life that their controllers have defined for them.

These women cannot integrate because they are held back by their men. Their religion does not want them to integrate. It is that simple, and it is so ridiculous that we have this today in an apparently "free" "educated" country. Why do the feminist groups never mention these Muslim women in their pity speeches? It is because they think this is fine as it's just part of their religion, but why does religion have different rules than any other part of society? If I made my wife wear a mask because I didn't want her to show her face in the name of Matthew Santley, then I would be locked up, and rightly so; unless Matthew Santley was the name of a popular religion, that is. So why is that different in the eyes of the law? It's because the law is complete bollocks and the people making the law are imbeciles – or they are frightened.

After she retired, my mum continued to work as a community nurse in some mainly-Muslim populated areas. She would often see Muslim women in their homes without their hijabs, so she actually got to know a few of their friendly faces, becoming friends with them. Later, she'd often hear a voice outside say, "Hello, Pat." She would then be confronted by a black figure – no face, no personality, and no real person in her eyes. My mum had no clue who was behind the veil and she actually knew that person, so what chance have they got with the rest of us, and us with them? It's so fucking basic this it's unreal.

It is so sad that women are held back like this, and the fact that our governments let it happen in today's world is unbelievable and shocking. They only allow this because they are scared to offend religion. Why is this? It's a disgrace and someone needs to speak up about this nonsense. These entire beliefs stem from a world before science; a world before intelligence. Religion was our first stab at trying to understand the world before we could put a fucking basic sentence together, so why does it still exist? Simple; it's because many people in today's world are still thick as fuck.

One more thing my mum said was that whenever the Muslim man in the family was dying, he always looked very frightened, as if to say he wasn't really sure there was anything waiting for him in the afterlife after all. If you dedicate your whole life to a religion, then surely you must have one hundred per cent faith in it; complete faith in there being all those virgins or whatever else waiting for you. I wonder how many are not really sure, yet they keep quiet their entire lives for the fear of being excluded from the family – or worse. How pathetic. Many of the wives often didn't seem too upset either, as if to say, "Thank fuck for that. Now I can actually get on with my life."

I accept that these are only observations of the few, but they are true nevertheless.

I find it disgusting that religion has such a big part to play in today's world, and especially within governments. Why is it that we could never have an openly atheist president of the USA, and probably never even an openly atheist politician in that country? As far as I'm aware, in 2018, there are still no openly atheist politicians in the US Congress. The reason being, that an atheist politician in the United States is digging their own political grave by coming out of the unholy closet. It's scandalous that religion has anything to do with politics at all. Let's face it; a religion is just a cult with some political clout. Cults are looked upon unfavourably because they are seen as being poisonous; even groups of crazy people. Religion is also poisonous, and the world would be such a better place without it. I know I'm ranting a bit but it's because it's fucking annoying. I know I'm right. You know I'm right. It's fucking bollocks. Religion is bollocks. Why can these people not see?

There are currently around four thousand two hundred religions alive and kicking in the world today. *Four thousand two hundred.*

What does that tell you? And why are the only ones laughed at those with no political backing? The small teams, if you like. People make a joke about Scientology, and this seems to be the only religion which you can have a go at right now, the reason being that it is a new religion. All religions started in a similar way, by people who either wanted to control society, make money, or for some other selfish or sordid reason.

After all the lucky escapes and coincidences I've experienced, you might have thought that I would believe in a god. Well, maybe I do, but I don't believe in a personal god who listens to prayers and grants wishes. Why would I? Why would you? Has he ever delivered?

I am a non-believer because I am a logical person. I choose to make this logical judgement based on scientific findings by some of the most brilliant minds to have ever lived, rather than believers who base their godly beliefs on hearsay, fantasy, and peer pressure. However, I am open to anything new. My mind can easily be swayed by some evidence of one god or another. This is why I don't believe, because I've just never been given a reason to believe that a god exists. I have, however, been given many reasons to believe that god does not exist.

Also, all I see from religion is evidence of division, segregation, control, grooming, prejudice, abuse, oppression, and conning people out of their fucking money, and their lives.

I've never really thought about this before now, but during my young religious days, seeing all those people crying over their loved ones in the morning before I went off to school can't really have set me up for a happy day of learning – maybe that's even where my schooling started to go wrong. I remember often feeling quite melancholy walking up to church before school. It was such a dreary, depressing place, and definitely not an environment for any child to be subjected to.

I did enjoy missing the first hour of school most mornings, though – literally a blessing which came as part of the job. This was no doubt one of the reasons I volunteered for this nonsense in the first place. However, my main reason for being an altar boy – I think – was because my mum had been quite a devout Catholic at one time, so much so that she even had thoughts of becoming a nun. Thank god she had a fucking family instead.

Ironically, she married a man who was not religious in the slightest. My dad was what is known as a Wesleyan, which is a form of Protestant, though he wasn't practicing. He was just yet another one who was born into his religion.

Wesleyan is a religion named after an actual man from the eighteenth century, John Wesley. He, along with his brother and some other cleric clown, founded Methodism. Now then, if all this doesn't make you realise that religions are a farce, then I don't know what will.

All religions are founded by people – people like you and me. They are man-made. The reason these people found/form a religion/cult is either for their own financial/sexual benefit, or because they are complete and utter fucking nut-jobs. The church of Scientology was actually created by science fiction writer L. Ron Hubbard. He wrote a self-help book which then became the basis of Scientology. Wouldn't you just know it; a writer of fiction creating a religion.

My dad actually converted to Catholicism when he married my mum. He only did this so that they could marry before the altar in a Catholic church – something my mum wanted. If he hadn't converted they could still have married in a Catholic church, though it would have had to happen at the back of the church, quite ridiculously. My dad obviously didn't give two fucks about what he had to do. It meant nothing to him. He would have agreed to anything for an easy life. He still does.

Rather than religion, my dad was into things far more important – music and clothes. At one point he even had a different-coloured suit for each day of the week, and he would make my mum sit and listen through hours and hours of songs by his hero – Bob Dylan. Like

354

me, even after all those hours of pain, my mum thankfully didn't become indoctrinated to Bob, choosing instead to stay faithful to her religion, which she was still practicing when I became an altar boy.

Becoming part of the church for me just seemed like the natural thing to do because I knew it would make my mum proud. I carried out my role on the altar for a couple of years, probably being the most experienced and reliable of all the boys by the time I moved on.

Not long before I left primary school, however, my mum saw something to "wake her up". This would have a dramatic effect on my future.

We were very lucky that the local bishop was visiting our church for an extra-special service. This only happens once every blue moon, so the whole school and church were especially excited about it. I was excited too, because I would obviously have an important role to play on this "wonderful" occasion.

However, for some reason, yours truly was not selected to serve for this "mass of the century". I remember being really upset about this at the time because it just didn't add up, even to my young mind.

As a ten-year-old boy, I just felt that I must have done something wrong not to be selected. I must have been naughty. I did used to dick around every now and again on the altar, like we all did, but I didn't think I'd been spotted. Maybe the almighty one himself had a quiet word in the ears of those that mattered? I mean, what else could it be?

I just couldn't fathom why probably the most senior and loyal of all the boys wouldn't be selected for such a big occasion. It wasn't as though I was going to bring a fucking grenade to the party or something.

My mum saw straight through this, though. Thank the Lord.

She knew exactly why I wasn't chosen, or more accurately, why others were chosen before me.

Coincidently, all the boys selected on that day came from families with money; families who were closely connected to the church and often donated generously. My family was not in this clique because my mum and dad didn't have money. They had to be careful with every penny they earned.

This would have really annoyed my mum. I bet she was seething.

However, what happened that day was probably one of the best things ever to happen to me and my family. Right there and then, my mum decided that the church was an absolute sham, later telling me and my brother that we didn't have to go to church again if we didn't want to. It was our choice from then on, as it should be for everyone, from the start.

Apart from weddings and funerals, I don't think I've been to a church service since I was eleven years old. Just imagine if I had been selected on the day the bishop came to town. We would probably have all been poisoned even further, and who knows where I would be now. By chance, and before it was too late, I was given the choice, and I am very thankful for that. Maybe this was the luckiest escape I ever had.

Despite not attending church, or believing in God, and despising every religion I know of – apart from Buddhism – though that lot does seem to do an awful lot of street begging – I actually do kind of believe in something; though I'm not sure I believe in anything spiritual. It's more scientific, though there may be a link between our spiritual and scientific journey. The fact that I say scientific rather than spiritual might confuse many, but please stick with it.

Something happened recently in the world of science that made me think there might be something scientific about having a positive outlook in life benefiting us. Something that means we may be able to help ourselves today in ways that determine parts of our future just by the way we think.

Please understand that this is only a theory – nothing more. It's just something that might explain how people somehow manage to help themselves overcome problems, and even illness, by having a positive mind.

Most theories are complete bollocks until they are proven to be correct by science, so just bear that in mind. It's a theory, and it's probably complete bollocks. However, without people thinking differently now and again, we would never move forward. So it's just my theory.

This theory concerns something that blows the mind of everyone – even all the best and most amazing minds in the world – quantum mechanics. If it doesn't blow your mind, then you just don't understand it.

I know that you are now probably thinking, "This prick has been drinking again while watching the fucking Discovery Channel," which isn't far from the truth – and that was actually how the poem 3.14 came about – but there is nothing else to explain this, so I am using this opportunity to have a go.

Quantum Mechanics

For those that don't know, quantum mechanics/physics is just physics on a very small scale, or on the smallest scale possible – particle level. For some unfathomable reason, these minute particles are behaving in a way not expected by normal science, and it's as though they can appear in more than one form or more than one place at the same time, and as though they don't become reality, and have a specific form or place in the world, until we actually look at them. Scientists' minds have been blown by this for years. Some have said that it's like the moon not being in the sky until you actually look at it. It hurts your head if you read too much about it.

However, some Australian scientists recently took this one step further. They proved that changing something in the future actually changed the way an individual particle behaved in the past. Yes, something done in the future changed the past. This has all been proven at a microscopic level by science.

Now then, our brains apparently work at quantum level, so this is what my theory is based on.

My Theory of Positivity

Could thinking positive thoughts actually have some part to play in how our future pans out? Could our thoughts harness these particles in a way that can determine our future? We have no idea what is going on in the "empty" space between us, which has been proven not to be empty space at all – that empty space weighs something so there is something else going on. Maybe the positive energy from particles within us somehow transmits to other particles around us in that space, causing the positivity to be passed on, just like your smile can

357

spread positive energy throughout a room of people, changing the whole atmosphere around you. Maybe this is why good things seem to happen to us more often when we are being positive. How? I don't fucking know. It's just a thought – a theory.

Now then, is my theory any more ridiculous than believing in a god that you pray to when something goes wrong, hoping he will answer your call for help? And still believing in him even when he never actually answers your prayers? I don't think so, because however slight, there is some science backing up my theory, unlike any god theory out there.

What I do know is that being positive helps, and I've definitely experienced my best moments when I've had a positive attitude. Not only this, it just feels better to be positive rather than choosing the easy option of moping around feeling sorry for yourself; something I've done far too much of in the past.

Where does science and all the building blocks of life come from? Well, maybe it does actually come from some god, but until he is proven to exist, I will not believe in anything other than being a decent human being. I don't need a commandment to tell me that, and neither should anyone else.

In my opinion, there are three things that separate believers from non-believers; intelligence, common sense, and courage.

1. People lacking intelligence won't question what they are being told about religion. They will just follow all the other lemmings - or as the bible calls them, "Sheep".

2. The intelligent ones will come up with the logical conclusion – religion is nonsense - but they might still reject and refuse to believe this if they lack common sense.

3. Those clever souls that possess both intelligence and common sense will only fail to accept their findings if they lack the courage to do so; the courage to admit and welcome the fact that this is the only gift of life they will ever get – the one they are living right here and now. The one they must make the most of.

There's just not enough love in this world for us to waste any of it on some fictional being; that's unless you are six years old and that fictional being is Santa Claus.

Heaven's Basement

If you disobey
And lie to me and others
You punch and put lights out
Of girlfriends, wives, and mothers
Then if this is your thing
Your form of entertainment
One day we'll hear your screams
From the realms of heaven's basement

If you con for a living
A lowlife piece of scum
Profit from others giving
You almost make me numb
You'd better change your ways
And find a new arrangement
Or one day you'll find yourself
Being mugged in heaven's basement

If you blame your ways
On your hardwired circuitry
You're not wired up correctly
And don't deserve to be free
You can blame your creator
For the coded byte displacement
While you sit forever head-tapping
In a dark corner of heaven's basement

If you are a killer
The worst that there can be
Then you're in for a thriller
In a place you won't find me
You'll prefer a return
To your coffin's deep encasement
Than to meet your evil match
In the pit of heaven's basement

If you treat others

As you wish those to treat yourself
Then you're sitting pretty
In a nice rich vein of health
If you stick to your guns
And don't become complacent
I'll see you on the rooftops
A million miles up, from heaven's basement

I Believed in Father Christmas

Some believe they should cut off their foreskin
Because it says so in an old book
Some believe they should ask for forgiveness
If they want god to give them a look
Some believe they must pray five times daily
To be considered a genuine being
And some must cover their faces
Their god says it's just not worth seeing

I believed in Father Christmas
I often left him a mince pie
But it was always still there in the morning
So I realised I'd been told a lie
I was six when my world fell apart
And I saw my dad scoffing his face
But if I'd followed the ways of religion
I'm sure I would still have kept faith

Muhammad Was a Paedophile

Muhammad was a paedophile
Yes, he had sex with a nine-year-old child
So just think about that for a while
And come to your own conclusion
Muhammad, the prophet they see
As an example of what man should strive to be
Was like Jimmy Savile to you and me
And deserving of execution

Jesus Christ rose from the dead
Miraculously prepared some fish and bread
For five thousand that were heartily fed
"They all ate and were satisfied"
Matthew 14:13–21
Explains it all, so he must have done
And that's why my mum wanted to be a nun
Before she realised it was all just a lie

Jewish believe that the Messiah will come
He will come down and save everyone
And all those people that have already gone
They will be resurrected
One plus about Judaism, I see
It is more about actions than about beliefs
But why need religion for people to see
Being nice and polite should be expected

Then we get to fucking Scientology
A businessman wants to make some money
A friend of his said the best way is that he
Should start a new religion
Then all these fucking idiots follow
Empty their pockets until they are hollow
They're just making coin from others sorrow
And feeding superstition

I lived amongst Buddhists for a year or two

And I loved how their calmness and peacefulness shone
through
But all they ever seemed to do
Was sit on the street and beg
They were treated like gods in the Far East
Others would pay for them all to feast
And all they had to do was not speak
So was I being misled?

Everyone has their own opinion
And has their right to choose a religion
But consider these texts that were written
And then regarded as "The Truth"
They were probably written by a normal bloke
Like me and you, who was pissed having a smoke
Then it somehow graduated from a joke
And used to brainwash and recruit

I'm not saying that there is no god
But if there is, then it would be quite odd
That he would want a great big wad
Of your cash at his disposal
And I'm sure he wouldn't want you to fight
Or for you to cover your face, whatever the sight
And now the sad fact is, after writing this I might
Need a course in bomb disposal

Amen

God did not create man.

Man created god.

He did this to help him deal with death, the unknown, and all the other bollocks that he couldn't quite get his head around.

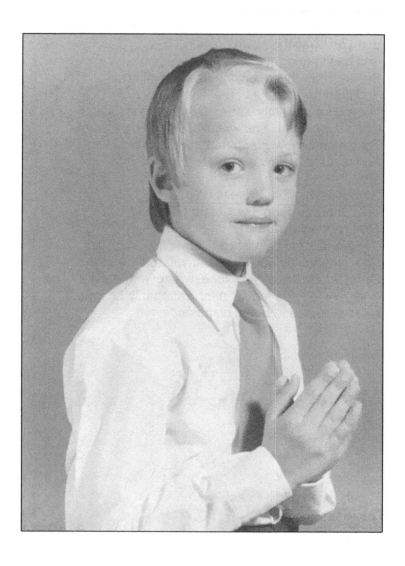

The Ten Commandments – A Shortened Version

1. Thou shall have no other gods before Me.

You just had to make the first one about you, didn't you? So what you're saying is, I need to worship You? Can I not just get on with my life and do my own thing? I don't even know who you are, pal. Is this spiritual spam?

2. Thou shall not make idols.

Hang on a minute. You've just made an idol – yourself – and I still don't know who the fuck you are. Can you give me a sign that you are actually real? I mean, I don't want to waste my whole life on something that seems to be a figment of imagination.

3. Thou shall not take the name of the LORD your God in vain.

Good fucking Lord.

4. Remember the Sabbath day, to keep it holy.

I promise to do absolutely fuck all on Sundays just for you. I'll even stay in bed all day with my head under the covers if that'll make you happy. Hang on. The Sabbath is Sunday isn't it? I once heard a rumour that it was a Saturday. If that's the case, it would really mess things up because Saturday is everyone's main day out on the piss.

5. Honour your father and your mother.

This is obviously to do with obeying your mum and dad when they tell you about the LORD your God. Even my mum now thinks your church is a sham, so I have no problem with this one.

6. Thou shall not murder.

Jesus! It took a while to get around to that one. I think this might have been at the top of my list. Then again, doesn't it go without saying? Do we really need to be told this?

7. Thou shall not commit adultery.

Does this apply to gay couples too, or do they have a free card? Oh, I forgot. You don't like gays, do you? You need to get with the times, pal.

8.   Thou shall not steal.

These are starting to sound like token fucking gestures now. You only need two more to make it a nice round number. The eight commandments sounds a bit shit really.

9.   Thou shall not bear false witness against thy neighbour.

This whole religion nonsense is one big lie. All those following it are believing a lie.

10.   Thou shall not covet.

So you are saying that I can't think about – or desire – something that doesn't belong to me? Last night, I confess that I thought about shagging my neighbour's wife. However, this was only because he actually did shag my wife, so it just came into my mind. I didn't mean to think it, and I'm not going to shag her. Does this mean that I'm going to suffer the same punishment as my neighbour and go to hell, even though he did actually shag my wife and I only thought about shagging his?

Oh, hang on. Forget it. I'll just go to confession tomorrow and tell one of your priests. Problem solved.

The Ten Alternative Commandments

1. Don't be a prick.

2. Be nice to everyone, unless they're a prick; then just ignore them.

3. Be honest with everyone, especially yourself.

4. Give everyone an equal chance, even vegans and cyclists.

5. Don't judge without knowing all the facts.

6. Don't be a smart-arse.

7. Please get drunk every now and again.

8. Do everything in moderation; too much of anything is not good for you, even alcohol, unfortunately.

9. Don't worry about things that are completely out of your control.

10. You only live once, and it doesn't last long, so please try to have some fucking fun.

Heaven Is a Dirty Brothel

Heaven is a dirty brothel
Only fit for certain "pure" souls
And getting to this dirty brothel
For some is their only life goal
They live a "pure" existence
Well, in their own mind at least
With their only reason for being
The end-of-lifetime sex feast

So what's a "pure" existence?
It's not what you would think
Not just about the food they eat
Or that which they don't drink
It concerns the women they "love"
Many of whom are persecuted
And certain words they can't utter
Or they may well be executed

The women who can't show their faces
To the likes of you and me
Are oppressed in many countries
Not even allowed to walk free
And if they show their faces
Their husbands will lose their free pass
Whereas she might be stoned to death
By "*men*" who appear en masse

Now here's a lovely thought
Female genital mutilation
Whoever would have thought
This could be a real situation
And honour killings no less
Where a daughter dishonours the family
So they agree that she must die
And they all do this quite gladly

But why is it always the women?
Who are raped and murdered and such?

While the "men" do all the killing
On the words of a typically male judge
Well it's quite obvious really
With their vision of the afterlife
Where they appear to be very happy
To be rid of their "darling" wife

Now if the "man" loses his pass
To the brothel of eternity
There is another way
That he can get one for free
He just needs to go and find
Then kill and maim an infidel
Now that's his vision of heaven
But to me that's quite obviously hell

Evolution

There was no Adam
There was no Eve
There is no basis
For which you believe

The first human was born gradually
With evolution and natural selection
Well before your mutilated vaginas
And your men with mini erections

Science is proving
Day in, day out
How we are here
Though you still have your doubts

But you continue to preach
And spout all your blurb
Which to those with a brain
Is quite frankly absurd

So carry on your path
Of awaiting your final breath
While I'll happily use my time living
My actual time before death

When?

When were your prayers last answered?
When did your dreams last come true?
When were your hopes last shattered?
Whenever did your god think of you?
When are you going to wake up?
When are you going to see through?
The nonsense, the lies, the hypocrisy?
The death of which is long overdue

As The Chinese Say, "Oh My God!"

Quite worryingly, while writing this chapter I've spotted a spooky coincidence in these very pages. This is the kind of chance occurrence that some people would see as a "sign from God" – a miracle.

The chapter consists of nine sections. The first three sections contain poems I've written over the past two years, as do the last three sections. These are the only religion-based poems I have ever written, and most were written before I even came up with the idea for this chapter.

The title of these six sections is just the name of the associated poem.

The other three sections were written and given titles before I even considered adding any poems to this chapter.

If you read downwards, picking the first letter of each section title, it just so happens to spell out the greeting, "Hi, Matthew."

- Heaven's Basement
- I Believed in Father Christmas
- Muhammed Was a Paedophile
- Amen
- The Ten Commandments
- The Ten Alternative Commandments
- Heaven Is a Dirty Brothel
- Evolution
- When?

So I write a chapter about religion – in a book describing many coincidences in my life – and how I don't believe in God, and God speaks to me.

I am not so clever to have made this up. I just wrote about things that sprung to mind, not even thinking about the book when I wrote any of the poems, and it all just miraculously fell into place.

Also, many of these poems have only come into being by chance. Heaven's Basement was written because my artist friend, Chris, was in a band called Heaven's Basement for years until he recently left to concentrate on his art, and I just liked the sound of the name. The Muhammad poem was written after my friend Alan (Mike) randomly said to me, "Muhammad was a paedophile", as we were stood at the bar in my local pub waiting for a taxi. Heaven is a Dirty Brothel was written after the terrorist bomber in Manchester in 2017 was found to be a jihadist looking to kill infidels and therefore gain his place in 'paradise'. I've no idea where the others came from, but I probably wrote them in bed after drinking too much at the weekend.

Spooky, isn't it?

Did I make this happen by having it in my subconscious thoughts? Am I a lying bastard? Who knows? I just know that I didn't plan it consciously. Should I now believe in God? Should I bollocks. It's just another coincidence, isn't it?

Anyway, people will always believe what they want to believe. What do you believe?

"Sometimes, not getting what you want..

...is a wonderful stroke of luck."

Dalai Lama X1V

Chapter Thirteen

Full Circle

My first experience of something going wrong in my life actually being a major slice of luck was when I was eight years old. I wrote a letter to *Jim'll Fix It*, and Mr. Jimmy Savile himself – the now deceased well-known celebrity paedophile – sent me a reply, but at the time I was disappointed that I received a letter of rejection.

This was even more amazing than it sounds, because my daftness, even at such a young age, meant that my letter was asking Sir Jim if he could fix it for me to smoke his fucking cigar. Now then, now then, what a massive stroke of luck, because when would this pervert ever otherwise refuse such an offer from a child of my age?

My latest experience of not getting what I wanted being a good thing, regarded my job. It was January 2017, and I'd been working back at my old haunt in Lytham for one year on a project that, by all accounts, was set to go on for another year or two.

However, I was getting quite bored and fed up again at work, so I decided to interview for another, much better paid job, and I was convinced that the role was mine. I couldn't see anyone else having the particular specific but varied knowledge and skills needed; otherwise, I would have known that person. Also, there were several roles up for grabs, so I thought I would definitely be offered one of them. Fortunately, I wasn't.

At this time of rejection, I was again feeling lost, and I wanted to break away from my day-to-day routine. I thought getting a new job in a new environment would help me with this, but it seemed I was stuck again, and would be for the next year or two unless I did something drastic.

At the same time, I was also becoming aware that I didn't have an ending for my book. I felt as though I was just waiting for something to happen to help me out. I even thought I might need to go away on my own again at some point to try to manufacture an ending, though I knew deep down that forcing it wasn't the best way to finish it. I hadn't forced anything else in the book, so why should I start now? Everything so far had just seemed to bloody happen.

One morning at work, towards the end of January, I remember looking out the window and thinking that I was back where I'd been fourteen years previous, just before I went travelling.

On that government site in Lytham, there were now many new houses being built to replace all the old buildings in which I'd previously worked over the past twenty-two years, with my current office also set to be demolished within the next couple of years.

I realised I had so many memories lying within those plots of land – both good and bad – and with it being a typical wet dreary Lancashire morning, it felt quite sad to see those buildings being replaced. It was at that point I realised I'd come full circle, and I'd done so just to see the end of an era. That was the moment I decided that the title for my final chapter should be "Full Circle", though I still had no idea what I was going to write about. Something else really did need to happen.

Although so much had happened in the fourteen years since my escape to the Far East, I still almost felt as though I hadn't gone anywhere in my life.

Those years that had past felt like a dream at this moment. I couldn't quite comprehend that I used to live in Taiwan – and recent experiences like my drive to Belgrade felt like a bit of a blur in my memory. I'd picked up so many things on my journey over those years though; things that I would previously never have imagined.

Since leaving Lytham in 2003 to embark on my adventure, I'd travelled the world; loved – and lost – two amazing girls; learnt to read and speak Mandarin Chinese, then forgotten much of it; achieved a BSc (honours) degree in computing in my spare time; studied music for a while; written countless poems; and even started a videography business which didn't make me any money.

When I'd started to take the video-editing business seriously in 2004, I even used to put my own films online, and I had an idea of doing this on a wider scale for other people. However, I assumed that I would have to edit all the videos myself first, thinking that nobody would ever want to sit through an unedited video. This would be around twelve months before a certain YouTube appeared online. I thought this idea would never work; that's because I'm an idiot.

Looking out the window at that moment, I should have been feeling proud and happy about those years past, not least because I'd actually managed to write a bloody book about them – a book that I was sure would entertain. But I didn't feel proud; I felt a bit hollow, like something was still missing; like something needed to be finished off.

My health was also deteriorating at this time. I put this down to what happened to me a few months before – that crazy drive to Belgrade and back. The months leading up to the drive had been quite a healthy time in my life, but in the months following the experience I began to suffer – though it was all self-inflicted. Ironically, and very stupidly, I turned to drink myself.

In addition to drinking with my mates in the pub, I was drinking every day at home, alone, and I was drinking far too much – a lot more than anyone knew. It's funny, or depending how you look at it, "worrying" how things can turn in a heartbeat, setting you on a totally different path. That ridiculous Belgrade ordeal affected me so much more than I'd thought possible, and I think a lot more than anyone could ever understand.

After arriving home in the early hours on that Sunday morning in September, I felt like a different person. Something inside me had changed. It was as though part of me had died. I felt quite numb and nothing really seemed to bother me at all – nothing apart from the flashbacks that is. It was as though I'd put a protective shield over my senses – blocking everything out. This was no doubt what I'd done subconsciously for the whole trip, and is probably what led me to being a bit crazy the entire time; what led me to do what I did without thinking of the consequences. I probably wouldn't have attempted it or succeeded otherwise.

The problem I was now stuck with was that the protective shield was still there and I had no idea how to rid myself of it.

Whenever I drove to work in the subsequent weeks and months I was reliving parts of the experience over and over again. I couldn't get it out of my head – not just the drive and my emotions at the time but also the pathetic but haunting image of my brother. That destroyed me each time it jumped into my mind.

I'd fill-up with tears at the thought of him, and sometimes with my mind elsewhere, I didn't even realise how fast I was driving – all over again. The M55 on the way to Lytham is typically a fast motorway, often being quite light in traffic. This is similar to many of the European roads on my journey to Serbia. You'll remember I was driving home on the motorway that night, when, quite worryingly, after falling asleep at the wheel, I looked up to see that I was doing just 20 mph. Well, driving along the M55 to work I'd often look up and see that I was driving at 120 mph (50 mph over the speed limit), and I'd think, "How did that happen?"

It was quite frightening. I mean, how does that happen? My mind just kept returning to the days and nights of the drive through Europe over and over again, and my foot would often respond without me even knowing it. It was crazy.

Every now and then I'd hear a song on the radio that would seem to fit with a particular part of the journey, and each time I heard that song I would relive it. I even made a playlist of the whole journey this way, and that is how the screenplay sections of the book came about. In my mind the journey was a film, and the playlist became the soundtrack. This probably sounds ridiculous to many, and I even feel slightly embarrassed writing about it – like men generally do – but I have to tell the story to be true to myself and to be true to the book.

I think, because it was such an intense and emotional three or four days, certain parts of it just kind of tattooed itself onto my brain. I was still experiencing all this six months after the bloody event too. I hadn't told anyone about it either. I was just hoping it would go away sooner or later, but it didn't. I did eventually mention it to my mum and a few friends, and just getting it out in the open seemed to help a bit – but only a bit.

I was in a terrible state of mind, and the only escape seemed to be having a drink and getting on with writing my book – at least some good came from the drinking situation because I didn't half write a lot over those months. I didn't touch the chapter on Belgrade, though. I'd written those words two weeks after the event when it was fresh in my mind, and I couldn't read it afterward. I didn't want to relive it yet again. I was already reliving it daily anyway.

Then, out of the blue, something happened to help me – again.

Another Blessing in Disguise

On Monday, January 30th, 2017, I called in sick to work. I'd probably had one or two gin and tonics too many on Sunday night while writing a few tales. Around 4.30 p.m. that Monday afternoon, when I was lying on my sofa – a couple of hours after moving from the pit of my bed – I received a phone call from my employment agent.

I was shocked to be told that I was being given two weeks' notice on my job, and I would therefore be out of work. This really was completely unexpected. I'd assumed I'd be working in this contract for another twelve months at least and maybe even a year or two after that, and after not getting the other job I'd applied for two weeks earlier, this really was a massive kick in the bollocks.

At first, I thought that it was only me who'd been fired, but that was me being paranoid, and the whole project had been scrapped. It was yet another piece of work in a long line in which the government would waste up to £100 million by deciding that it wasn't going anywhere. Does this sound familiar?

However, although I didn't realise it at the time, that phone call about my job was to be the next blessing in disguise.

On hearing the news, after the initial shock – which lasted a couple of minutes – I opened a bottle of Bollinger. This champagne had been in my fridge since before Christmas, so I can't have had that much of a drink problem really. I'd been saving it for a special occasion, though; I just didn't know what that occasion was going to be until now.

Two hours and one bottle of champagne later, slightly tipsy, I booked a flight to Singapore. This would be leaving three weeks from that day and returning three months later. I'd saved up some money from my two years "hard labour" on the doomed project, so I decided to put it to good use and travel again. Uncannily, this was something I'd done almost fourteen years ago to the day; the trip which ended up with me later living in Taiwan and changing my life in so many ways.

I'd be travelling around the same part of the world all over again, and without even realising it, I would be flying out at the same time of year – it was the actual same week of the year in which I flew to Singapore in 2003.

Now this really was full circle.

Again, luck seemed to be on my side. Yes, I lost my job, and most people wouldn't see this as luck, but I really needed to lose my job so that I could get myself back on track. I needed to get away from that routine and get that mad journey and those awful images of my brother out of my mind. Living the same day over and over again wasn't helping me at all. In fact, it was killing me.

This was the perfect scenario. On the surface something bad happening, but yet again it was happening for a greater good. It was a major blessing in disguise.

The added bonus was that I could now spend all this time finishing my book properly, and maybe finding the ending I was searching for. I was going travelling again like I thought I might have to, but I hadn't forced it; the unplanned ending of my contract had determined the timing of it all over again, so I just went with the flow, and started to get excited about what I hoped would be another experience of a lifetime.

It would be different this time, though.

Another Lucky Escape

On February 28th 2017, I set off on my second great escape of a lifetime.

Just as I'd done previously, I spent the first three days in Singapore, before flying to Kuala Lumpur in Malaysia for two days, where I would decide on my next move – again similar to the previous trip.

For the first four weeks, as I travelled around Malaysia and Borneo – although I'd written loads and improved a lot of the book – I felt as though I was still looking for my ending rather than letting it happen. It seemed as though I was hoping something crazy might take me somewhere, like it did in 2003. I'd meet someone who would change my life all over again.

However, I hadn't realised until I was having a quiet moment in the middle of a thunder storm in a rainforest in Borneo – where there was fuck all else to do – that I probably already had the ending all along. All over again, I just couldn't see the wood for the trees, yet I saw it in a moment when I could see nothing but trees around me.

I'd been looking outwardly for something to happen, but having that time alone in the middle of nowhere forced me to look inwardly instead. That's when I met someone on my trip that could change my life all over again – me. Nobody else could help me, and this was the moment I realised that. Nobody else was going to stop me being a prick, stop me drinking every day when I just didn't need to.

I even realised that I'd tried to tell myself about drinking too much almost two years earlier – that morning I was walking to work in Newcastle with my balls hanging out and dog shit all over my suitcase. However, I'd ignored my own warnings even then, the day I'd started to write the book. Maybe now, while finishing the book, I could actually make a point of heeding my own advice. Maybe that was the whole point of the book; to warn myself and others of their alcohol abuse?

People really do need to help themselves more before they put their problems onto others, and although I totally agree that we must share our problems more when we can't find a way of helping ourselves – don't suffer in silence like me – we must also do more ourselves in the first place rather than relying on others all the time. I'm obviously thinking of my brother while writing these words. He has relied on other's help for years, lying to everyone and himself too often – and look where that has got him.

He didn't change after we got home from Belgrade. I thought his experience in the Balkans and what I did for him might actually wake him up, but it had no effect. Seeing him in the same state months after Serbia really did hurt me because I'd put my life on the line to rescue him and give him another chance and I felt like I'd been betrayed. He was still getting too much help from my mum and dad, his ex-wife Deb, and the authorities, without whom he would definitely have already been dead, but I stayed out of the way. I did my small piece to help, but I couldn't continuingly help someone who threw that help back in my face. I needed to get on with my own life. If only my mum and dad could be left alone to get on with their lives too.

This might now sound contradictory, but it was immediately after my wonderful wake-up call in the rainforest that I realised, in the first four weeks of my trip – the trip on which I was supposed to be putting my life back on track – I'd continued to drink every fucking day, so that problem of mine was no nearer to being fixed.

However, this is not contradictory in the slightest because although I feared that I might be going down a similar path to my brother at one point, I'd never asked anyone for anything in my life. This was my problem, and only I was going to fix it. This was completely the opposite philosophy used by my brother – an unselfish one.

I had a choice. I could control my drinking or I could continue on this same path. It was all down to me. I'd been presented with this opportunity to help myself but it still depended on me making the most of it, which I quite clearly wasn't doing at the time. I was still being a prick.

On April 10th 2017, while in a hotel in Ao Nang Beach, Thailand, I made a decision. I promised myself that I would spend the next forty days and forty nights of my adventure alcohol-free – just like biblical *Jon* apparently did when he fasted in the New Testament. The day on which I decided to stop drinking was actually two weeks after my initial brainstorm in Borneo, where I'd told myself I needed to control my alcohol consumption, so it still took a further two weeks after I'd admitted that I wasn't in control to actually stop drinking. What an absolutely massive prick I am.

From that day in Ao Nang Beach, I managed twenty-three days without alcohol on some of the most beautiful beaches in Thailand, before finally succumbing after spending a full night locked in Langkawi airport alone in the dark, and then having to catch three uncomfortable flights to my final destination – Mauritius. I had a few wines on the plane and got drunk when I landed in Mauritius.

People who drink too much always have an excuse to drink, but I felt mine was quite justified. I mean, how do you get yourself locked in a fucking airport overnight alone? I will explain.

I was leaving Thailand to travel to Mauritius, and my journey would involve one boat and three flights. I left the Thai island of Koh Lipe by boat at around 4 p.m., arriving at the Malaysian island of Langkawi around 6.30 p.m. My flight from Langkawi to Kuala Lumpur was around 7.30 a.m., so I thought it was pointless getting a hotel for what would be around ten hours. I would therefore go for dinner, arrive at the airport quite late and just wait there until the morning.

However, around midnight in the airport, a security guard told me that I had to leave because he was locking up. I hadn't realised that the airport would close so I was now in a bit of a pickle. There was nothing near the airport; all the taxis had gone and I really didn't fancy sleeping on the floor outside with all my belongings.

I said to him, "My flight is at 7.30 a.m. Can I not just stay here until the morning?"

He looked at me strangely, before replying, "I check with big boss."

He was soon back, saying that I could stay on one condition. I had to give him my passport, which he would take home with him. When he returned at 6 a.m. he would give it back to me.

Not really having any choice, I succumbed, gave him my passport, and off he went. Then, a few minutes later, all the fucking lights went out.

It then hit me what I was doing. I was alone, in the dark, in a locked airport. I'd been very good on the first nine weeks of this trip, managing not to do anything typically me (stupid), and staying out of trouble, but I was now at it all over again.

I sat in silence for a while outside the barely lit Starbucks café. Thankfully the coffee shop had left their Wi-Fi connected overnight, so at least I had some contact with the outside world – my phone hadn't been working for the previous five weeks.

I then decided to explore; to check if I really was locked in all by myself. I crept around the large check-in hall, hearing noises everywhere, feeling as though I was in some kind of Blare Witch horror film, and I started to become quite scared.

I recorded myself walking around and posted the film on Facebook to let people back home know what was happening. Quite rightly, they thought I'd lost the fucking plot. I mean, who does this?

I then stayed awake most of the night, sitting with my back to the Starbucks window while constantly scanning the hall for movement and shitting every minute of it.

Then, all of a sudden, something touched me on the shoulder.

It was the fucking security guard with my passport. I'd finally fallen asleep, and he'd kept his promise of returning with it at 6 a.m.

My flight was then delayed one hour. This was a bit of a problem because it meant I would land in Kuala Lumpur just twenty-minutes before my flight to Singapore was due to take-off, and the gates closed twenty minutes before take-off.

On landing, I thought there might be someone greeting me to help me catch my connection, but there wasn't, so I assumed I'd missed it. I ran around, looking for the right gate, then realising I had to catch a fucking monorail to the other terminal first. I couldn't believe it. I now thought I'd definitely missed my flight, but I still kept trying.

After a five-minute monorail ride, I ran like mad for what felt like a mile to my gate, arriving exactly one minute after the take-off time. I then somehow managed to board the plane and find a seat, only to find some prick from Bangladesh already sitting in mine who I couldn't be arsed arguing with. Then, they immediately closed the doors and we were off.

Everyone had looked at me when I'd boarded, like I'd been holding them up, so maybe my name was being called out. They'd all looked at me again when I'd discovered Mr. Bangladesh in my seat and I'd exclaimed, "I'll find my own fucking seat then, shall I?" The stress of the situation had obviously got to me.

I didn't even have a drink on this flight. I really was being very good.

We landed in Singapore and all disembarked before boarding the same plane to Mauritius with additional passengers. It was only when I found the same prick in my seat again that things started to really annoy me. I asked him to move, and he did, but he decided to sit in the seat next to me – still not his seat.

I hadn't realised it, but he was in a party of around thirty from Bangladesh, and when we were airborne, they all seemed to congregate around my seat, panicking about the simple immigration forms they needed complete.

They obviously didn't understand the forms, and for at least three hours, they were all just pottering around, helping each other out, and more importantly, invading my fucking space.

This was why, feeling even more stressed, when the stewardess came by, I just shouted, "Wine, please!"

I had one sip, and I relaxed immediately. At that moment, I realised that my life just wouldn't be the same without the odd alcoholic beverage.

I was disappointed that I didn't manage forty days, but I really enjoyed those drinks, and this was the lesson I'd learnt from this short break. Like most of us, I drink because I enjoy it, but we need to realise that there becomes a point when it is not enjoyable – it becomes a habit. That is when you need to take a step back and take control of the situation.

Six days later, I realised I'd drank every day again, and I really wasn't enjoying it. I was in a lovely hotel with a great cool bar, and being at the bar with a cocktail just felt like the right thing to do – but I was going too far again. Therefore, I took another step back and decided to have another week without alcohol.

I think that's all you can do, just take a look at what you are doing and be honest with yourself.

I was no alcoholic. Not everything has to have a label put on it. I was just drinking too much, which is a big difference. Labels are used far too often for things which are just part of life. They are not illnesses, they are just part of life – things that we all go through; things that we can help ourselves through.

Alcoholism is obviously an illness, but just drinking too much is not an illness; it is a choice. When you don't have that choice, then it has become an illness, though it all begins with a choice – your choice.

That day in Ao Nang Beach when I decided to stop drinking, something else happened – my iPhone 7 suddenly stopped working. Now the strange thing about this is that I hadn't had a phone die on me for fourteen years, and that had been the last time I'd been in Ao Nang in 2003. It really was quite spooky and near impossible that this could happen fourteen years later in the same fucking place.

This freaked me out even more because the last time it had happened was just before I'd travelled to Koh Phi Phi Island, where months later all those people died in the tsunami, and I was travelling there next.

While on Koh Phi Phi island, I walked to the beach on which I'd stayed in 2003 to have a look if it was as badly hit by the tsunami as I had initially thought; part of me had hoped that it was going to be one of the very few lucky areas of Koh Phi Phi.

I couldn't find my old hotel (hut), but twenty metres behind where it had been was a new brick building – a tsunami shelter. My heart sank when I saw this, and when I asked one of the locals about what had happened; it sent shivers running down my spine.

He said that everything and everyone on this side of the island that day just vanished; there was absolutely no trace of anything or anyone afterward. It had been one of the worst hit places of all – anywhere.

This was a very sad moment which stayed on my mind for a few days. How lucky I really had been, and those poor people who were on holiday like me or living there. That poor little girl, too.

The rest of this second three-month holiday was quite strange but perfect at the same time. I didn't meet many people really. It seemed as though I had a tattoo on my forehead at times, saying, "Fuck off," because almost everyone I spoke to just wanted to keep to themselves, which I suppose is a sign of the times.

I did meet some lovely people, but mainly I was left to relax and write my stories, which was actually fine. The time I had alone really helped me become better as a writer, and I was able to take the book to a completely new level; something I don't think I could have done without having those months to myself.

It was so coincidental and perfect how that time was given to me.

Just like the book started when my car broke down, and I happened to be at work when I should have been at home, it would end with that phone call on Monday afternoon when I was at home, 'sick', but I really should have been at work.

That initially depressing phone call informing me that I'd lost my job was soon translated by my crazy mind into, "You go and use this opportunity to sort out your mind and your liver, and while you're at it, go and give your book the time, attention, and the ending it deserves."

On returning from my trip with the book still unfinished, albeit twice the size, I started to think about the overall message I was trying to get across in the book.

Is it that if you are a decent person, then everything will work out fine? No, because there are an awful lot of decent and all-round lovely people who have terrible things happen to them.

Is it that you should just let things take their course and things will be fine? No, because that obviously doesn't always work. Sometimes you need to take action.

I think part of my message is that you should just be yourself and not worry about stuff that is out of your control. These things are going to happen anyway, so what is the point in worrying about them?

Also, don't overthink things like I have done in this book. It has been a great journey for me, but I would recommend that you just leave things in the past and look forward instead, unless you want to write a book, in which case you will need to be prepared to go over things that you really don't want to – things you have forgotten for a reason.

I think I've also shown that bad things can happen to us for the best, so don't give up when something awful unexpectedly turns your world upside down. It can often be an amazing stroke of luck.

I now understand that my main goal for writing has always been to make people smile for a bit at my expense, and hopefully for them to take something positive away with them from reading my stories. I might have the odd rant along the way, but I mostly try to do it with a hint of humour, and much of it really is tongue-in-cheek, but what is the real message?

Well, I find it amazing how strange things seem to happen for the best when you least expect it, and how we somehow meet the right people at the right times who end up transforming our lives from then on. This especially seems to happen more often – though not always – when you are feeling positive – which I know isn't always possible; but it's just better.

With this in mind, I started to think about my lucky escapes from earlier, and one of them really stood out.

I then thought about the question I'd asked myself on that crazy day in Taipei all those years ago; the question I'd never really got around to answering; the question at the very start of the book.

"How the fuck did I end up on the top of a building in Taipei, overlooking some mountains, in the middle of an earthquake, holding some shopping bags, after attending a Mandarin Chinese language class, while my tap-dancing Taiwanese girlfriend is dancing in New York City?"

I thought I'd try to answer it in one breath.

I obviously only ended up in Taipei due to meeting Ling. I met Ling during my Asian travel experience in 2003, the timing of which was triggered by Adele's suicide. On this trip, I decided to escape Thailand on one particular day after having some bad experiences – first being very ill, and then after being pestered constantly by local slags and dickheads. I made a snap decision to go to Bali of all places, only returning to Kuta because of those terrorist attacks the previous year. Ling just happened to be in Bali at that exact time because a newspaper company paid her to go at that time. Thorsten also just happened to be in Bali at that exact same time, and it was him who brought us together. I almost missed Ling that morning in Bali by taking the wrong turn, before I decided to take the other route to my hotel room – otherwise I would never have seen her again. I stuck to my principles and said no to all those lovely girls wanting payment for their services, and luckily, the girl from Java had already arranged the Mexican bloke for the one evening on which I cracked, otherwise I would have been with her, and I would have missed Ling and the others altogether. My emails to Ling went missing, almost ruining everything, but she happened to have met Aline at the airport in Bali, so I was able to contact Aline, who gave Ling my message. Aline also being in Bali was therefore crucial – the final cog, if you wish.

Going further, I only stayed at that very hotel in Bali because my ex-girlfriend Karen had taken me there when I went to meet her in Australia – so you could say I only really met Ling because I'd met Karen. Karen had only gone to Australia because her sister had married an Australian and moved there to live. I met Karen at work in the job I'd fought to get in Lytham. Me and Karen only got together because we were forced to work in a team consisting of just the two of us. I only got the job in Lytham because I had the trainee programmer job at British Gas previously. I was only offered that job because I did badly in my exams and left school at sixteen years of age. Was failing my exams all down to my miserable early school years when I was more interested in God? Is God responsible after all? Who knows, but I might have only got my first job because I was motivated by the prick from Farnworth – the prick who punched me in the face – being interviewed for the same job. Therefore, being punched in the face that Sunday morning as a teenager might well have started the whole turn of events leading me to be there on that roof in the middle of an earthquake; the turn of events that would eventually lead to that miserable morning in the office car park when my fucking car broke down – all of which leading me to write this book.

All this leading to *you* reading these words right at this very moment.

Without me writing the book, right now you'd be doing something else instead. There would be no book to read.

391

Everything that's happened in my life has therefore determined what you are doing right now. Isn't it amazing how the things we do can touch and impact other people's lives? Right now, I am either making you feel happy, sad, bored, tired, drained, emotional, or even relieved that you are finally near the end of this fucking book.

The book has obviously been all about me, the strange coincidences, the lucky escapes, and crazy situations I've gotten myself into, but all these occurrences are only down to the people I have met who have influenced or touched my life in some way.

I really don't want the end of the book to be about me too. I want it to be about you. I want to make you think how much your actions influence those people around you.

The small things you do in your life can ripple throughout the world and have a massive effect on so many others – but even if what you do just stops at one person, it still touches them in some way. It can affect how they are feeling or even how they live the rest of their lives from that moment onward – and how they are with others; one small example being my primary school teacher Mr. Marr telling me not to wear my watch on my right hand. His words stuck with me and changed what I did from that day onward for the rest of my life. However minor that was, he bullied me into that.

Bearing in mind that your actions can have such an effect on other people, isn't it better to have a positive effect?

Make up with the person you're not speaking to. Apologise to the person you've upset. Give the money back to that person you owe it to – you tight bastard. Try to move on from things that hurt and upset you – there is no other way because the smile you find will have a positive effect – both on yourself and others. Give your partner a hug – or if you're like me, your pillow.

If you now want to call me a condescending prick, then do so, but do it with a fucking smile on your face.

If I've made just one person smile from all this, then that is enough for me.

I hope that person with the smile is now you.

Try to make the next chapter of your life a positive one. There really is no point being any other way.

My mum and me on our last night in Mauritius - June 2017.
She joined me for the final nine days of my trip. Her luggage arrived on day eight.
Later that night I wrote much of the final chapter.

"Right, I'm going. You can all get lost!"

– *Dave "The Leg" Hartigan*

The Final Coincidence

I had thought that the previous passage was the end of the book, but on Saturday, August 19th, 2017, everything changed again.

I was even going to send the manuscript to my editor for a final copy edit that week, but we decided I might as well leave it one more week because she was going on holiday. Also, the job I'd had that was so conveniently cancelled in January was ultra-conveniently restarted again, and I would now have just one more week of leisure before returning to work. I therefore decided to go away again for a few days while I had the chance.

I booked three nights in Annecy, France, and on the evening of Tuesday, August 15th 2017, I drove the eight-hundred miles to this beautiful place on the French-Swiss border near Mont Blanc.

There was another reason for me driving all this way. I was still having trouble getting the awful Serbian nightmare experience out of my head – even one year later – so in some way I thought if I did a similar trip, only making it a much nicer experience, then it might replace the repeating bad memory I had.

I did enjoy the drive through France, and had a lovely time in Annecy, but after two lonely nights, I changed my mind. Instead of staying the third night that I'd paid for, I decided I'd spent enough time on my own over recent months and I wanted to be home for the weekend. I therefore set off from Annecy at 4.30 p.m. Friday after booking the 12.20 a.m. ferry from Calais to Dover.

Whilst on the ferry, it soon hit me that this was the same vessel I'd boarded with my brother the year before, and it brought everything back from that trip; the place where he sat trying and failing to eat a messy hot dog; the toilets where we had to go and clean the ketchup and mustard from his face; the banging door we were sitting beside when I saw the lonely tear drop from his eye. There was one big difference though – Chris was missing.

I had ninety minutes reflecting and wondering about Chris and the state he'd managed to get himself into. Although he was now a mess to look at and had been going downhill for years, I still remembered that even on that trip home we had some lovely moments together; just a few minutes where he became himself again;

where he became my brother again, the brother I felt had departed this world in many ways years earlier. It was so sad to see his deterioration, knowing that there was nothing anyone could do to stop it. That was why I stayed away from him after the trip, only seeing him a couple of times and realising there was still no hope in my mind. He was getting all the help he needed, but his mind wasn't there to help himself.

The morning after arriving home, when I was in bed, I received a phone call from my mum. It was lovely to hear her voice, but there was a tone in her delivery which I'd never heard before.

This was the call I'd been expecting and dreading for quite some time now – the call telling me that my one and only brother had died. My dad had found him at home in bed – the worst possible thing for any parent to experience.

Chris was just forty-eight years old.

Ironically, it was the withdrawals from the drug he'd craved too often lately that killed him; trying desperately again to halt his own decline. He'd been due to enter a rehabilitation clinic for three months the following Thursday, a place where his withdrawal from alcohol could have been monitored, giving him a better chance of survival, but it just wasn't to be.

Chris obviously hadn't always been like this, and I have no idea what happened to start his downfall. What triggers a person to do this? Also, at what point does the problem cease being one you can fix yourself and start to be a problem over which you have no control? It can obviously happen to anyone – like you and me – because it does. If we haven't been to the depressing depths of despair and suffered the cravings that people like Chris have, then it is difficult for us to understand their predicament. Yes, he had started it all off, but I know he desperately wanted to escape his situation because that was all he would really talk about. He'd just got to the point where his body needed alcohol to survive in much the same way it needed water. What was previously a mental problem had become physical. Is that the point of no return, I wonder?

We had all been preparing for this, but no matter what you prepare for it is still a terrible shock when it comes. You think you are ready for it, but you really are not.

It was strange that I cut my trip short by one day, because it made all the difference to me personally. It also coincidentally meant the timing of his passing was approximately the same time I had been on that same ferry home that I'd shared with him the year before, and it meant my parents didn't have to tell me the news before what would have been a sixteen-hour drive home alone on the Saturday. I think that would have destroyed me even more than the last trip.

It's so sad what happened to Chris, though in a strange unfortunate way I suppose it is the fitting ending to the book that I feared, and that we all didn't want, but was probably always going to happen. Maybe it was even meant to happen? I'm also sad that he will never get to read this, because I was hoping parts of it might trigger something inside to stop him being a fool to himself – though I think we're all honest enough to realise he'd already gone past the point of no return.

I am happy though that he got to read the chapter on Belgrade, and if his whole experience in Serbia, or reading about my experience didn't make him sort himself out, then I don't think anything was ever going to. Maybe it was all just too late.

You're probably now thinking, "Well, there goes that fucking happy ending." And you are right, but such is life, and life goes on for the rest of us.

If you are reading this right now, then it means you are alive and kicking, so realise what a gift you have and make the bloody most of it – and be careful not to hurt those close to you in the process.

Also, don't be a prick; and that includes not being a prick to yourself.

I think it's crazy, and very fitting, that I could have started to write this book at any point over the past ten years, but writing it at this time just happened to coincide with two of the most interesting and distressing years of my life, and that finishing it then sadly coincided with the passing of my brother. It even feels as though Chris left me with his story as a gift, for me to tell the world on his behalf – possibly helping the odd person along the way - because it wouldn't be half the book it is without him playing such a major role in it.

He often told me that he felt we could create something amazing together – either a song or a funny story – and though I laughed at him then, I hope this book can now go some way to being that something.

I'd previously said that I wrote the book in an attempt to make people smile for a bit, especially my mum and dad, but now I feel there was always a hidden reason for writing it: to help me and my family through what is probably going to be the toughest period of our lives – it's already helped me a great deal.

I've written about trying to stay positive, especially through the hard times, because during these testing periods you can either choose to go one way or the other. Now is the time for me and my family to follow this advice, however difficult that might be.

Writing the book has also selfishly kept me occupied over some difficult months in the past couple of years, while my mother and father dealt with the day-to-day problems of my brother's situation. However, I take solace in that they've already found some joy and a little bit of comfort from reading my stories and I know they are as excited as me about my book's completion and what follows next.

Now, after what has happened recently, if I hadn't written it, and I didn't have the excitement of the impending book launch to look forward to – and what might come after – then in these sad times, I think more than any other time in my life I really would be *Lost in the Crowd*.

Lost in the Crowd

Lost in the crowd
For crying out loud
This happens more often than not
I thought they were my friends
But were they pretend?
Or have they just forgot?

Lost in the crowd
I am screaming so loud
But no one around can hear me
They're too busy Facebooking
Or talking about fucking
This just doesn't entertain me

Lost in the crowd
Am I covered by a shroud?
That only I cannot see
Because I'm so unnoticed
I could be in the remotest
Place that I ever could be

Lost in the crowd
In my own black cloud
The people around me are draining
They can't see me for toffee
But why should this hurt me?
When in my own mind it's not raining

Lost in the crowd
But through it I ploughed
And I started to see the sunlight
I started off gently
Before it became elementary
And now, I'm the one in the spotlight.

The End

Sometimes it is the people you can't imagine anything of who do the things no one can imagine.

Alan Turing

In Spite of it All

He lived in a world of Viz comics
With his humour a taste unto itself
But in the last couple of years
He did little to aid his own health

The laughter was constantly there
With no room for a sense of reflection
It was as though life was all just a joke
Maybe he felt this was his only protection

But he had help and support from all corners
That he tapped into more and more every day
Though he wouldn't take that advice given
Just choosing to do things his own way

In the end there was only one outcome
A prediction not too hard to call
But it's still hard to come to terms with
And we love and miss you, in spite of it all.

For my brother x

01/01/2017, 03:22

I cry myself to sleep over you
Chris. What else can I say x 🖤

I'll get sorted. It's. Not easy but I
will get there. X

My chat with Abi: To Belgrade and back.

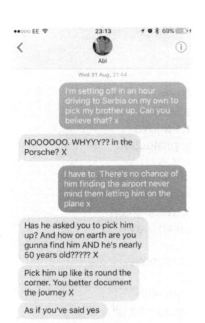

Wed 31 Aug, 21:44

> I'm setting off in an hour driving to Serbia on my own to pick my brother up. Can you believe that? x

NOOOOOO. WHYYY?? in the Porsche? X

> I have to. There's no chance of him finding the airport never mind them letting him on the plane x

Has he asked you to pick him up? And how on earth are you gunna find him AND he's nearly 50 years old????? X

Pick him up like its round the corner. You better document the journey X

As if you've said yes

> He didn't ask me. I have just told him. I know where he is and it's an opportunity cos Sam is home Sunday so he wants to get back to see him x

> He's lost 7 phones and been in hospital 5 times since he's been away x

I don't understand how this has even come about. For the record I think it's a terrible idea. ASIF you're going half way round the world to 'collect' your brother. I can't take it in. And I'm nervous. Is this not a dangerous plan. Well in that case he needs driving to K2 X

How has he got any money I thought he was poor? X

Why you setting off so late? Where are you driving to? X

> He will die there if I don't go I can't see another option. I've only decided in the last hour and my ferry is 6:40 from Dover. He needs to see a doctor soon and get help. He's a prick and doesn't deserve me going getting him but I have to as my mum is in bits x

Awwww is she. What's up with him? X

> Drink but his head has really gone he's fallen so many times think he's done some damage he's got cuts all over his head and face x

Bloody hell. Go and sort him out but remember talking to him like he's stupid don't work with him. Arm round him and look after him. Good luck X

Keep me updated. X

> Will do. Pray for me  x

Thu 1 Sep, 13:56

Hello? Are you alive? X

 where are you? X

402

Still alive? X

> I know and it's got a lot worse lately. I only came here for my mum not for him x

Awwww don't be like that X

Ok, right, please stay safe. I'm nervous 🙈🙈 how's Germany? X

Thu 1 Sep, 20:52

> Sorry I was driving. Nothing to be nervous about I'm not nervous in the slightest. Germany is so much fun this car belongs here it's like the best car racing game ever 😊 😵 x

> I overtook a police car at 125mph and then someone flew past me 😵 I didn't realise the police cars are green x

Fri 2 Sep, 11:09

> I'm just sat having a cold beer on a main road looking out for him. I asked the barman if he'd seen him and he said he was here yesterday. That's just 1 person I've asked. He's going to ring me if he sees him around x

Bloody hell 🙈🙈 how do you feel about the situation. Are you getting a hotel or something? X

> Well I don't want to stay in that fuckin hostel but the lads are brilliant so I might have to. I feel annoyed but I'm too tired to

OMG did they not pull you over? X

> No they don't care I don't think there is a speed limit on the autobahns there didn't used to be x

> feel too much. I've not told my mum yet she is driving home from cornwall with my dad so will wait til they get home x

> I went to try and have my haircut but the woman didn't understand me so we both just said fuck it 😂😂😂 x

Right. Well make sure you get enough sleep X

So is he not answering your calls either? X

Fri 2 Sep, 08:52

> I've arrived and he's not here been missing since yesterday afternoon. He's just a cunt x

> He doesn't have a phone. He's lost 7 in 6 weeks x

Omg you're joking. Missing from where his hotel? X

What a gobshite X

Have you slept? X

Remember when you do see him give him a big hug. Don't be mad. There's something wrong with him in his head X

> He will never have any idea what I've been through in the last 36 hours for him. After Germany it was awful and frightening and I also got done by the first fucking speed

403

camera in Austria because I still thought I was in Germany x prick

He's in a police station. Will explain all later

I have to go and see the judge when she found out I was here she just said thank god for that because she got no sense from him. He had wounds and refused treatment so she couldn't do anything until he had his wounds sorted. He owes the hostel 20000 about 180 euros I think so I said I'd pay that and he will have a very small fine for his crime which I will sort out. His crime? Climbing into the fucking Canadian Embassy!!! (!)

OMG how do you know? X

Judge called the hostel x (!)

Not Delivered

Holy fucking shit. X

Fri 2 Sep, 19:30

I sat in the mini court hearing with him paid a £70 fine and ducked off with him. He was a mess shaking and tried to run off when we were waiting for a taxi. Better now he's asleep x

He tried running off what do you mean?? Literally. How's his head? So you're driving back now? X

Running to find s drink I mean. It was as if he was possessed. It's a mess. Yeah on way home x

Fucking hell. 🙈🙈 I thought he went to rehab not long back?

Anyway it's done now. Just be safe on way home. And good luck. Where you going to take him? X

Fuck knows yet x

Top 10 Annoying Twats

1. Chris
2. Darren
3. Michael
4. Jack
5. Stephen
6. Dave
7. Simon
8. Richard
9. Dale

😂😂😂😂😂

Sat 3 Sep, 13:37

Are you back? X

Few miles from Calais x

How is he? X

What times your ferry? X

Ok but needs about 4 shots every 4 hours otherwise he's shaking and gets very nervous acting very strange like a different person x not got one yet x

He's properly fell of the waggon then ain't he 🙈 you taking him to your house or his mums? X

404

Sun 4 Sep, 12:53

Hey you back? Safe? X

> Yeah thanks. The hardest thing
> I've ever done that x

Thank god, how is he? X

> He is ill. Drink is only half of it.
> He starts shaking needs a drink
> and that's it sometimes. Other
> times it transforms in into a
> different person and he can't
> remember what he's done.
> He's been in hospital 7 times in
> 6 week x

Through injuries? X

> Yeah falling. Happened once
> when I was with him. He got
> the shakes and tried to walk
> and his left leg just gave way
> he didn't trip so think that is

> he didn't trip so think that is
> what happened every time. He
> is going to hospital today x

Ok good, did he stay at yours?
How do you feel now you've
seen him? X

> My mums. Glad he's home and
> shattered beyond belief. I now
> realise he is ill and so does he
> sometimes. Can't really think
> I'm too tired x

Ok well I'm glad it's on track
for getting better and I hope he
realises what you've done for
him. Go and get in bed and
watch F1 😊 😊 x

> I've been in bed since 2am and
> slept most of but feel like I
> need w month now. F1 is
> rubbish apart from the first lap
> 😊 x

I fucking know! 😂 😂 😂

> Haha I didn't mention my sleep
> deprivation. I was hallucinating
> much of the time I was driving
> seeing strange faces, dancers
> all sorts of stuff. No idea how I
> survived that x

Jesus Christ!! That's awful! Go
to bed now. Are you going work
tomorrow? X

> I'm off I just mailed them x

At least you've got a good
excuse X

> I know. I emailed last week
> saying I won't be in I have to
> drive Serbia pick my brother up
> 😂 😂 😂

I still can't believe you've done
it! X

> Nobody can including me. It's
> all a daze now staying awake
> on adrenalin and coffee. 3
> hours sleep out of 92 hours I
> had x

Fucking hell

Shocking that X

Sun 4 Sep, 19:56

Samantha Peacock-hilton and Billy Gornall
shared a link.

Gin lovers are probably all psychopaths, say
experts

Samantha Peacock-hilton

Janet Bolton

Belgrade – The Recurring Soundtrack Playing in My Head

My Way – Sid Vicious

Driving home from work bored.

Will You? – Hazell O'Connor

At home, wondering what to do. How on Earth can I help?

This One – Bubble Toy

Geeing myself up to make the journey. Making and drinking countless cups of strong espresso. I start driving, but after one minute the music stops dead when I see the fucking roadworks and diversion.

The Only One I Know – The Charlatans

I'm on the M6 motorway two hours into the journey. I decide to turn up the music and try to enjoy myself.

Voyage Voyage – Desireless

I'm on the ferry to Calais, then driving in Calais. The music stops dead again when I open the car window and a big bumble bee hits me hard in the throat, killing itself and shitting me up in the process.

99 Luft Balloons – Nena

I'm enjoying driving along sunny country roads in Germany. The music stops dead again when I'm halted by what turned out to be a three-hour fucking traffic jam.

Seven Cities – Solar Stone

I decide to say "fuck it". I then drive like a maniac, covering one thousand miles in twelve hours - somehow.

What Took You So Long? – Courteeners

Arriving in Belgrade; lost, looking for the hostel. I'm excited but apprehensive about seeing Chris.

Stella Maris – Moby

Chris isn't there. I am in bits, totally lost, aimlessly wandering around Belgrade in disbelief with tears in my eyes.

Temptation – Moby

Still lost and still wandering around but I've now come to terms with the situation. I have a cold beer and consider my options.

In The Aeroplane Over The Sea – Neutral Milk Hotel

I get a surprising call informing me that Chris has been found. I am over the moon. I run back to the hostel and am quickly put in a taxi to the police station. My joy is short lived. The music fades when I see the state of Chris. It was a horrendous shock to see him like that.

We Do What We're Told (Milgram's 37) – Peter Gabriel

The surreal, heart breaking, but hilarious court experience. It was so serious, but then so funny and ridiculous at the same time.

Imagine – Pentatonix

The opening scene is revisited, only now played in slow motion to explain how things pan out. Chris and I leave the police station and attempt to get a taxi. We are laughing and joking one minute, but then he disappears. I panic, but then see him in the distance and chase him. The song ends with us in the taxi. I am wondering what chance I have of getting him home, but more importantly I am wondering whatever happened to my brother. He is ill. He is spaced-out; gone.

The Answer – Kodaline

We begin our journey home as I'm trying to make sense of what has become of Chris. Where did it go wrong for him? How did it get this bad? Should we have seen it coming long before it arrived? Could we have done more to help? Will he ever recover? Will we ever make it home? I wasn't confident about the final two points at the time.

Two-Headed Boy – Neutral Milk Hotel

The long journey home continues. The Belgrade rush-hour starts to subside. We stop to buy alcohol as we near the border with Croatia.

Bang My Head – David Guetta

We are stopped at the Serbian border and prevented from passing, but then overjoyed when finally allowed through. The music stops dead yet again when the Croatian police stop me for speeding.

(Song For My) Sugar Spun Sister – The Stone Roses

We are now both enjoying the last of the sunshine. The scenery in Croatia is beautiful, and for a short time I feel like I'm on a driving holiday with my brother. It was only brief, but it was wonderful.

A Day in the Life – The Beatles

Driving in the dark when the hallucinations start. The music changes and I find myself in a different world/dimension where everything is fluffy and nice. Chris is the younger, nicer, scar-free version of himself. The music soon reverts back and so does Chris and my real world.

By My Side – INXS

I'm really struggling; slipping in and out of consciousness while driving. Words can't really explain how exhausted I was, but just one look at Chris in the passenger seat was enough to make me carry on.

Osez Josephine – Alain Bashung

The situation has become quite comical. It's now daytime and everyone just stares at the pair of us when we get out of the car. We must look like comic criminals or smack-heads. We are now in France and nearly get arrested for pissing on French soil. That is the height of our criminal activity, but it's yet another run-in with the law.

Everyday Is Like Sunday – Morrissey

We drive through the shithole that is Calais. It is like driving through a fucking dirty prison.

Sign Of The Times – Harry Styles

We board the ferry to Dover, trying to find somewhere out of the way to sit. Chris is a mess. A single tear rolls down his cheek. He wasn't always like this and he knows it. It's heart-breaking to watch.

Nothing Left To Say – Imagine Dragons

We are now on the M25 motorway in the pissing rain at night. I don't know where I am. Driving is now very dangerous. My reaction time is non-existent. We see flashbacks of Chris's life, him growing up, getting married, having kids, taking them on holiday. We drum home that he wasn't always a prick. He was a decent lad at one point; a good brother, a good son, a good husband, and a good father. We realise what happened to him can happen to anyone. The music stops dead when I wake up driving 20mph in the middle lane of the motorway. Chris has woken me up, probably saving us both from disaster.

Manchester – The Times

We are driving up the M6 motorway on the last leg of the journey. Both our faces must be a terrible sight. We finally see a sign for Manchester and I look like I'm about to cry tears of joy and relief. The tears stay inside for the time being. We see a sign for Bolton. The music stops. We arrive at my mum and dad's. Chris has another funny turn as we park. My dad says, "You're a Saint, Math" as I exit the car.

Where Is My Mind? – Maxence Cyrin

I drive the short journey home. I arrive and collapse on my floor in tears. I cry my eyes out. What had just happened?

That's The Way God Planned It – Billy Preston

I get myself a beer and collapse on the couch - finally. I fucking did it.

Sunscreen – Sun Tan

"Your choices are half chance, so are everybody else's."

Forget the book; this trip was my greatest achievement of all time.

Was it worth it?

Of course it was; every last painful, worrying, tearful, ridiculous, dangerous, crazy, brotherly inch.

Chris with Sam and Liv. Love you all xxx

Thank you for reading to the end.

I wonder what happens next.

www.litcbook.com

xxx

Made in the USA
Columbia, SC
27 May 2018